Reader's Digest Paperbacks

Informative.....Entertaining.....Essential.....

Berkley, one of America's leading paperback publishers, is proud to present this special series of the best-loved articles, stories and features from America's most trusted magazine. Each is a one-volume library on a popular and important subject. And each is selected, edited and endorsed by the Editors of Reader's Digest themselves!

THE EDITORS OF *READER'S DIGEST*

ORGANIZE YOURSELF

A BERKLEY/READER'S DIGEST BOOK
published by
BERKLEY BOOKS, NEW YORK

ORGANIZE YOURSELF

A Berkley/Reader's Digest Book, published by arrangement with Reader's Digest Press

PRINTING HISTORY
Berkley/Reader's Digest edition / August 1982
Fourth printing / November 1983

ISBN: 0-425-06580-4

A BERKLEY BOOK ® TM 757,375
The name "BERKLEY" and the stylized "B" with design are trademarks
belonging to Berkley Publishing Corporation.
PRINTED IN THE UNITED STATES OF AMERICA

Grateful acknowledgment is made to the following organizations and individuals for permission to reprint material from the indicated sources:

"Ten Tips to Help you Manage Your Time" from the book GETTING THINGS DONE by Edwin C. Bliss, copyright © 1976 by Edwin C. Bliss (New York: Charles Scribner's Sons, 1976). Reprinted with the permission of Charles Scribner's Sons. Margaret Blair Johnstone for "The Most Valuable Thing a Man Can Spend" by Margaret Blair Johnstone, copyright © 1957 by the Reader's Digest Association Inc. McGraw-Hill Book Company for "Work Less, Accomplish More" from the book WORKING SMART by Michael LeBoeuf, copyright © 1979 by Michael LeBoeuf. Curtis Brown Ltd. for "To Do More Work With Less Fatigue" by Judith Chase Churchill, copyright © 1953 by Crowell-Collier Pub. Co. *Money Magazine* for "Bring Your Budget Back to Earth" by Jeremy Main, copyright © 1974 by Time Inc. *Money Magazine* for "Signs of An Ailing House" by Jerry Edgerton, copyright © 1975 by Time Inc. "42 Ways to Make Your Houselife Easier" from the book MARY ELLEN'S BEST OF HELPFUL HINTS by Mary Ellen Pinkham and Pearl Higginbotham, copyright © 1979 by Pearl Higginbotham and Mary Ellen Pinkham. Reprinted by permission of Warner Books, Inc. "Supershopping: How to Save 50% at the Checkout" from the book CASHING IN AT THE CHECKOUT by Susan Samtur and Tad Tuleja, copyright © 1979 by Susan Samtur and Thaddeus Tuleja. By arrangement with Stonesong Press, a division of Grosset & Dunlap, Inc. "How to Shop for Food" from the book SYLVIA PORTER'S MONEY BOOK by Sylvia Porter, copyright © 1975 by Sylvia Porter. Reprinted by permission of Doubleday & Company, Inc. Macmillan Publishing Co. Inc. for "A Strategy for Daily Living: Define Your Goals" from the book A STRATEGY FOR DAILY LIVING by Ari Kiev, M.D. copyright © 1973 by Ari Kiev, M.D. *Psychology Today Magazine* for "Why You Make Mistakes" by Donald A. Norman, copyright © 1980 by Ziff-Davis Publishing Company. Lester Velie for "Should You See a Career Doctor?" by Lester Velie, copyright © 1966 by

Contents

PART TWO:
ORGANIZE YOUR MONEY

PART ONE:

ORGANIZE YOUR TIME

CHAPTER 1

How to Get Your Act Together

HOW TO GET MORE WORK DONE

by JOHN KORD LAGEMANN

WHENEVER I meet anyone with a special flair for getting things done, I make a point of asking, "How do you do it?" The answers, I have found, are rules of thumb which belong in the category of practical wisdom rather than scientific research—but they work. Here are the techniques that busy men and women in a wide variety of professions have told me are most helpful.

• *Get started.* "There are two steps in getting any task done," said the late Adlai Stevenson when I asked him how he managed to write all his own speeches in addition to carrying on his official duties as U.S. ambassador to the United Nations. "The first step is to begin. The second is to begin again. The first is the hardest."

Making a good start on any new project is like taking your first parachute jump—it requires boldness. At 40, Winston Churchill took up painting as a hobby. "Very gingerly," Churchill recalled, "I mixed a little blue paint with a very small brush, and then with infinite precaution made a mark about as big as a small bean upon the affronted snow-white shield." At that moment, a friend who was a painter's wife entered the room and exclaimed, "But what are you hesitating about?" Seizing a brush, she walloped the canvas with large, fierce strokes. "The spell was broken," Churchill concluded. "I have never felt any awe of a canvas since. This beginning with audacity is a great part of the art of painting." It is also a large part of tackling and mastering any new job.

Just getting into the posture for work may put you in the mood. Pianist Ania Dorfman said that the hardest part of practicing was sitting down at the keyboard. After that, habit and discipline took over and set her in motion.

The hardest part of writing a letter is the first line. A publisher who carries on a tremendouse correspondence once told me: "When I am in doubt about how to start a letter, I begin with one of six words—who, when, where, what, why or how. It never fails to start the flow."

• *Choose a pacesetter*. Every coach knows that the best way to improve the performance of a player is to expose him to pacesetters—outstanding players who set high standards of skill and endurance. In tennis, for example, it is impossible for even an ace to show what he can do if he is matched with a dud. Dennis Ralston, three times the top-ranking U.S. amateur tennis player before turning pro, says, "In training, the main problem is to find the opponent who's a little better than you are, and learn how to beat him at his own game."

In every office, in every endeavor, there's at least one pace-setter. Just watching him work can inspire you to do more. Financier James Ling, who expanded a small electrical-contracting business in Texas into the multimillion-dollar Ling-Temco-Vought Corp., once told a reporter, "The first thing I do when I take on a new enterprise is to single out the best man in the field. My initial challenge is to catch up with him. The second is to overtake him. The better he is, the faster we both move."

• *Manage your time*. Time is our working capital. "Managing it is everybody's No. 1 problem," said the well-known management consultant, Peter F. Drucker, in his book, *The Effective Executive*. "Those who really get things done don't start with their work; they start with their time."

Like money, time has a way of disappearing—a dribble here, a dribble there, until you find yourself asking at the end of a busy day, "Where did it go?" It's only by budgeting the hours and minutes of the day that you can have time left over for your own personal use. It's this "discretionary time" that buys freedom from harassment and a sense of mastery in getting a job done.

One of the most effective techniques of time management is the simple one of setting a deadline. Once my two sons and I spent a week by ourselves in the country. We had to do all the housework, but we put off doing the domestic chores until the house was a mess. One night I bet the boys a dollar I could do the supper dishes in ten minutes. They took me up on it, and I finished just under the wire. Next night, my sons shaved two minutes off my record. We assigned time limits to the other daily housekeeping tasks, and found that we could keep things shipshape with no more than an hour of concentrated work. The rest of the day was ours to do with as we pleased.

• *Leave it and come back to it*. One of my first jobs after graduating from college was on the research staff of a national magazine. When the editor gave me my first big chance to write an article, I worked night and day, trying one approach after another. The harder I tried, the more confused I became.

One day the editor dropped in to see how the work was going and realizing that I was getting nowhere, said, "Did you ever notice that one of the first things that strikes you about a girl is her perfume? After you've been with her a while, the perfume seems to disappear. But if you leave her and come back, the scent is as vivid as ever. Maybe that's what you should do with this article. Leave it for a while and do something else. Then come back to it."

I took his advice, and the article was finished. Since then, I've noticed that most people who work with ideas use this same device. They work on one problem until they start losing the feel of it, then turn to something else. Later they return to the first problem with fresh interest.

• *Filter out the irrelevant.* Imagine yourself surrounded by an invisible bubble within which you are shielded from distraction. The outside world is still there, but the wall of your bubble filters out everything irrelevant to the task at hand.

Concentration doesn't mean a narrowing down of interest. It means the widening out and fullest use of all one's powers— a comprehensive awareness of all the aspects of the problem under consideration. Emerson called this kind of concentration "the secret of strength in politics, in war, in trade—in short, in all management of human affairs."

• *Find your own work rhythm.* The conventional way of breaking up the day is so many hours for work and so many for play, relaxation and sleep. But if you feel like working after dinner— or, for that matter, at 3 a.m.—why not? A lot of creative work can be done at odd times and places.

The great Canadian physician Sir William Osler, between his teaching, his medical writings and practice, had very little time to pursue his lifelong interest in books. However, he set aside 15 minutes every night to compile an annotated bibliography of his huge library. When he died his ambitious *Bibliotheca Osleriana* contained 7787 entries.

• *Finish the job.* Jobs, like stories, have a beginning, a development and an end. Having started work on a project, many of us don't know when or where to stop. The solution is to plan your work in advance so that when you come to the point where your plan is fulfilled, you can say, "That's that."

Don't be like the futile politician of whom philosopher

George Santayana once said, "Having lost sight of his goal, he redoubles his effort." Define your goal precisely, so that once it is attained you can move on to other projects.

For many of us, work is just a "happening"; the secret is to turn it into a production. The exciting thing is that this approach makes work a most stimulating, rewarding and satisfying part of life.

TEN TIPS TO HELP YOU MANAGE YOUR TIME

by EDWIN C. BLISS

I FIRST BECAME INTERESTED in the effective use of time when I was an assistant to a U.S. Senator. Members of Congress are faced with urgent and conflicting demands on their time—for committee work, floor votes, speeches, interviews, briefings, correspondence, investigations, constituents' problems, and the need to be informed on a wide range of subjects. The more successful Congressmen develop techniques for getting maximum benefit from minimum investments of time. If they don't, they don't return.

Realizing that I was not one of those who use time effectively, I began to apply in my own life some of the techniques I had observed. Here are ten I have found most helpful.

Plan. You need a game plan for your day. Otherwise, you'll allocate your time according to whatever happens to land on your desk. And you will find yourself making the fatal mistake of dealing primarily with problems rather than opportunities. Start each day by making a general schedule, with particular emphasis on the two or three major things you would like to accomplish—including things that will achieve long-term goals. Remember, studies prove what common sense tells us: the more time we spend planning a project, the less total time is required for it. Don't let today's busywork crowd planning-time out of your schedule.

Concentrate. Of all the principles of time management, none is more basic than concentration. People who have serious time-management problems invariably are trying to do too many things at once. The amount of time spent on a project is not what counts: it's the amount of *uninterrupted* time. Few problems can resist an all-out attack; few can be solved piecemeal.

Take Breaks. To work for long periods without taking a break is not an effective use of time. Energy decreases, boredom sets in, and physical stress and tension accumulate. Switching for a few minutes from a mental task to something physical—

6

isometric exercises, walking around the office, even changing from a sitting position to a standing position for a while—can provide relief.

Merely resting, however, is often the best course, and you should not think of a "rest" break as poor use of time. Not only will being refreshed increase your efficiency, but relieving tension will benefit your health. Anything that contributes to health is good time management.

Avoid Clutter. Some people have a constant swirl of papers on their desks and assume that somehow the most important matters will float to the top. In most cases, however, clutter hinders concentration and can create tension and frustration—a feeling of being "snowed under."

Whenever you find your desk becoming chaotic, take time out to reorganize. Go through all your papers (making generous use of the wastebasket) and divide them into categories: 1) Immediate action. 2) Low priority. 3) Pending. 4) Reading material. Put the highest priority item from your first pile in the center of your desk, then put everything else out of sight. Remember, you can think of only one thing at a time, and you can work on only one task at a time, so focus all your attention on the most important one. A final point: clearing the desk completely, or at least organizing it, each evening should be standard practice. It gets the next day off to a good start.

Don't Be a Perfectionist. There is a difference between striving for excellence and striving for perfection. The first is attainable, gratifying and healthy. The second is often unattainable, frustrating and neurotic. It's also a terrible waste of time. The stenographer who retypes a lengthy letter because of a trivial error, or the boss who demands such retyping, might profit from examining the Declaration of Independence. When the inscriber of that document made two errors of omission, he inserted the missing letters between the lines. If this is acceptable in the document that gave birth to American freedom, surely it would be acceptable in a letter that will be briefly glanced at en route to someone's file cabinet or wastebasket!

Don't Be Afraid to Say No. Of all the time-saving techniques ever developed, perhaps the most effective is frequent use of the word *no*. Learn to decline, tactfully but firmly, every request that does not contribute to your goals. If you point out that your motivation is not to get out of work but to save your time to do a better job on the really important things, you'll have a good chance of avoiding unproductive tasks. Remember, many people who worry about offending others wind up living according to other people's priorities.

Don't Procrastinate. Procrastination is usually a deeply rooted habit. But we can change our habits provided we use the right system. William James, the father of American psychology, discussed such a system in his famous *Principles of Psychology*, published in 1890. It works as follows:

1) Decide to start changing as soon as you finish reading this article, while you are motivated. Taking that first step promptly is important.

2) Don't try to do too much too quickly. Just force yourself right now to do one thing you have been putting off. Then, beginning tomorrow morning, start each day by doing the most unpleasant thing on your schedule. Often it will be a small matter: an overdue apology; a confrontation with a fellow worker; an annoying chore you know you should tackle. Whatever it is, do it before you begin your usual morning routine. This simple procedure can well set the tone for your day. You will get a feeling of exhilaration from knowing that although the day is only 15 minutes old, you have already accomplished the most unpleasant thing you have to do all day.

There is one caution, however: Do not permit any exceptions. William James compared it to rolling up a ball of string; a single slip can undo more than many turns can wind up. Be tough with yourself, for the first few minutes of each day, for the next two weeks, and I promise you a new habit of priceless value.

Apply Radical Surgery. Time-wasting activities are like cancers. They drain off vitality and have a tendency to grow. The only cure is radical surgery. If you are wasting your time in activities that bore you, divert you from your real goals and sap your energy, cut them out, once and for all.

The principle applies to personal habits, routines and activities as much as to ones associated with your work. Check your appointment calendar, your extracurricular activities, your reading list, your television viewing habits, and ax everything that doesn't give you a feeling of accomplishment or satisfaction.

Delegate. An early example of failure to delegate is found in the Bible. Moses, having led his people out of Egypt, was so impressed with his own knowledge and authority that he insisted on ruling personally on every controversy that arose in Israel. His wise father-in-law, Jethro, recognizing that this was poor use of a leader's time, recommended a two-phase approach: first, educate the people concerning the laws; second, select capable leaders and give them full authority over routine matters, freeing Moses to concentrate on major decisions. The advice is still sound.

You don't have to be a national leader or a corporate executive to delegate, either. Parents who don't delegate household chores are doing a disservice to themselves and their children. Running a Boy Scout troop can be as time-consuming as running General Motors if you try to do everything yourself. One caution: giving subordinates jobs that neither you nor anyone else wants to do isn't delegating, it's assigning. Learn to delegate the challenging and rewarding tasks, along with sufficient authority to make necessary decisions. It can help to free your time.

Don't Be a "Workaholic." Most successful executives I know work long hours, but they don't let work interfere with the really important things in life, such as friends, family and fly fishing. This differentiates them from the workaholic who becomes addicted to work just as people become addicted to alcohol. Symptoms of work addiction include refusal to take a vacation, inability to put the office out of your mind on weekends, a bulging briefcase, and a wife, son or daughter who is practically a stranger.

Counseling can help people cope with such problems. But for starters, do a bit of self-counseling. Ask yourself whether the midnight oil you are burning is adversely affecting your health. Ask where your family comes in your list of priorities, whether you are giving enough of yourself to your children and spouse, and whether you are deceiving yourself by pretending that the sacrifices you are making are really for them.

ABOVE ALL ELSE, good time management involves an awareness that today is all we ever have to work with. The past is irretrievably gone, the future is only a concept. British art critic John Ruskin had the word "TODAY" carved into a small marble clock that he kept on his desk as a constant reminder to "Do Now." But my favorite quotation is by an anonymous philosopher:

> Yesterday is a canceled check.
> Tomorrow is a promissory note.
> Today is ready cash. Use it!

WHAT'S SO SMART ABOUT BEING LATE?

by DON WHARTON

WHEN, AS a boy, I made my frist trip to New York, I headed
for the Polo Grounds to see a big-league baseball game. I was
impressed by the size of the stadium and the number of peanut
vendors. But what really amazed me was the fact the game
started *exactly* on time. In my small Southern town, nothing
ever began promptly. From that day on, boyishly assuming that
this was the way people of the world lived, I began being as
punctual as snapbeans, which come up eight days after planting.

Years after that game I landed a job on a New York newspaper, and was assigned to cover Jimmy Walker. That debonair
mayor was celebrated for always being late. And today there
are thousands of people like him, who make a fetish of tardiness, at both business appointments and social engagements.
Apparently they believe that being "fashionably late" is smart
and blasé. They fail to consider that they are forever upsetting
other people's schedules.

Being "on time" means arriving at an engagement precisely
at the hour you are expected. I cringe when I hear someone
say he will come to dinner at "sevenish," which means no one
will arrive until "eightish" or get food until "ninish." It is my
observation that no one is ever late when asked to lunch with
his boss. And, of course, everyone would make every effort
to be punctual if invited to a White House dinner. True courtesy
in keeping engagements asks that all persons be treated as
though they were our bosses and all homes as though they were
the White House.

Sam Rayburn, before his death Speaker of the House of
Representatives and one of the most courteous of men, was
always irritated by tardiness. D. B. Hardeman, his research
assistant, told of an occasion when Rayburn found he was
behind schedule for an address he was to make at an American
Medical Association meeting. Rayburn exploded, "I loath
being late! And I loathe people who are late!"

After serving as U.S. ambassador to India, Chester Bowles
brought home the story of a political meeting which had taken

place there some years before. The meeting began 45 minutes late. Gandhi, sternly consulting his watch, remarked that India's independence would also be delayed 45 minutes.

In Botkin's *Treasury of New England Folklore,* Dwight Morrow, diplomat and financier, told of a weekend he spent at the White House with President Coolidge, a great believer in punctuality. One Sunday Morrow called across the hall, "Cal, what time is church?"

"Eleven o'clock."

"What time do we start?"

"Seven minutes to 11, from upstairs."

Sometimes crises arise to make even the most punctual person late. But there's always the phone, and a call saying you have been delayed underlines your intention to honor the appointment. Any thoughtful gesture will show that you realize the other person's time is important. Once when I was to meet H. L. Mencken, known for the fierceness of his pen, I was hardly seated in the reception room of his office when he came out, shook hands and said he regretted he would have to keep me waiting, but it would be for only a few minutes.

Usually we have no recourse when others are tardy, but an architect I know found a way to sweet revenge. He had an appointment with a doctor, arrived on time, waited for two hours without getting any more attention than a shingle on a barn. He then got up, walked out, returned to his own office and sent the doctor a bill for two hours' time.

Washington, D.C., according to Eleanor Elliott, former social secretary to John Foster Dulles, is the most punctual of U.S. cities. The tone is set by the members of the diplomatic corps. "Often, before a dinner," Mrs. Elliot said, "I have seen diplomats being driven round and round the block in their limousines, to avoid being a minute too early or a second too late."

One of the most thoughtful hosts I've known was a Frenchman who recognized the difficulty of getting a taxicab in Paris at dinnertime. When he set the hour, he said to me, "Don't worry if you're a bit ahead. We'd rather people be early than late."

Bernhard, Prince of the Netherlands, is pictured by his biographer, Alden Hatch, as a man who takes seriously the saying that promptness is the courtesy of kings. "If a luncheon invitation says 12:30, you can absolutely count on Prince Bernhard arriving at 12:29 and a half."

Social customs vary, of course. Edward T. Hall, the anthropologist who directed the State Department's Point Four Training Program, said, "In Mexico, where time is treated rather cavalierly, one commonly hears the expression, 'Hora americana, hora mejicana?' 'Your time or our time?'" In Manila, dinner guests may wander in an hour late without explanation, whereas in Stockholm one must be really prompt. "The trick there," says a businessman I know, "is to be ringing the doorbell exactly as the clock strikes eight. If you're two minutes late, you're supposed to apologize."

Being late is a habit—but no one can cure himself of it until he determines the cause of his tardiness. Most people are continually attempting to crowd too many chores, amusements and social or business engagements into an inexorable number of hours and minutes. Some people have stopwatch minds; some are sundial beings to whom time is a fuzzy thing, particularly after dark.

There are others who are deliberately late, to make a dramatic entrance or to show an imagined superiority. In Hollywood, it's been said, everyone important is usually late for everything but studio conferences. At a party, each star arrives late—in order of status. The top box-office attraction is allotted the final arrival.

A psychiatrist tells me that sometimes tardiness is a form of subconscious sulking, an attempt to get even with another person. It is also a sign of immaturity. People who are habitually late are in a sense still infants to whom time and the other person's convenience mean nothing.

Some unfortunates will always be incapable of being punctual. A movie star noted for continually being late was invited to christen a destroyer, and pointedly informed that the Navy does things on time. She arrived promptly, then kept the admiral and his staff waiting while she spent almost an hour in the powder room. Subsequently she decided to undergo psychiatric treatment to correct her habitual lateness. But she had to give up the sessions. She was always too late for her appointments with the psychiatrist.

Fortunately, being punctual, like being late, is also a habit—easy to cultivate once you have decided what has made you so careless of time in the past. It is a most rewarding habit; after you have attained it you will find how greatly it simplifies living.

"THE MOST VALUABLE THING A MAN CAN SPEND"

by MARGARET BLAIR JOHNSTONE

WHILE I was on a lecture tour recently my train arrived at one station late, allowing me less than five minutes to make a connection. As I rushed to the other train, red-faced and breathless, a Pullman porter signaled me to slow down and said: "Lady, you better take it easy or you goin' to come down with Americanitis."

"What's *that*?" I gasped.

"I can't rightly say what it is, but I can tell you how it acts—Americanitis is somebody runnin' up an escalator."

What an apt description of our flurry-scurry pace these days! So many things to do—meetings to attend, schedules to meet, records to smash—these are our goals and, all too often, our gods.

"Time," said the Greek philosopher Theophrastus, "is the most valuable thing a man can spend." Yet how often, instead, do we let time spend us?

But, you say, I've *got* to rush; "Time is money," you quote old Ben while nervously keeping your eye on Big Ben. I do not quarrel with Franklin's adage. Time *is* money. But we need to remember also that time is a fixed income. And, as with any income, the real problem facing most of us is how to live successfully within our daily allotment.

Sooner or later every phase of living through which we rush turns into a physical and emotional treadmill unless we stop and ask: What can we do about it? How can we *really* live within 24 hours a day?

I have found four simple rules which have helped me, and which I worked out the hard way—while flat on my back during an enforced rest. My basic discovery, which I think all of us must eventually make if we are to lead calmly useful and happy lives, was that *no one is totally indispensable*. Having admitted that—as I had to when I found that things I thought

13

only I could do seemed to be getting done quite well without me—I began to work through some new rules for my life.

My first rule is: Wherever you are going or whatever you are doing, *start in time*.

I once had a parish comprising several churches which meant that we had an elastic schedule for our services. This lent itself to an interesting experiment. One choir member, who was consistently late complained of our ten o'clock service. "If you had church at a decent hour," she said, "I'd be on time."

Soon after this, we scheduled services in that church for 11:15. The choir member arrived each Sunday at 11:20. But that winter we held services at 2 p.m., and, true to form, in she came at 2:05 without fail!

As parents most of us would not think of rearing children without teaching them how to tell time. But how many of us teach them timing? How many of us have learned timing ourselves?

My second rule is: *Do it now!*

It's not what we do but what we don't get done that wearies us. Procrastination not only wastes minutes but saps our emotional energy by adding dread and dislike to chores which should be routine.

Many a postponed job could be completed in those stretches of time which come to all of us every day—unused waiting time. A University of Wisconsin analysis showed that the average individual spends three years of his lifetime just waiting. And a Gallup poll which sampled 100 persons at random reports that every one of them expected to do some waiting during the next few hours, but only one out of eight had any plan for doing something constructive with the time.

Some of the world's great have been those who used their waiting time well. Thomas Edison set up a laboratory in the baggage car and, between peddling sandwiches on the train, conducted experiments. Robert Louis Stevenson seldom left home without two books in his pocket—one to read and one in which to jot down notes. William Lyon Phelps carried on a voluminous correspondence in the chinks of time between appointments.

According to the U.S. Bureau of the Census, there are comparatively long stretches of waiting time in more than 100 occupations—which indicates that many of us could do *now* small tasks that clutter up other hours.

This doesn't mean that we are never to be inactive. So my

third rule is: *Learn when to say "No," and when to say "Yes."*

Channing Pollock once said, "I've got to decide whether I want to be a famous author or an infamous diner-outer. I cannot be both."

And Anne Campbell, in one of the loveliest bits of verse ever dedicated to a daughter, writes of the choice most parents must make:

> You are the trip I did not take.
> You are the pearls I cannot buy.
> You are my blue Italian lake.
> You are my piece of foreign sky.

Because our time income is fixed, we must learn to be selective in spending it. In reading or TV viewing, for example, one can ruin one's eyes on trash or use them to increase knowledge.

So the next time someone asks you to head the hospital drive or help with the PTA and you are tempted to say, "I don't have time," ask yourself first: to what am I giving first claim on my time? Am I putting first things *first?* Could I curtail some of the time I spend foolishly and invest it more wisely?

"Time stays long enough for those who use it," Leonardo da Vinci once said, and certainly the last rule can help us "stay" time both wisely and well: *Take time out.*

An eye surgeon who was stationed at Fort Devens once attended our church. When I called on his family I was surprised to see painting after lovely painting on the walls. "Who did these?" I asked.

"I did," said the surgeon.

Knowing of his long hours on duty and his heavy responsibilities, I said, "But how on earth do you find time?"

"Find it!" he sputtered. "I don't *find* it, I *take* it."

Then he told me how at one time the dread thing happened. Toward the end of an operation he noted a slight tremor in his hand. He took some leave time immediately, but the tremor persisted. "From sheer boredom I turned to painting," he explained. "I just couldn't sit around doing nothing with my hands. Then as my skill with the brush grew I found the tremor lessening. Now when I get overtired, I turn to my painting *before* my hand starts to shake."

A change is as good as a rest, the old saying goes. You don't have to be a surgeon, or a statesman like Churchill, to paint. Nor need you have Bernard Baruch's busy schedule in order to find that 15 minutes a day spent on a park bench, simply sitting quietly watching the squirrels and thinking, can refresh you for the rest of the day. No, you may be just an office worker, like a friend of mine who stops in a record booth every noon hour and plays a favorite recording.

But take time out—in which you do something that restores the lilt and zest to your living. For, as John Ruskin put it, "There is no music in a 'rest'—but there's the making of music in it. And people are always missing that part of the life-melody."

SIMPLIFY YOUR LIFE!
by MARTIN E. MARTY

"I MUST STRIP MY VINES of all useless foliage and concentrate on what is truth, justice and charity," wrote Pope John XXIII in his *Journal of a Soul*. "The older I grow, the more clearly I perceive the dignity and winning beauty of simplicity in thought, conduct and speech; a desire to simplify all that is complicated and to treat everything with the greatest naturalness and clarity."

John's simplicity gave his actions the force of parables. As Pope from 1958 until 1963, he was driven by one grand and simple idea: peace. He was a reconciler. His Catholic people had stood apart from Jews for 19 centuries; but when Jewish leaders visited him he did not quote intricate doctrines to overcome the distance. He simply acted out the Bible story of a man separated from his family. John reached out to his visitors and said, "I am Joseph your brother."

All the truly deep people have at the core of their being the genius to be simple or to know how to seek simplicity. The inner and outer aspects of their lives match; there is something transparent about them. They may keep the secret of their existence in a private preserve, but they are so uncluttered by any self-importance within and so unthreatened from without that they have what one philosopher called a certain "availability"; they are ready to be at the disposal of others.

Part of genius *is* simplicity, in the sense of oneness of life, of gathered force. We sense an affinity between Albert Einstein's admiration of childlike simplicity and his own powers of wonder and concentration. We sense a connection as well between simplicity and profundity. Albert Schweitzer was musician, philosopher, historian, physician; but his profundity lay in one simple idea, the focus of his years of service in Africa: reverence for life.

Successful living is a journey toward simplicity and a triumph over confusion. Many use the term "spirituality" to describe the route for this journey. Some cherish a spirituality of ecstasy. Like the prophets and mystics, they find their center in God, in the All. They reach a sudden enlightenment that reorders their lives. Others experience a spirituality of agony, on the more barren landscape of loneliness and doubt. But it, too, can give clarity to life. And activists possess what I call spirituality materialized; we see it in Schweitzer and others who change the world.

In all these approaches the common thread is the genius to be simple. Dietrich Bonhoeffer, a pacifist who was in on the plot to kill Hitler, tried to explain before he died on Nazi gallows how simplicity can be one's guide. "To be simple," he wrote, "is to fix one's eye solely on the simple truth of God at a time when all concepts are being confused, distorted and turned upside down. It is to be single-hearted."

Even when genius explains itself, there is force, there is unity, in an underlying simplicity of thought. Karl Barth, the Swiss theologian, was another who saw clearly during the Nazi era. The world could not corrupt his faith. Asked years later by an American audience to summarize the gist of his enormous books on theology, the learned man charmed them by quoting from a Sunday-school song: "Jesus loves me, this I know, for the Bible tells me so."

What assets await those who achieve this inner grace? French mystic François Fénelon wrote, "When we are truly in this interior simplicity our whole appearance is franker, more natural. This true simplicity makes us conscious of a certain openness, gentleness, innocence, gaiety and serenity."

Though the search for simplicity is, at any time, a difficult journey through a wilderness, we can learn from guides ancient and modern. In a way, the American sect called the Shakers had the right idea when its members sang of the "gift to be simple." It often looks like a grace to be enjoyed more than a goal to be sweat over. Nature is not stingy with this gift, but it exacts some effort, so the Shakers called for a conscious act, a need to "turn, turn."

People who despair because their calendars are so crowded and their duties demanding have to turn, to put a premium on simplicity. Some find a way by clearing a special room and a certain hour in which they can strip away what matters finally in their lives from all the things they have to take very, very seriously—but in the end not *too* seriously.

The guides on this journey advise others to follow exemplars. Some find them through reading; the religious may do it through meditation and prayer; the thoughtful often keep journals of their souls' journey.

In Western culture more people claim to find simplicity in

Jesus of Nazareth than in any other figure. Scholars have written millions of books about him, but people first followed him because they saw in Jesus a life covered in five words: "He went about doing good." Those who admire a modern such as Mohandas Gandhi know that the great Hindu leader was a cunning politician who upset empires, but they see how he focused his life with passion on people he called "the last, the least, the lowest, and the lost."

The lives of such leaders offer clues, not codes, for the simple way. Each individual has to discover and nurture the appropriate path for himself. Searchers often band together for the journey. Some have tried communes, only to find them complicated. Others have found both freedom and communion in congregations, clubs or causes.

Sooner or later, the searchers learn to live in harmony with nature. But the genius of simplicity has to do with more than the material world, so the seekers have to prune and sort ideas until the lasting ones alone survive. At this point they come to a crucial step; they learn to be suspicious of simplism. The advice of English philosopher Alfred North Whitehead to natural scientists is well placed for all thinkers: "Seek simplicity—and distrust it."

I came to this theme while writing a history of 500 years of American religion. Wherever I have looked in the national past it became clear that citizens use faith to simplify life. Modern American existence is especially bewildering, but we still have to endow our joys and sorrows with meaning, refusing to let them "merely happen." Millions turn to the life of the spirit to sort out the complexities of life. This search for order and simplicity is a constant in religion and may be close to a definition of it.

Simplicity does not call for anyone to turn back to the good old days, or even back to nature. And true simplicity demands no commune or cult. For most of us it will mean life in the company of others who can judge us and nudge us. In community we can follow the trajectory of our belief and develop the core of our being.

One man who was on the path of true simplicity was, according to the Talmud, a certain Rabbi Zusya. He once said, "In the coming world, they will not ask me: 'Why were you not Moses?' They will ask me, 'Why were you not Zusya?'"

WORK LESS, ACCOMPLISH MORE!
by MICHAEL LeBOEUF

MOST OF US work harder than we have to in order to reap the benefits life has to offer. When that thought first crossed my mind, I began to focus on the question: "How can I get the greatest return on my investment of time and energy?" My research has proved fruitful, and for several years I have been conducting seminars on how people can make the most of their time and effort.

It turns out that improving your effectiveness is much like playing golf. Theoretically, the perfect golf score is 18, a hole in one on 18 consecutive holes. Obviously, no one will ever come anywhere near that score, but this doesn't stop avid golfers from trying to improve their game. As you strive to work less and accomplish more, take a similar approach.

Set daily goals. Making action lists should be as habitual as brushing your teeth. The minimal time and energy you invest will repay you many times over. As Thoreau stated, "It's not enough to be busy. The question is: What are we busy about?"

Consultant Ivy Lee once offered the following advice to Bethlehem Steel president Charles Schwab, who was searching for ways to make better use of his time: "Write down the six most important tasks that you have to do tomorrow. Number them by importance. First thing tomorrow morning look at item one and start working on it until you finish it. Then do item two, and so on until quitting time. Don't be concerned if you haven't finished them all. If you can't by this method, you can't by any other. Try this system every working day." Schwab reportedly called the advice the most profitable he ever received.

Make the most of your best time. You can accomplish more with less effort if you schedule important tasks at the time of day when you perform them most effectively.

For many of us, a task requiring solitude and concentration is best performed before 9 a.m., whereas a task involving socializing should be scheduled later in the day. I have one close friend who barely functions before 3 p.m. Fortunately, his career in broadcasting enables him to take advantage of his late-night prime time, 10 p.m. to 2 a.m.

You can discover your best time for a given task through trial and error. When I began writing I tried picking up the pencil at various times. I found that in the morning my ideas were good, but I had trouble getting them on paper; early afternoon was my period of highest writing productivity. So, now I think about the topics I want to cover in the morning, then jot down my ideas and put them aside until early afternoon, when I write them out fully.

Capitalize on committed time. Sometimes you can put time committed to routine daily essentials to a second use. One friend of mine working toward a business degree records his class notes on a cassette tape recorder and plays them back while dressing and driving to work. A salesman friend uses commuting time to memorize the names of his customers and salient details about each one.

Another type of committed time most of us simply write off is waiting time. With a little effort, however, you can squeeze all sorts of activities into the minutes you spend waiting for doctor or hairdresser. You can plan your weekend, pay bills or write letters. You can even nibble away at a major project: planning your dream home or outlining that novel you always wanted to write.

Distinguish between urgency and importance. The two seldom go together in our daily lives. Fixing a flat tire when you are late for an appointment is a matter of great urgency, but its importance is, in most cases, relatively small. Unfortunately, many of us spend our lives fixing flat tires and ignoring less urgent but more important matters.

When you are faced with a number of problems, ask yourself which are the truly important ones, and make them your first priority. If you allow yourself to be governed by what's urgent, your life will be one crisis after another. A little foresight—taking steps to prevent potential problems—may ensure that you spend your time achieving your goals rather than reacting to crises.

Master the art of deskmanship. Many of us perform some or all of our work at a desk. A desk is a tool that aids in the processing of information, *not* a place to conduct a paper drive, a storage depot for non-job sundries, or a flat surface on which to stack items you want to remember. Merrill Douglass, a time-management consultant, kept a close time log on one executive with a stacked desk and found that he spent an average of 2 hours and 19 minutes per day looking for information on the top of his desk!

Most desks only bury decisions. Try reorganizing your desk for effectiveness by asking, "What's the worst thing that will happen if I throw this away?" If the answer doesn't suggest a serious consequence, throw the item away.

Learn to say NO. Success at working less and accomplishing more depends on knowing what *not* to do. Overcommitment is one of the most frequent ways to dilute our effectiveness. Unfortunately, many of us just don't know how to refuse someone else's request for our time and energy. Two of the reasons we say yes are: (1) we are afraid someone else will have a lesser opinion of us; (2) a request for our help indulges our ego by giving us a feeling of power. Saying yes in either case is self-defeating.

Don't misunderstand me; I'm not against helping people. I'm referring to the times we say yes when we know we could be putting our time to better use.

When you mean to say no, say it rapidly and directly. Answers such as "I don't know" or "Let me think about it" only raise false hopes. And don't feel guilty about it. You have the right to say no, and you don't have to offer a reason every time you politely turn down someone's request.

Make the telephone work for you. The telephone can be a terrific labor-saving tool. It can get you information in minutes that a letter could take weeks or months to acquire. It can save you the time and expense of trips. Yet telephonitis is a disease that can lead to gigantic wastes of time, energy and money.

It's often fun to be interrupted from the task at hand by a ringing phone. So we take the calls as they come and allow our work to be randomly disrupted. Don't let this happen. Establish a period of time each day for placing and receiving telephone calls. For most of us, the best time is in the morning, when people are most likely to be at their offices. Buy a three-minute hourglass and put it by your phone. See if you can successfully complete every call in three minutes. Don't rush, but keep a score card and try to reduce your telephone time each week.

Rid yourself of effectiveness-killing emotions. Picture yourself as a container in which liquid time and energy are stored. Negative emotions are holes in the bottom of the container. To the extent you are able to plug up the holes, you will have more time and energy to do the things that are fulfilling to you.

Of all negative emotions over not getting more done, guilt is one of the most useless. Regret, remorse and bad feeling can't change the past and they make it difficult to get anything done in the present. A prayer I once saw posted in a store offers a healthy perspective: "Lord, there's never enough time for everything. Help me to do a little less a little better."

Worry, which is future-oriented, is another useless emotion. As Mark Twain once said, "I have known a great many troubles, but most of them never happened."

Here are two ways to help get worry out of your life: First, confront your concern head on. Ask yourself, "What's the *worst* that could come from this?" When you answer that question, the need for worry usually vanishes. Second, replace worrying with action planning. Set yourself meaningful goals and go right after them. You'll soon get so absorbed in their pursuit that you won't have time for worrying.

Ridding yourself of negative emotions can make you a new person. Suddenly, you will find you have time, energy and abilities you never dreamed you had. An unknown philosopher summed it up nicely: "Most of the shadows in this life are caused by standing in one's own sunshine."

GET THE MOST OUT OF ODD MOMENTS

by JEAN BRADFORD

TIME AND TIDE wait for no man. Maybe not—but all the rest of us do, and we don't only wait for men but for women, children and dogs. We wait in crowds and we wait alone; we wait to go somewhere and we wait to come home again. And what do most of us do as we wait? Nothing!

Recently I killed the hour and a half my husband's plane was overdue by determined pacing, in ever-widening circles, through a big air terminal. When he did get in, I was traversing an outer loop and missed him. It was several days before we were able to speak civilly to each other, but I did a lot of thinking in the somewhat strained quiet of our home, and decided that it was time I learned how to watch my wait.

None of us would think of throwing away the nickels and quarters and dimes that accumulate in our pockets. But almost all of us do throw away the small-change time—five minutes here, a quarter hour there—that accumulates in any ordinary day. I figure I probably threw away a full working day in the dentist's office this past year, flicking sightlessly through old magazines. And it is sobering to make yourself add up the time you spend waiting for children to get out of Little League or ballet lessons or for the 5:47 to creep slowly into the station at 7:05.

I became a wait-watcher very modestly at first by putting notepaper and a pen in my pocketbook. It delighted me to discover that, practically overnight, I became the kind of person who wrote letters. Not only long ones to old friends with whom I'd meant to keep in touch, but even the short, spur-of-the-moment notes of appreciation to people who'd done something good in our town. Finally I progressed to where I was writing stand-up-and-be-counted messages to our representatives in Washington.

Terribly proud of myself, I began to brag here and there about how cleverly I was employing my odds and ends of time—only to discover, as braggarts will, that I was only an

24

amateur. Others had come up with some far cleverer ways to use idle moments.

One friend always carries scrap paper for making lists for marketing and errands. But she also carries a regular notebook for the kind of lists that grow gradually and improve with age— like the list of presents that people around her have casually said they wanted. That spring her husband had shouted in frustration as he got out the lawn mower that all he wanted in his life was a sharpening stone; she noted it carefully, ensuring a successful Christmas gift for him that year.

Another neighbor reported that orthodontics had come suddenly into her life this past winter. Twice a week, she had had to wait for half an hour or more while her son had his braces worked on. So she began an incredibly ambitious afghan requiring 367 handwoven white-and-yellow daisies. She's past the 200 mark already and figures that by next Christmas her son will not only have beautifully straight teeth but her mother-in-law will have a present she'll never forget. And lately I haven't seen a business friend of my husband who always carried a French phrase book in his pocket to study at odd moments. He's now running his company's Paris office.

Inspired by these success stories, I got out a strong shopping bag and settled down to assemble a waiting kit to go everywhere with me. I filled it with yellow pads, pencil stubs, notebook, and sewing gear. Then I looked at the cluttered, tattered collection of cross-outs in my address book and dropped it in my kit. Less than a week later I came home in triumph from the usual routine waiting stints with a brand-new, tidy address book.

Right at this moment my kit holds a bulging manila envelope of all the recipes I've been tearing out of magazines since I was married. Winnowing as I go (that marshmallow mousse that caught my eye as a bride is nothing I'm going to try as a matron), I intend to bring that confusion into an orderly collection of gourmet gambits. And while I'm at it, I'll make a list of those friends who would go together well at the dinner parties I'm finally going to find the time to give.

I hadn't realized that my husband was playing the same game until the other day when I found a little celluloid "Guide to Successful Bidding" in the pocket of a suit I was taking to the cleaners. I *had* noticed that he had recently developed a breezy kind of confidence at the bridge table, however, and so I borrowed the guide. I want to be worthy of him the next time he opens with "three clubs." In return, I replaced it with a card describing simple isometric exercises you can do without anyone knowing you're doing them.

Some businessmen might want to have a folder in their briefcases for the things they'll use to make their waiting time productive. Others will need no more than a suit pocket. I once sat next to a friend who travels a great deal by air. He reached into his pocket and brought out a slip of paper on which he had spent odd hours constructing a treasure hunt for his daughter's 14th birthday. "Just got one more clue to go," he said cheerfully. "I've been working on this for a week."

As we hurry toward, and away from, the diverse business of our lives, we are all very apt to spend the moments in between thinking of the people we love, and of things we would like to do for them. My friend on the airplane had found a way to show how much he thought of his family. My neighbor with the afghan fitted her affection for her mother-in-law into the waiting time she would have wasted otherwise.

Try it yourself in spare moments. It's easy to turn the "thinking" of people you love into "doing" something for them. Instead of waiting *for* something to happen, it's a lot more fun to *make* things happen.

CHAPTER 2

How to Overcome Time Pressures

TENSION'S LITTLE TRIGGER MEN

by RICHARD H. HOFFMANN, M.D.

As told to Clarence W. Hall

I SAW Bill Jones's picture staring at me from the obituary columns the other day. A highly successful executive in his early 40s, Jones had come to me a few months before. He had the symptoms of several diseases—headaches, insomnia, loss of appetite, rising blood pressure. Yet examinations showed no organic disruption. A few days later I dropped into his office, spent a half-hour observing his work habits. Then I said: "There's nothing wrong with you, Bill, that you yourself can't cure. You're simply allowing yourself to be riddled by three of today's most potent killers—the Telephone, the Clock and the Calendar. They can be the trigger men of your death."

They were.

I volunteered the same warning to a harried housewife. When she came to my office she was a museum of complaints for which careful diagnosis could reveal no physical cause. From the description of her average day, I got the picture of a civic do-gooder furiously dashing about between kitchen stove, an ever-jangling telephone and endless deeds of mercy. She somehow found time to fret constantly over her limited household budget, worry over appointments and entertain an almost paranoiac fear of the future.

"Right now," I told her, "you are nothing more than a victim of your telephone, clock and calendar. As such, however, you have made yourself a likely candidate for any of a number of real diseases."

She listened impatiently to my advice on how to revise her manner of stressful living, then flounced out, annoyed that I had not uncovered an interesting psychiatric condition or prescribed some glandular injection. Six months later she was taken with a severe—and fatal—kidney ailment.

Both she and Bill Jones, like many of the hundreds of thousands of other middle-aged Americans who this year will succumb to stroke, hypertension, angina pectoris and gastrointestinal diseases, were active accessories to their own killing.

More than half our hospitals are occupied by people with nervous troubles—most of them caused by such out-of-hand emotions as anxiety, despair, discontent, fear, frustration. By our own habits we heckle our nerves with minor irritations, reduce efficiency of body and mind, sour our dispositions and turn existence into a rat race.

After 40 years of general and psychiatric practice, I am convinced that tensive states, being self-induced, must be self-cured. I am further convinced that worriers would do well to start with those despots, the telephone, the clock and the calendar.

The telephone's peculiar tyranny is that of *interruption*. People in public life are not being arrogant when they refuse to have their phone numbers listed. They won't allow themselves to become victims of the telephone's conversational shrapnel.

Few of us can afford the luxury of a secretary who acts as a buffer, yet we can learn to live more calmly with the phone. Have the instrument placed as far from your usual base of operations as convenience will allow. Before answering, relax, take a few deep breaths, compose your suddenly aroused nerves. Don't run; *walk* toward it. When phoning others, ask: "Are you busy now? Will it be more convenient if I call back later?" Make your calls as brief as possible. The dawdlers and gossips who tie up a line indefinitely provoke needless resentment.

The clock's despotism is the tyranny of *appointment*. Safety experts estimate that nine tenths of the accidents on streets and in homes are caused by careless rushing. Bent on beating a deadline, tens of thousands of us every year jaywalk to our deaths, accelerate our cars into fatal smashups, fall down stairs or skid on skittery rugs.

Resolve to make your whole day less dominated by the ticking tyranny of clocks. Get into the habit of starting a few minutes earlier to work; the same in keeping an appointment. Avoid making your day's program too tight with successive engagements. Pad your time budget with little chunks of extra minutes to rediscover what Don Herold calls "the lost art of doing nothing." Leave some leeway for emergencies. You will be amazed how this increases your efficiency and conserves your vitality.

The tyranny the calendar exercises is that of *apprehension;* it gets in its most killing licks when we allow the morrow to saddle us with unreasoning fears. I have a patient who regularly goes into an emotional tailspin with the advent of each income-tax day. Other calendar dates produce repeated tensive states—such as the first of the month, a time for paying bills.

The fear of growing old is perhaps the calendar's sharpest thrust. Scores of people are plunged into mental and physical upset by fear of future insecurity, loneliness, failure, sickness. Our American cult of youth has created the silly concept that in youth alone is beauty and excitement and achievement. Now, happily, a host of individuals are demonstrating the fallacy of that notion.

Only a few years ago a star of stage and screen brought me her woes. She wailed that she was a has-been, with glamour gone, youth long past. I scoffed at her: "Why not be your age—and act your age?" She accepted the leading role in a dramatic production featuring a has-been, and rose to popular acclaim. Now, healthy in body and spirit, she boasts about grandchildren whose existence she had kept hidden before.

No better advice was ever given the calendar-cowed than that offered by Sir William Osler: "Waste of energy, mental distress, nervous worries dog the man who is anxious about the future. Cultivate the habit of a life of *day-tight compartments*"—with each day sufficient unto itself.

You will have taken one of the longest steps toward the achievement of serene living when you tackle these tyrannies of the telephone, the clock and the calendar. Three simple rules will start you:

Look *inside* yourself. The human body is a delicately adjusted mechanism. Whenever its even tenor is startled by some intruding emotion like sudden fright, anger or worry, the sympathetic nervous system flashes an emergency signal and the organs and glands spring into action. The adrenal glands shoot into the blood stream a surcharge of adrenalin which raises the blood sugar above normal needs. The pancreas then secretes insulin to burn the excessive fuel. But this bonfire burns not only the excess but the normal supply. The result is a blood sugar shortage and an underfeeding of all vital organs. So the adrenals supply another charge, the pancreas burns the fuel again, and the vicious cycle goes on. This battle of the glands brings on exhaustion.

The body can handle a reasonable number of emergency calls. But if they are repeated too often, your nerves and organs and glands, fatigued from trying to keep up with all those confusing false alarms, finally quit—and you're in for a nervous breakdown.

Look *at* yourself. If we who rush and worry needlessly could see ourselves as others see us, simple pride would stop us. Let any morbidly distraught woman consult her mirror when she is under the lash of our trinity of tyrants, her face ugly with frowns, her jaws clenched. Cosmetic tricks won't banish those beauty destroyers.

A candid survey of ourselves might also make us cease calling our stressful commotion by such flattering names as "diligence to duty ... love of getting things done ... wise provision for the future."

Look *away* from yourself. Practice lifting your mind, every now and again, above the rush and confusion around you. Take time out during your busiest day to think of something pleasant. Said Edwin Markham: "At the heart of the cyclone tearing the sky is a place of central calm." Each of us, in cyclonic situations, has his own place of "central calm." One secret of living above the tensions of the day is finding that place—and repairing to it often.

Paste a skull-and-crossbone label on your telephone, clock and calendar. Then sit back and say—as did the late Mahatma Gandhi—"There is more to life than increasing its speed."

HOW TO BYPASS FATIGUE

by JUDITH CHASE CHURCHILL

IF YOU want to accomplish more and tire yourself less, it will pay to know whether the following statements are true or false. Some of the answers may explode your pet theories.

A half-hour nap can equal three hours of night sleep.

True. Nap after lunch or before dinner, and you can do with a lot less sleep. Experts say that for some people it is equivalent to the three hours of sleep just before waking in the morning. Chances are, people who boast that they sleep only a few hours a night are nap-snatchers.

How well you rest means more than how long you sleep.

True. Relaxed rest is effective in restoring energy. If you sleep only a few hours but relax the rest of the night, you'll be refreshed in the morning. The insomniac rarely relaxes, however, because he worries about not sleeping—and worry keeps him awake.

Small tensions wear you down as much as large ones.

True. Mostly because you can't identify and attack them, a lot of small worries will thoroughly exhaust you. So will continuous nagging. But in a big crisis of which you're fully conscious, all your resources come to the rescue.

Elevate your feet to rest them.

True. A daily ten-minute rest with your feet at hip level does refresh you.

Quiet entertainment relaxes you best.

Not necessarily. For long-term relaxation many experts advise supplementing passive pleasures like TV and radio with

32

active ones that involve your mind and body. Try gardening, sports, home decoration or any other "participating" hobby.

Don't trust evening decisions.

True. Postpone them till morning when you're refreshed. Chances are, your opinions then will be different from what they were the night before, when you were fatigued.

Extravagance tires you.

True. Fatigue often follows on the heels of buying something you can't afford. Uncertainty and doubt produce muscle and nerve exhaustion every bit as tiring as strenuous physical exercise.

Early to bed and early to rise—.

Not an infallible rule. There are two types of people. A's peak efficiency is early in the day; he gets his best sleep during the early part of the night. B's maximum efficiency is in the afternoon or evening; he sleeps best during the last part of the night. B's best bet is late work and late rising.

Standing is more tiring than walking.

True. When you walk, each leg rests half the time; when you stand, neither leg rests. And the stress and impatience of waiting in line are likely to tire you more than simply standing.

Do worst chores first.

True. Plow into them. Dodging a job gives you double fatigue—from dreading the work and then from doing it. Tackling the tough jobs first will make the others seem easier.

HOW TO SAY NO
by VANCE PACKARD

MANY OF US are harassed in daily life by an inability to utter a firm but gracious no. Often our difficulty is caused by a desire to be a good person.

A relative of mine, Edgar Wright, is a small-town businessman. Edgar is serving on 17 committees, mostly because he just can't say no. He goes to bridge parties which bore him. When his hostess offers him chocolate cake, for which he has an allergy, he eats it politely and is sorry later.

Edgar's wife, Ella, is just as bad. A few weeks ago an acquaintance who sells cosmetics by home demonstration asked her to sponsor a "cosmetic party." Ella tried to say no, but the woman kept coaxing until she said yes. Ella persuaded 20 of her friends to come; they couldn't say no either. Edgar estimates that the "party" cost him and the other husbands $148.

Almost every day many of us are caught in positions where we should logically say no, but don't. However, there are several reasonable and friendly ways of saying no. You may find one of them useful the next time you are faced with the problem.

Put it on an impersonal basis.

One of the most serene housewives I know says she achieved her serenity when she licked the problem of saying no. She explained: "I go by rules."

When an acquaintance asks her to wrap packages for unfortunates in Mozambique she says simply: "Sorry, I can't. This year I'm confining myself to two things, the Girl Scouts and the polio drive, and trying to do them right."

When a salesman knocks at her door, she is polite but firm: "We make it a rule not to buy anything at the door."

Make it clear that you would like to say yes.

My friend Tim is in charge of adjusting claims made against clients his company has insured. Though his office approves millions of dollars in payments each year, Tim often has to say no. However, he always shows sympathy for the claimant. He explains that morally he may agree with him, but legally his hands are tied. In this case the company's legal department has ruled that the insured has no liability. He adds, regretfully, "We are unable to make a voluntary payment."

"People usually go away," he says, "feeling that at least we would like to be helpful."

Show that you have given the request real thought.

And *do* give it real thought. It is the brush-off that causes resentment. Clarence Lyons, formerly of the Bank of Commerce, once explained, "You must make the person see that you understand his problem, even if you have to say no."

Joe Stauffer, while at N. W. Ayer & Son, had to turn down many amateur ideas submitted for radio and television programs. He observed, however, that "most of the people seem satisfied if they simply get a chance to tell their story."

Say no by helping the person say no to himself.

One of my neighbors is an interior decorator. He never says no to clients when they want to incorporate impractical ideas into their homes. Instead he educates them to say yes to what he wants them to do.

He told me about a couple who built a modern home with floor-to-ceiling windows and open layout. The day came when the wife was to pick curtain material. She preferred flowery chintz—most inappropriate to the house.

The decorator suggested: "Let's go through the house and see just what you want your curtains to do." As they walked he talked about the functions the curtains would serve in each room, and what fabrics would harmonize best with the modern *décor*. By the time they were through, the woman had forgotten her enthusiasm for chintz.

In saying no, show what needs to be done to get a yes.

Should you try to cash a check at a Statler Hilton Hotel without sufficient identification, the clerks will not merely say no. They will helpfully suggest some way that you can cash the check locally.

The late Dr. William Reilly, author of *Successful Human Relations*, was a management consultant. Here is how he advised business executives to handle the person who wants a raise but doesn't deserve it.

"Yes, George, I understand your need for a raise. However,

to give it to you we will have to make you more valuable to the company. Now let's see what we need to do...."

Say no by showing that the request isn't reasonable.

By asking questions you may turn up circumstances which give you a legitimate excuse for saying no. Asking questions also gives you time to think up a graceful refusal.

Here is how a smart executive will say no, gently, to a poor idea without discouraging future ideas: "John, your suggestion has merit, but what would you decide if you were in my place?" He then weighs the pros and cons to show why the answer must be no.

Most important, say your no in the nicest, warmest way you can.

I learned one of my best lessons in the art of saying no nicely from my four-year-old daughter, Cindy. A few days ago a rather effusive elderly woman decided to become Cindy's pal. After fussing over the child a while she asked: "Cindy, would you like to come up to my house and play tomorrow?"

I held my breath as Cindy considered the proposal. I would have stumbled all over myself trying to reject such an invitation. Cindy's face broke into a big warm grin as she gave her one-word answer. She said, "No."

Her no was friendly and appreciative and good-humored. But it was so unmistakably firm that the woman did not pursue the matter.

SLOW DOWN!
by MEYER FRIEDMAN, M.D.

I SUSPECT that the most careful diet and best exercise program won't do much to check heart disease in America unless we do something, too, to check the frenzy of our lives.

My associates at Mount Zion's Harold Brunn Institute and I first came to that conclusion back in 1957—that it wasn't just the American diet, cigarette smoking or even lack of exercise that could account for the huge increase in heart disease. We knew that our ancestors ate about as much meat, milk and eggs, that they also smoked, and that not all of them kept in Olympic trim. But they were spared one trauma we are exposed to: the ever-accelerating pace at which we live.

What I am saying—and though it's controversial we have much data to support it—is that whenever a man struggles *too incessantly* to accomplish too many things in too little time, whenever he struggles too competitively with other individuals, this struggle markedly accentuates the course of coronary heart disease. If this struggle is not abated, I suspect that it does little good to alter one's diet, smoking or exercise habits, because the biochemical forces generated by this internal unrest are quite capable in themselves of bringing on cardiac arrest. They do this by elevating blood cholesterol, flooding the body with adrenalin-like substances and depleting normal reserves of life-sustaining hormones.

Would anyone dare to race the engine of his car, hour after hour, day after day, and expect this engine to endure as long as a machine more gently treated? Yet millions of Americans race their engines at a frightfully increasing pace—and leave survivors who are shocked at their abrupt breakdown. If, then, a reduction in the heart-attack rate is to be won, each person must cease to suffer from "Type A Behavior Pattern."

How can a person identify the presence of this pattern in himself? First, if he worries about being dreadfully behind in all the things he believes he should do. Or if he frets at delays in traffic and restaurants. Or if he frantically strives to obtain the things *worth having*—a lovely home, a better position, a college education for his children—at the expense of the things *worth being*—a lover of the arts, a devotee of the wonders of nature and mankind. Or if he finds himself obsessed with the acquisition of numbers—number of clients served, number of cases of merchandise sold. Or if he is irritatingly dissatisfied with his socio-economic status, no matter how high it might be. Or if he pays service with his lips but not with his heart to the ideals of love and friendship.

Many men will protest that, if they are to survive financially, it is absolutely necessary to accelerate ever more zealously the pace of their living. But after interviewing thousands of executives, shop owners, physicians, professors, clerks, truck drivers and salesmen, I am convinced that the only solid approach to socio-economic success and security consists of judgment, creativity and love. Who really ever went bankrupt because of an airplane's delay? Who ever lost a fortune because he used a calendar rather than a stop watch in making important decisions?

This Behavior Pattern A is doing far more than hastening the onset of coronary heart disease among many men. It is also "depersonalizing" them. It releases its victims from their jobs every afternoon to be slaves on parole to return to their homes, where they endure—but have forgotten how to enjoy and thrill to—the events of the day. Their children, sensing that their fathers are not hearing and feeling life as they are experiencing it, grow silent and too often sullen. Can we wonder that our young sometimes do not wish to emulate these harassed slaves, that somehow they rather pity them? Are these children really naïve in resenting a system that makes their father vice president of a bank but takes away his joy in the cherry tree that he himself planted a decade ago?

Is a surcease possible from the buffeting that this Behavior Pattern A administers to its sufferers? I believe it is, but the process of freeing oneself is difficult. Perhaps the first faltering step consists in a frank avowal of one's addiction to a mode of life which has been distorted by wanting too many things in too little time. Let one dare to ask himself, "Who will attend my funeral?" In his frenzied quest for status, this Type A man so denigrates himself that at his death few if any will feel his passing, and some—only too often his wife and children—will actually be relieved. He must begin to value friendship again. And the friends he seeks must be people who don't necessarily admire him as much as they love him.

But an almost lifelong pestilence cannot be expelled merely by a recognition of its presence and the acquisition of true friends. One must "re-see" one's family as a relevant and magnificently important aspect of the real life. Thus if a wife talks about her welfare activities, or if a child relates an anecdote that stirred him, the would-be convalescent from Pattern A must recognize that their affairs have as much importance as—perhaps even more than—his own activities.

Important, too, is the need to reevaluate one's use of time. One must ask repeatedly such questions as: What difference will it truly make in five years if the departure of my plane is delayed? Am I making so many appointments each day chiefly to achieve a greater mass of numbers? And at what particular number do I quit harassing myself?

Finally, there must be encouraged the search for beauty, and daily activities should be inspected with this question always in mind: Has anything happened to me or have I done anything which will have memory value? Asking this question is the first step toward the approach of beauty in life, because only beauty carries true memory value. I have repeatedly asked patients to bring me a list of those events which they frequently recall with pleasure. Not one of these lists ever contained a reference to the acquisition of numbers.

I believe that if each man would begin each day as if it were to be his last, he would search diligently for various essences of beauty and would not exclusively seek them out in the corridors of banks, stock exchanges and industrial plants. It is not too late, whatever your age, to attempt this quest.

KNOW THE RIGHT MOMENT
by ARTHUR GORDON

I SHALL never forget an interview I had with that late, grand old actor Charles Coburn. I asked a stock question: What does one need to get ahead in life? Brains? Energy? Education?

He shook his head. "Those things help. But there's something I consider even more important: *knowing the moment.*"

I remember staring at him, pencil poised. "What moment?"

"The moment," he said, "to act—or not to act. The moment to speak—or to keep silent. On the stage, as every actor knows, timing is the all-important factor. I believe it's the key in life, too. If you master the art of knowing the moment, in your marriage, your work, your relationship with others, you won't have to pursue happiness and success. They'll walk right in through your front door!"

The old actor was right. If you can learn to recognize the right moment when it comes, and act before it goes away, the problems of life become vastly simplified. People who repeatedly meet with failure are often disheartened by what seems to be a relentlessly hostile world. What they almost never realize is that time and again they are making the right effort—but at the wrong moment.

"Oh, these quarreling couples," I once heard a family-relations-court judge say. "If only they'd realize that there are times when everyone's threshold of irritability is low, when a person can't stand nagging or criticism—or even good advice! If married partners would just take the trouble to study each other's moods, and know when to air a grievance or when to show affection, the divorce rate in this country would be cut in half!"

The judge was saying what Charles Coburn had said: know the moment. Once, in a penitent mood, I asked my wife which of my smaller failings annoyed her most. "Your tendency," she said promptly, "to wait until we're about to walk into a party before telling me that my hair is mussed or my dress doesn't look quite right."

Good manners are often nothing but good timing. What is more annoying than to be interrupted in mid-anecdote? Who has not been trapped for what seems a lifetime by the bore who never knows when to leave?

Good timing sometimes means doing the unexpected. Down in Georgia a doctor who had arranged for a childless couple to adopt a baby was making some late night calls with his wife. Suddenly he said, "The adoption papers are all in order. Let's go to the hospital and get the baby for Ruth and Kenneth."

"At this hour?" cried his wife. "Why, they're not supposed to get the baby for several days. They'd be scared to death!"

"Ha!" said the doctor. "New babies have a way of arriving late at night—and first-time parents are always scared to death. It'll give them a good, normal start. Let's do it!"

So the baby was "delivered" in the middle of the night, the parents were flustered and excited, and it was indeed a memorable beginning.

For a long time I thought that timing was a gift, something you were born with, like an ear for music. But gradually, observing people who seemed blessed with the gift, I realized it was a skill that could be acquired by anyone who cared to make the effort. To master the art of good timing, keep five requirements in mind:

First, keep yourself constantly aware of how decisive timing can be in human affairs, of how true Shakespeare's insight was when he wrote, "There is a tide in the affairs of men which, *taken at the flood,* leads on to fortune." Once you have grasped the full importance of "knowing the moment," you have taken the first step toward acquiring a capacity for it.

Next, make a pact with yourself (a pact you will undoubtedly break at times) never to act or speak when driven by the whirl-winds of anger, fear, hurt, jealousy or resentment. These emotional monkey wrenches can wreck the most carefully developed timing mechanism. At a turbulent public meeting once I lost my temper and said some harsh and sarcastic things. The proposal I was supporting was promptly defeated. My father, who was there, said nothing, but that night, on my pillow, I found a marked passage from Aristotle: "Anybody can become angry—that is easy; but to be angry with the right person, and to the right degree, and at the right time, and for the right purpose, and in the right way—that is not within everybody's power and is not easy."

Third, sharpen your powers of anticipation. The future is not a closed book. Much of what is going to happen is determined by what is happening now. Yet relatively few people make a conscious effort to project themselves beyond the present, gauge future probabilities, and act accordingly.

This look-ahead capacity is so important in business that many corporations make it a main yardstick for job advancement. But it is just as important in running a household. Will Saturday be a good day for a trip to the beach? Better have cold cuts and sandwich bread on hand just in case. Is your widowed mother-in-law's health beginning to fail? Better face the possibility that she may have to move in with you or be placed in a nursing home. The art of good timing includes knowing the moment when present action will eliminate future trouble or gain future advantages.

Fourth, learn patience. You just have to believe, with Emerson, that "if the single man plant himself indomitably on his instincts, and there abide, the huge world will come round to him." There is no easy formula for acquiring patience; it is a subtle blend of wisdom and self-control. But one must learn that premature action can often spoil everything.

The final—and most difficult—step is learning to get outside yourself. Each moment is shared by every living creature, but each person sees it from a different point of view. Really knowing the moment, then, includes knowing how it looks to other people.

A great philanthropist, the late Mrs. John Dibert of New Orleans, told how one night in midwinter, as she was riffling through a magazine, her eyes were caught by a cartoon. In it, two ragged old women were shivering over a meager fire. "What you thinkin' about?" asked one. "About the nice warm clothes the rich ladies will be givin' us next summer," answered the other.

Mrs. Dibert, supporter of hospitals, donor to many charities, looked at the cartoon for a long time. Finally she went up into the attic, unpacked trunks, made bundles of warm clothes to be distributed the next day. She resolved to time her charity better, to give, as she put it, "to the ones whose needs are now."

As the Old Testament says, "To everything there is a season, and a time to every purpose under the heaven."

CHAPTER 3

Make Time For the Things That Count

MAKE TIME FOR LOVE

by JEAN BRADFORD

THAT Friday night, when my husband and I began to remember what we had begun to forget, seemed quite ordinary at first. He came in, hung up his coat, looked around the kitchen. Suddenly, he asked, "Where *is* everybody?"

I looked up from the six baked potatoes I was buttering. "They must be around somewhere," I said. "I've been tearing around so much today that..."

He disappeared, and I heard the record player click off. Then the phone rang, and I took a message that his meeting for that night had been canceled. He appeared again, nodded thankfully when I told him about the meeting, and peered once more into the corners of the kitchen. "There's nobody here," he announced flatly.

I stopped putting the potatoes on a platter and thought for a moment. "Oh—I'd forgotten. Jim's gone on an overnight with the Scouts. And didn't Ted tell me this morning he was going to Billy's for the night?" I took two potatoes off the platter.

"Bobby is at the Howes', and...and Jane is..." I stood absolutely still, counting in my head. "You know something?" I said weakly, looking over at the man I'd been married to s... e forever. "There's just the two of us...."

My husband and I are in what I suppose the sociologists would call our "middle period." You know: children half-grown, house half-paid-for; half the time we feel like young marrieds, half the time we feel we've never not been married. Actually, if we weren't so harried *some* of the time, we'd realize how happy we are *most* of the time.

Marriage starts out as a private affair, but it sure doesn't stay that way for long. That quiet country lane you strolled together, hand in hand, leads all too quickly into a kind of Times Square, where if any man and woman hold hands at all, it's more for mutual protection than for romance.

In this period of your life together, your early vow to "forsake all others, cleaving only unto thee" gets rewritten by business trips, car pools, committee meetings and fourth-grade plays. Now, for the sake of a lot of others, you're leaving more than cleaving. Before you know it, your intimate dinners for two have turned into boarding-house meals for a crowd. It's an exciting life, maybe, but a long, *long* way from the tea-for-two, me-for-you point you started from.

So, that "ordinary" evening when we found ourselves suddenly alone together turned out to be far from ordinary. We talked about a lot of things we don't usually talk about, and we didn't talk at *all* about the things we usually talk about. After our second cup of coffee, my husband leaned back in his chair and said happily, "I *needed* this. Both of us did."

So, ever since that fateful Friday we've been on the lookout for every kind of unexpected way to Get Alone Together. Which is very different from the everyday being alone together. *That* happens, for example, when you and your husband get up early some morning to put him on a plane. The house is quiet, but the outside world is still coming in strong. The plumber has to be called again today, as your husband reminds you; and the town planning board meets tomorrow night, as you remind him. There's a report card that needs discussion, and a development at the office that needs a decision. You are alone together, but you aren't really Alone Together. See the difference?

There are plenty of easy—and expensive—ways to get Alone Together. You can, for example, go off on a trip around the world, or take a few weeks at some resort hotel. But if these ideas seem too exotic, try doing what my husband and I have done: discover a couple of simple ways to Get Alone without blitzing your bank account.

Our children, once they got over their ill-concealed amusement at the thought that any two people as old as their mother and father would even want to be Alone Together, have been a great help. They often make an effort to synchronize their nights out—after we explained what an odd and pleasant feeling that simple coincidence had given us. And our oldest boy invented another successful technique, which we call the Don't Go to Meeting game.

He created it on the spot one night when I had fed everyone early because there was an important meeting that my husband and I were supposed to attend to learn something important about something or other. I had dressed up in my meeting clothes, and my husband had resigned himself to another dull evening, when my son said casually, "There's a great movie downtown. And since you're all ready to go out anyway . . .".

We went to that movie. We stopped for a hamburger afterward. It was quite late when we came home. We had a wonderful time, and we've done it often since. Maybe we haven't been hearing as much about whatever it is that they hold meetings to tell us about—but we've been hearing a lot more from each other, and we think that's important.

Of course we feel a little guilty when we sneak off this way. But it's good to feel guilty when you sneak off with your husband to Be Alone with him. A friend of mine, for example, told me that she once was with her husband on a weekend business trip that promised to be nothing more than just ordinary being alone together until something happened that turned it into the other kind of thing.

It was all because she began to giggle, for no reason at all, as she watched her husband sign the hotel register. The room clerk glanced up in some surprise, which made her giggle all the more. Her husband, embarrassed, practically pushed her into the elevator in so obvious a desire to get her out of sight that even the bellboy snickered. By the time they actually shut the door to their room, they felt practically unmarried. Which is a very good way for the very married to feel once in a while. In fact, to feel sinful without actually being sinful is one of the best and most unexpected pleasures of Being Alone Together. It's a little like getting the best of both worlds.

Though we can't often go on weekends together, my husband has come up with a simpler way to feel sinful without actually sinning that can make any housewife feel that she has left her household far behind. He takes me out for Saturday-morning breakfast. Now, we all know what Saturdays are like, what with the children and the chores and the concentrated chaos. But try starting your Saturday by walking into some steamy diner at 7:30 a.m., leaning possessively on your husband's arm, meeting the truckers' bored stares with your most womanly smile. All the rest of the day you can be a humdrum housewife, but during that warm hour in the diner you'll color yourself scarlet, and that's a good color for any housewife to be, just once in a while.

It takes practice, this Being Alone business. It's a little like riding a bicycle. You never really forget how, but if you haven't done it for years, you may wobble a little at first. When we are Alone Together, I still have to discard the first three things I think of to say. I mean, these are *not* the times to discuss the

dentist's bill or the burned-out motor in the washing machine
or the booth you said he'd build for the church bazaar.

Whenever I start on subjects like those, my husband just
smiles and doesn't answer, and I catch on. And *he* sometimes
forgets, too. For example, when he slows for an intersection,
he's likely to reach over and backhand me smartly against the
front seat because he thinks he's driving the nursery-school car
pool on his way to work. When that happens, I just hold his
arm and smile, and he begins to catch on, too.

The important thing, of course, is that we've *both* started
to catch on. We've caught on to the fact that our life together
is filled with more joy than either one of us deserves, but unless
we take time to be Alone Together we'll forget to appreciate
what we've got. You only need a little time. Time to listen,
and time to talk; time to love, and time to be loved; time to
remind yourselves that this busy, bewildering, crowded, crazy,
exciting and exhausting life you share began with just the two
of you. And it will end with just the two of you. And isn't that
the way you planned it to be?

WHERE HAVE ALL THE FATHERS GONE?

by LESTER VELIE

BECOMING a father is easy. *Being* a father is difficult. Ask these fathers. They know:

Commuter: Bruce M, a young advertising executive, rises at 6 a.m. while his two toddlers are still in bed. He travels 30 miles to his New York City office and returns about 7 p.m. When a big ad campaign is being mapped, he may return as late as 10 p.m. On many weekdays, the most he can do as a father is to look wistfully at his sleeping children before and after work. Weekends? Every other Saturday or so, Bruce locks himself up in his study with a bulging briefcase of work—or, to escape wife and children, flees to his office. Along with millions of other young husbands who follow the commuter way of life, Bruce is an "invisible father."

Pawn: Bill W, father of two adolescents, is a pawn in a corporate chess game. Every few years, he is moved to a new square in a new city, by a company which considers this "good for the company and for the career development of the individual." What this does to the development of Bill's uprooted children, the company doesn't say. Of course, Bill doesn't have to move if he doesn't want to. But Bill is a willing pawn, because he believes this is the way to become a corporate knight.

Good Citizen: Henry S, father of two pre-adolescents, heads his town's school board. He is on the board of the Community Chest and is a chief money-raiser during annual fund-raising campaigns. Henry also umpires Little League games and helps raise money to fight muscular dystrophy. At one point, Henry's wife said to him, "Do you realize that you haven't been in the house for ten consecutive nights, and I haven't been *out* of it?"

Henry's natural inclination to do good is exploited by his company, which tells its executives that such efforts are "good for our image." Unions also pressure members to "get involved," and so do most people's neighbors. Result? Millions of Henrys are involved with everybody's business except that of their own children.

48

Moonlighter: Joe H, father of five, pounds a policeman's beat by day and drives a cab by night to keep his family in groceries. Joe has lots of company, especially among those who work in low-paid industries. The Labor Department tells us that well over four million workers are holding down two or more jobs. The kids? "That's the old lady's job."

Low Man: Homer J, father of four children ranging in age from nine months to nine years, is low man on the job totem pole. Because of the color of his skin and his lack of salable skills, he is the last to be hired when jobs are plentiful and the first to be fired when jobs are scarce. Since the welfare laws of his state bar Aid to Families with Dependent Children if there's a man around the house, even if unemployed, Homer has vanished so that his wife and kids can eat. With unemployment over seven percent, there are a million fathers who are unable to bring home the bread—and therefore are unable to be fathers.

The father is the forgotten man of our society.

Not so long ago, sociologists and psychologists turned out reams of research papers on mothers virtually ignoring the father. Anti-family critics ignored him, too. They told us the family itself was outmoded and that new models—group marriage or permissive "kiss-and-tell" marriage—worked better. None of them suggested that the going model, which has served us for centuries, would work better if only the father had more of a chance to help.

Now, however, reports show the father's importance.

"The father's influence begins before the baby is born—by keeping the expectant mother in a good frame of mind," said psychologist Henry B. Biller of the University of Rhode Island. And it remains crucial, said Biller, even in those early years when the mother supposedly is the key parent. "In fact," Biller pointed out, "the father is probably more important than the mother to the healthy sexual development of both boys and girls.

"The father tends to differentiate considerably more than the mother between his sons and daughters and to reward his children's sex-appropriate behavior more than she does. Thus the father-deprived child is more likely to have problems in his relations with the opposite sex—stemming from a lack of a secure sex-role orientation. Studies of the family backgrounds of both male and female homosexuals reveal a very high incidence of father-deprivation."

Lack of adequate fathering may damage a child's school progress, too. Biller and a colleague studied 44 third-grade boys in the Cape Cod, Mass., area, whose involvement with their fathers ranged from two hours or more a day (high father presence) to less than six hours a week (low father presence). Biller reported: "The high-father-present group demonstrated a much higher level of academic achievement."

Why? Principally because, Biller believes, a warm relationship with a father fosters the self-confidence needed for achievement.

The family has the job of socializing the child, teaching him the values of the society and the rules of the game. Cornell University researchers found, in a study of middle-class boys, that when one or both parents are frequently absent from home, adolescents are likely to turn to each other for their values. Such children are more likely, said the Cornell report, to be "pessimistic about the future, rate lower in responsibility and leadership, and are more likely to engage in anti-social behavior."

In a companion study, Cornell psychologist Urie Bronfenbrenner added: "Perhaps because it was more pronounced, relative absence of the father was more critical than that of the mother."

Looking at evidence like this, behavioral scientists are beginning to tell us that the neglected—and neglectful—father is a root cause for many of our social headaches: youth crime, drug abuse, the counterculture's rebellion against marriage and the family—and, indeed, what the most recent White House Conference on Children called "a breakdown in the process of making human beings human."

To arrest this breakdown we must strengthen the traditional functions of the family. This in turn requires, as Prof. Lawrence H. Fuchs of Brandeis University puts it, "the restoration of father."

The American father's authority inside the family has been downgraded, Fuchs argued, because of the pressures on him from outside. Pressure on the American male begins in boyhood, when more is expected of him than of his sister, continues throughout college and graduate school, and reaches a killing pace in early manhood and middle age. At the turn of the century, the average man died two years and ten months earlier than the average woman. Today's average male dies six years earlier than the female.

While father is killing himself to succeed, authority inside the family devolves to the mother. It is she who must civilize the little savages; it is she who insists that they go to bed on time and get up in time to catch the school bus; that they pick up their things, help set the table, live in relative peace. And it is the mother who confers with the teacher, attends PTA meetings, arranges for doctor appointments.

The authority-relinquishing father does more than deprive his children of the strong hand needed in their upbringing. His preoccupation elsewhere may be interpreted as indifference by his children, and so stir up the bitterness that leads to alienation and rebellion.

What the American family needs most, says Fuchs, is a strong father—not an authoritarian tyrant, but a sympathetic, listening, authoritative parent. And one who is around to deliver the fathering services in person.

How do we bring father back into the lives of his children? Well, for openers, the father might try self-help.

For instance, a young Assistant U.S. Attorney I know, Frank C, whose job often keeps him at his office nights and weekends, manages, nevertheless, to be a visible father. He invites his wife and three-year-old son to town for periodic lunches and, on working weekends, takes them to his courthouse office, where the boy charges up and down the corridor on his tricycle. Or, during a break, father takes son to a nearby courtroom, sits the boy on the judge's bench and watches happily as he hammers away with a toy gavel.

Research reveals that it isn't only the quantity of time a parent spends in the home that counts; it's also the quality of involvement with the child.

One significant and unexpected force that is at work to bring fathers into the lives of children is the feminist movement. While the primary objective is, of course, to liberate the neglected mother, we are forced to do something about the neglected father, too.

For example: Maternity benefits are already here, and more companies are adopting them, thanks to a decision by the Equal Employment Opportunity Commission that pregnancy and giving birth are a disability, to be paid for by disability insurance. Now, feminists—and sociologists, too—are asking: What about "paternity benefits" as well?

Sociologist Alice Rossi of the University of Massachusetts put it this way: "Some changes have to be made regarding the father's role at birth time. Perhaps the concept of sick leave has to be expanded to allow a man to spend more time at home after his children are born and while they are very young."

Some American Federation of Teachers' locals in New Jersey have proposed parental-leave contract clauses that will permit a husband a reasonable amount of leave without pay when his wife has a baby. And the International Union of Electrical, Radio and Machine Workers has a contract with Textron, Inc., at Rochester, N.Y., which permits either parent—or both—leave-without-pay to care for a new child.

Perhaps if the feminists could breach that male stronghold, the company board of directors, they could put still more fathers to work on fathering. Inevitably, women directors would soon be asking such questions as, "Is this convention trip necessary?" Or, "What, transfer young Jones again? His kids have barely settled into their *present* school!"

The White House Conference on Children reported that business and industry, more than any other institutions in our society, determine the life-style of the American family—and so have the opportunity to determine the fate of the American family and the American child.

Employers alone, of course, can't be blamed for the American phenomenon known as the "rat race." The individual has his own drives, nourished by a lifetime of conditioning, to achieve. Nevertheless, there are some things the employer can do to help a man be a father.

Urie Bronfenbrenner suggested for example, that corporations could improve their chances of attracting executive talent by offering a new kind of fringe benefit: more leisure for family matters, created by reducing job obligations that require absence from home on weekends and evenings. Bronfenbrenner also suggested that employers should create more part-time jobs and give these jobs more status—so as to permit parents to spend more time with their children.

Fathers and fathering can be restored to the American family. The first step is to realize that healthy family life, and the health of our society, depend on it.

MAKE TIME FOR THE SIMPLE THINGS

by ELIZABETH STARR HILL

"TEACH US delight in simple things," wrote Rudyard Kipling years ago. Today, in our fast-paced world, we might add, "And help us simplify our lives to make room for them."

One evening I got home at 5:30 feeling tense and rushed. I was late starting dinner, and my husband and I planned to attend an early meeting. "Set the table!" I called to my teenage daughter as I walked in the front door.

At that moment, the lights went out—all over the neighborhood.

It was November 9, 1965, the night a great power failure darkened much of the northeastern United States. My daughter and 12-year-old son and I had no idea what had happened. Only when we turned on the car radio did we learn. "I guess Dad won't be out from the city for a while," my daughter said. "The trains aren't running." So, we would be more rushed than ever. . . .

But then I realized, with relief, that there would be no meeting if the blackout continued. I began to relax. Our spirits rising, the children and I found candles and lighted them. We made a fire, cooked hot dogs on a stick.

Without the distractions of radio or television, Andrea and Brad settled down right after supper to study by candlelight. I browsed through a beloved book of poetry I had been "too busy" to look at for years. My husband, Russ, got a ride out from the city and joined us happily in our cozy lair.

Later, after the children had gone to bed, Russ and I lingered by the fire, watching castles in the coals, reluctant to give up this unexpectedly lovely evening. "Do you suppose it could be like this more often?" he asked me wistfully.

"Of course," I assured him. "We'll just make an effort, and—"

"Maybe what we need is to make *less* effort," he suggested thoughtfully. "That meeting we were going to tonight, for example—we had nothing to contribute to it. We merely thought we should show up. I wonder how much of our time we fill

53

with things that don't count—things not important enough to justify the effort we spend on them."

Was it possible that if we slowed down the merry-go-round we might take new delight in the scenery? I decided to try.

Next morning, facing a complicated mélange of errand-running, drawer-straightening, silver-polishing, I realized that although November was more than a week old, I had not driven once into the countryside, as I loved to do in autumn. On impulse, I got in the car and headed north. The drawers would wait, but not the last golden leaves; not the bittersweet, nor the red berries of dogwood.

On a winding, wooded road, I stopped and got out to walk. The brush was dry beneath my feet, the sky very blue overhead. It was quiet, except for my footsteps.

A sudden rushing sound startled me. I drew back, frightened. Something ran across my path. My fright changed to delight: it was a magnificent pheasant, plumage gleaming iridescent in the sun, button-eye bright. The bird plunged into the brush and disappeared. In that moment a contentment filled me. I felt kin to every living creature, alive as I was meant to be.

It had become my habit to think of happiness in elaborate terms: the expensive evening, the distant trip. Now Russ and I began giving first place to tranquil recreations that our hectic pace had denied us: long weekend days of fishing, evenings spent reading aloud. Soon it seemed incredible that we had ever allowed such easily found joy to be squeezed out of our lives. Instead of a rare blessing, relaxation now became our natural climate, the fair weather in which the simple marvels of life are discovered and appreciated.

We Americans are inclined to overcomplicate happiness—and to risk losing it in the process. We deceive ourselves with countless pursuits that *should* be fun—the book we *should* read, the play we *should* see. Like the legendary opera-goer who mutters, "I'm going to enjoy this if it kills me," we tend to force so-called pleasure upon ourselves as though it were punishment.

Once a very kind, childless friend of mine took my boy off for a day of treats. He was about five at the time, and she planned everything conceivable for his enjoyment. They went to an amusement park in the morning, a circus in the afternoon, a fabulous restaurant for dinner, all with hardly a pause. When she returned him to me, well after his usual bedtime, he thanked her for a wonderful day. But as soon as she was gone, he added to me, "If I'd known what a wonderful day it was going to be, I'd have stayed home."

Children are wise enough to take happiness as it comes, without much contrivance—and they leave plenty of room in their lives for it. Writing about her childhood in *We Took to the Woods*, Louise Dickinson Rich recalled "a hole in the ground among the roots of a maple tree that grew in front of our house. It was moist and smelled of earth and water when I lay on my stomach and thrust my four-year-old face into it. It was everything that was mysterious and marvelous to me then, and somehow it still is."

Mrs. Rich determined that her own little boy would learn patriotism not through lofty precepts, but by knowing his country as "the place where he walked with his father down a woods road one evening and saw a doe and twin fawns; or the place where he came in from playing in the snow and found the kitchen warm and fragrant and his mother making popcorn balls." Homely memories, nothing grand about them—yet any child would cling to them with love.

We sometimes forget, as we grow older, the magic that is all around us. We let petty distractions blur our vision of enchantment. "Life is frittered away in detail," Henry Thoreau wrote. "Simplify, simplify . . ."

We have friends whose marriage was in grave danger last summer. They were quarreling increasingly; their one hope was that a vacation away from the city might bring them closer. Looking in the paper, they found an ad for a summer rental that sounded ideal: "Choice location, desirable road, all conveniences, easy living—"

When they went to see the place, they could hardly believe their eyes. It was a ramshackle old house at the end of a tiny dirt road in the middle of nowhere. The inside, although clean and neat, was downright primitive.

"What is this?" our friends stammered to the genial, pipe-smoking owner. "You advertised conveniences—location—desirability—"

"Yes, sir," the old man replied proudly. "You'll go a long way to beat this place for them things. Why, look out there! No main road for miles around. Sleep like a log, no traffic noises. As for conveniences—you got a broom, a couple of pots, and a stove that don't hardly work. No chance for heavy housekeepin'. No chance for gardenin', either—it's berry bushes and roses all over the garden, gone wild. That's what makes the livin' so easy," he beamed.

On a wild impulse our friends decided to take the house. They wrote us, saying no doubt they would be bored and back in town within a week.

But they did not come back. Halfway through the summer, we received a surprising letter from them, describing their life in that little house. They told us how they sat together on the porch in the evening, under the scramble of sweet-blooming roses, and talked—because there was nothing else to do. "We haven't talked like this in years." By day, they picked berries, sat lazily in a patch of sun to eat them, held buttercups under each other's chins.

The best news of all was scrawled large at the end of the letter. "We never would have thought of leaving each other if we had got *really* acquainted before. . . . Bless this house."

Bless any house where the things that count are not pushed out by those that don't.

Years ago, newly arrived in a strange town, I was invited through a friend to a dinner party at the home of a woman famed locally as a hostess. As I approached the handsome house, I wondered nervously if my outfit was appropriate, if I could hold my own in the knowledgeable conversation.

At my ring, the door was opened by a casually dressed, merry-faced young woman who put me at ease at once. "Come on out to the kitchen and keep me company," she urged. In the kitchen I found six other guests: one was making a salad, others were carrying dishes out to a prettily set table on the terrace. Before I knew it, I was pitching in, chatting and laughing with the others.

The dinner was delicious, the conversation gay. After we had eaten, Elsa, our hostess, brought a record player out to the terrace. Smiling, she asked us to listen "with our whole selves," and played a record of haunting flute music.

We gave ourselves up to the sweet thread of sound. Gradually we became aware of the flower scents from the garden, the slow upward sail of a great white moon, a gathering intensity of stars; of the night, the magnificent night of summer.

When the music ended, we resumed a soft conversation, our companionship strengthened by the rare experience we had shared.

"What a magical evening Elsa has given us," I murmured to one of the other guests.

"She always does," he answered. "Elsa understands the simplicity of joy."

The simplicity of joy...a precious understanding, and one which can belong to anyone, rich or poor, young or old. As Robert Kahn puts it in his book *Lessons for Life:* "When life is spent and all added up, what are the memories that warm our hearts? The happy laughter of a child as we swung him high; the joys of an after-dinner hour when we put aside the dishwashing for a bit and just sat and talked; the movie we saw together and the ice cream we enjoyed after it."

Fleeting fragments of wonder that can come to every one of us—delight, delight in simple things.

NOW...
WHILE THERE'S TIME
by ED BARTLEY

"MISSY," I called to my wife, "did you smear Vaseline on the top of my desk?"

"No, honey. Meghan probably did." Just like that. Calm. As I feared, she had missed the carefully honed, double-edged irony of the question. I *knew* she hadn't put it there. The question was rhetorical; its only function was to make clear to her that she hadn't done her job: defend my desk against the aggressor.

I abandoned the conversation. I would deal with Meghan, our 22-month-old daughter, later.

All that was yesterday. Today I sit here at that same rolltop desk, which I salvaged from a friend's attic two years ago, and stare at the blank sheet inserted in the typewriter. I wait patiently for ideas to come to me, exam questions on Herman Melville for a test I will give my English students tomorrow. My wife is off to a reunion somewhere, but I am not alone. Our two children keep me company. Ten-month-old Edward cooperates to some degree; he spends most of his day poring over a seemingly endless array of cards, tags, assorted pieces of paper, and a Sears, Roebuck catalogue which he tears apart page by page. Occasionally he leans out and flails madly at the piano, which he can just reach.

But it is Meghan whose plans have been destined from all eternity to clash with mine today.

She follows a daily routine that is both time-consuming and challenging. It includes certain basic tasks: Watching the "grop." (That would be the fish; I cannot explain the derivation of the word beyond that.) Sweeping the rug in her room and her crib. (Yes, Meghan sweeps her crib.) Sitting for a few minutes on the bottom shelf of the bookcase to determine whether or not she still fits there. (She fit yesterday and the prospects look good for tomorrow.) Checking periodically on Edward—joining him, perhaps, in a brief duet. Climbing in and out of the stroller for practice. Testing the sofa springs

Her constant companion through all this is Dumpty, a shapeless rag doll whose best days are far behind him. A year ago he was well-stuffed and bursting with good cheer. His perpetual smile endeared him to Meghan immediately. She provides his transporation; he provides her security. The filthier he grows, the more she seems to rely on his wisdom and homespun philosophy.

About a week ago my wife put Dumpty into the washing machine, hoping at least to make him recognizable. We were not ready for the emaciated creature that emerged. Dumpty had been disemboweled during the rinse cycle. My wife spent 20 minutes picking his foam-rubber intestines out of the machine. We thought that Meghan might discard this mere shell of a Dumpty. We were wrong. There was no detectable difference in her relationship with him, except that she found him easier to carry while performing her chores.

I can do my own work fairly well during most of these chores, and so I concentrate on Melville. ("Discuss the similarity of the alienation theme in *Bartleby the Scrivener* and Kafka's *Metamorphosis*.") I am on my way. Unfortunately, I had not counted on the arrival of the "bib-bibs." ("Bib-bibs" are birds. Again the derivation eludes me.)

"Bib-bibs, bib-bibs!" shrieks Meghan, her eyes alive with expectation. She insists that I come with her to the window.

"In a second. Just let me finish this question. Have you read Kafka's *Metamorphosis*, Meghan? You haven't? You'd really enjoy it."

The sarcasm leaves no mark, and she pulls me by the hand (two fingers actually) toward the bedroom window. I see myself as a slow-wit in some Southern novel, being led oaf-like to watch the bib-bibs. And we *do* watch them. They chatter incessantly and leap abruptly back and forth on the lawn just outside our apartment window. Meghan is absorbed, but as I watch them I wonder whether I parked the car under a tree last night.

Suddenly she bolts from the room (she seldom walks) and I hear her naked feet slapping against the wooden floor outside. She returns with Dumpty. She holds him up to the window, stretching him out by his two pathetic, triangular arms and whispering into his non-existent ear, "Bib-bibs, Hindy, bib-bibs!" Dumpty smiles. It's a much wider smile than it used to be.

I leave them in conversation and return to my desk. Within five minutes she appears before me, wearing her mother's shoes. She reaches up to the typewriter keys and depresses four of them simultaneously.

"No, thank you, Meghan. Daddy's seen your work. He'll do it himself."

She backs off. Out of the corner of my eye I can see her in the kitchen, watching the grop swim around in his circular world. I can see that the water in his bowl needs to be changed.

Back to the test. Determined. ("Discuss illusion and reality in *Benito Cereno*.")

"Don't even ask, Meghan. Not today." She stands in front of me with her shoes and socks in her hand. I know the pattern. First the shoes and socks. Then the stroller. And pretty soon we're in the park. She'll want me to pick her a dandelion, or a leaf from that tree the hurricane knocked over but didn't uproot a few years ago. And she'll clutch that leaf or dandelion the way she always does when we walk to the park. Oh, yes, I know the pattern.

She rests her head on my leg, just as she did when she first learned to walk. She used to bring her plastic comb or her hairbrush (once it was a toothbrush) and rest her head on my leg while I combed her hair. That ritual, however, ended after only a few months—much too soon for me.

Finally she leaves, and I watch her frustration as she sits on the floor and tries for several minutes to put on one of her socks. The art proves too elusive. In years to come she'll put on stockings or leotards with the ease and grace of a ballerina. But today a tiny pair of socks defeats her.

She sees me looking! Back to work. ("What is the significance of the motto carved on the bow of Benito Cereno's ship?")

She pats the wicker chair, the comfortable one we sit in together to watch TV or to read, and she hastily gathers her books—*The Poky Little Puppy*, *The Magic Bus*, *The Cat in the Hat*, even that ancient copy of *National Geographic* with the penguin on the cover... Good Lord, she's got them *all*.

With her free hand, she tugs at my sleeve.

"No, Meghan," I snap irritably. "Not now. Go away and leave me alone. And take your library with you."

That does it; she leaves. She makes no further attempt to bother me. I can finish the test easily now without interference. No one trying to climb onto my lap; no extra fingers helping me type.

I see her standing quietly with her back against the sofa,

tears running down her cheeks. She has two fingers of her right hand in her mouth. She holds the tragic Dumpty in her left. She watches me type, and slowly brushes the tip of Dumpty's anemic arm across her nose to comfort her.

At this moment, only for a moment, I see things as God must—in perspective, with all the pieces fitting. I see a little girl cry because *I* haven't time for her. Imagine ever being that important to another human being! I see the day when it won't mean so much to a tiny soul to have me sit next to her and read a story, one that means little to either of us, realizing somehow that it is the sitting next to each other that means everything. And I see the day when the frail, loyal and lovable Dumpty will vanish from the life of a little girl who has outgrown him.

I resent Dumpty for an instant. He's consoling *my girl*, and that is my concern, not his. She and I have few enough days like this to share. So the paper slips gently into the top drawer, the hood slides over the typewriter. The test will get done somehow. Tests always get done.

"Meghan, I feel like taking a walk down to the park. I was wondering if you and Edward would care to join me. I thought maybe you'd like to go on the swings for a while. Bring Dumpty—and your red sweater too. It might be windy down there."

At the word "park" the fingers leave the mouth. She laughs excitedly and begins the frantic search for her shoes and socks.

Melville will have to wait, but he won't mind. He waited most of his life for someone to discover the miracle of *Moby Dick*—and died 30 years before anyone did. No, he won't mind.

Besides, he'd understand why I must go right now—while bib-bibs still spark wonder, and before dandelions become weeds, and while a little girl thinks that a leaf from her father is a gift beyond measure.

PART TWO:

ORGANIZE YOUR MONEY

CHAPTER 4

Put Your Money to Work

THE SAVINGS GAMES
PEOPLE PLAY

SOME U.S. families have no savings accounts at all, and most of us who *do* save are dissatisfied with how much. Obviously, advice to "be thrifty" and "save regularly" is far easier to give than to follow.

Talk to successful savers, however, and you often find that they have devised some "game" to enable them to live on less than they bring home. The gold-star savers, of course, are those who, at any income level, when they sit down to pay their monthly bills, relentlessly write the first check to their own savings accounts—and then live on a scale that permits them to leave the money there. If you aren't ready for the pay-yourself-first system, here's a roundup of other techniques that people are trying these days, or have used successfully in the past, to help themselves save more.

Branded money. This is a variant on the old practice of emptying all your change into a cookie jar. A librarian says, "When I have too much change in my purse, I put the excess into my jewelry box. Every other month or so, I have enough dimes there to fill a bank dime wrapper—$5. Or quarters for a quarter wrapper—$10. Nickels, too. I deposit the wrapped money in my savings account, and it adds up."

A designer says, "John and I have a bank shaped like an old man with a beard. We call it our 'FOR' bank—For Our Retirement. It gets only Kennedy half-dollars. If anyone in the family—including our three children—gets a Kennedy half-dollar in change, it has to be set aside for the retirement account."

Windfall. Once in a while you receive a windfall—unexpected money such as that from an inheritance. But there are other windfall possibilities that might not occur to you.

When you've paid the last installment for a car, furniture, appliance, or on the mortgage, for instance, continue the "payments," but put them into your savings account. You've been managing without; continue for a while.

Any time you win at bridge, poker, or a bet (election, golf, lottery), earmark the winnings for your savings.

How about refunds on your income tax, for returned purchases, for expense-account outlays? An office-supply salesman deposits in savings every check reimbursing him for travel expenses. "It's money I've already spent," he says. "I don't miss it."

Did you get a salary raise? If you've got along fairly well without, tag the increase for payday savings. Ditto with earnings from a second job. A retired couple banks all Medicare refund checks.

A Washington financial editor took advantage of a literal windfall. When a tree fell on his garage during a windstorm, the insurance check came to $3400. To rebuild the garage, which he didn't use, would have cost $5000. Instead, he paid $850 to demolish it and banked the remaining $2550 as savings.

Swap-a-habit. Choose a temptation that you'd like to resist. Then kick the habit and bank the savings.

A plump investment broker gave up pastry at morning coffee breaks. His saving: $125 a year. An economist quit smoking two packs of cigarettes a day, stows $1.50 in cash in his locked file cabinet every afternoon. He'll end the year with an extra $500-plus.

Self-service. Choose a chore you're now paying someone to do. What do you spend, for instance, at the car wash? For furniture slipcovers? To change a faucet washer? To paint a room? Learn how to take on the job yourself. Put the actual market cost into a savings account.

Women can find a do-it-yourself hairdo, skip the weekly hairdresser and put the price—*cum* tips, travel, etc.— in the savings account.

Hiding. A teen-ager puts a dollar bill from each baby-sitting job into a book on her shelf without looking at the book title. At the end of the school year she goes through her books to collect her savings fund. (If you try this scheme, don't lend your books!)

Such savings games, of course, lose interest while you are accumulating, but how much interest can you earn if you *never* accumulate? On the other hand, some hide-and-save games can earn interest as you go. Simply ask your bank to automatically transfer a set amount—from $10 up—out of your checking account into a savings account every month. This is a service at some commercial banks, and often gets the money into savings before you'd get to the bank yourself—so it picks up more interest. Or you can sign up for a payroll-deduction plan for savings, government bonds or your company's investment plan.

Crash-save—for emergencies. You decide that for 13 weeks, say, you'll buy only absolute necessities. You'll cut out, or way down on, movies, concerts, weekend trips, taxis, restaurants, desserts, steaks, liquor, etc. You'll bring sandwiches for lunch, walk rather than ride any distance under one mile, stay away from sales. If you've been drawing $150 a week for cash, keep drawing it but put the saved $45 or $50 a week into a new account.

At the end of three months, blow yourself to a congratulatory celebration—$75, or more, and then resume your usual routine. You'll have more than $450 in the savings account, plus interest.

WE ALL NEED, in today's economy, a liquid, cash emergency fund that could help carry us through the loss of a job, serious illness or some other financial crisis. A recommended cushion is a sum equal to about six months of take-home pay. (The self-employed may need more, since their income is usually not fixed.) After that, build special savings for specific goals: a vacation trip, college tuition, a remodeled kitchen—whatever provides the greatest incentive.

HOW TO MAKE CREDIT WORK FOR YOU

by SUSAN JACOBY

ANN AND CLIFF JOHNSON decided to replace their 15-year-old refrigerator when it broke down for the second time. Although minor repairs might have kept it running until they'd saved up for a new one, they decided not to risk it. They bought a new refrigerator for $500 on a bank credit card and spread the payments over five months.

Between July, when they charged the refrigerator, and December, when they made their last payment, the price of the appliance rose to $580—an increase of 16 percent. Their finance charges for the five-month period were slightly over $15. They saved nearly $65 by buying on credit instead of waiting to pay cash.

Like millions of Americans, the Johnsons have learned how to make credit work for them in an inflationary economy. "Knowing when to use credit is as important as knowing when to resist it," says Esther Wynn, founder of a New York group called Debtors Anonymous, a service arm of the National Council of Negro Women. "For some people, those little plastic cards are like a drug that makes them forget the connection between the items they charge and the bills that follow. But for most people, credit can be a tool for making the best use of their money—especially when prices are rising so rapidly."

Credit allows you to take advantage of sales and avoid future price increases. As recently as the mid-1960s, when inflation was less than five percent, a buyer was well advised to save and pay cash for a major purchase such as a refrigerator. But today, with inflation running at a yearly rate of about ten percent, saving for a major purchase—even for a few months—can cost you a substantial amount of money.

The apparent inevitability of price increases is not, of course, a valid reason for making unnecessary purchases. When the Johnsons bought their refrigerator, they considered replacing an old air conditioner as well. "It had broken down a couple of times, too," Ann said. "We decided we could just do without

67

it if it finally gave up on us. But you can't say, 'Oh, I'll manage without a refrigerator if it conks out again.'"

Careful timing of purchases allows you to save money with interest-free credit. On some credit cards and store charge accounts, you can obtain six to eight weeks of free credit by buying just after the billing date and paying in full just before the due date. Suppose, for example, your account lists the 15th of the month as the billing date. If you charge new clothes on September 14, the bill comes early in October. If you buy the clothes on September 16, the charges won't appear until your November bill—and you'll have until November 11 or so to pay before interest charges will be added.

It's wise to use credit, rather than your own money, for bills that will eventually be paid by a third party. Hospitals, for example, may demand a deposit of several hundred dollars—even though the bill will eventually be paid by an insurance company. Many accept credit cards, then settle directly with the insurance company without processing a credit card bill. Credit cards should also be used for automobile repairs covered by insurance, and for various business and moving expenses that qualify for reimbursement from your employer provided that you receive payment before interest is charged to your account.

Finance charges on credit cards and installment loans are tax deductible. Many people overlook this—partly because monthly charges seem so small. But $5 a month on each of five bills adds up to $300 a year. And if you're in the 25-percent tax bracket, you could save $75 by taking the deduction. (To take this advantage you must, of course, itemize deductions on your tax return.)

The advantages of using credit can be enjoyed only by consumers who keep their buying under control. Credit counselors have a standard rule: Most people can comfortably afford to devote 10 percent of their take-home pay to installment debt (not including mortgage payments). If you pay out more than 15 percent, it may be time to cut back. More than 20 percent, and you're probably heading for trouble.

To avoid becoming overextended, counselors recommend these techniques:

• Keep a record of credit purchases. A surprising number of people have no idea how much money they owe—or even how much they spend on installment debt each month. That's why so many families are in deep financial trouble before they realize they might be overspending. Says one credit counselor: "If your credit spending creeps up from $150 to $200 a month, you probably won't even notice unless you have the figures in front of you."

• Do not accept more credit than you need. It's a good idea to keep a reserve of unused credit—perhaps $250 to $1000—for emergencies. But it's equally important to turn down credit you don't need. The first reason is obvious: Even though you think you'll never use it except in an emergency, the temptation is always there. The second reason is obvious: *Unused* credit is sometimes counted against you as a debt when you apply for a loan.

Karen and Joe McCarthy, who always pay their bills on time, were turned down by a Washington bank when they applied for a $6000 auto loan because they had $3000 of unused credit on two credit cards. The loan officer explained that the credit line counted as a debt in the eyes of the bank. "You could charge $3000 on those cards at any time," he told the startled couple. "That would affect your ability to repay our loan."

You can avoid access to credit you don't need by simply not returning the application forms. If you already have a credit card and the company notifies you that your credit has been increased (without your request), you should write the company to reject the additional credit.

• Don't expand your use of credit simply because your income has increased. Inflated costs and higher taxes seldom leave much surplus for increased spending. This is especially true for families that have recently acquired a second wage earner— a second salary increases family income more than the usual pay raise, but it also increases expenses. It's smart, therefore, to use extra income to reduce your debt level or to make cash purchases—but not to increase your credit obligations.

• Keep your credit cards to a minimum. Credit-counseling services advise their clients to carry no more than two cards. The more cards you have, the greater the psychological tendency to overspend.

• Never charge any item under $25. Credit counselors agree that a significant portion of consumer debt—especially for middle-income families—stems from small purchases that probably never would have been made if the customer had to pay cash. It may hurt to be paying in December for a winter coat bought in September—but at least you're still wearing the coat. It is much more depressing to be paying in December for cosmetics or toys charged at a drugstore in September.

• Always figure out how long it will take to pay for any major credit purchase and the total cost, including interest. When the Johnsons bought the refrigerator, they planned to make five monthly payments of $100 each—a schedule that resulted in modest interest charges. If they'd been able to pay only $25 a month, however, it would have taken nearly two years, and they would have had to pay substantial interest charges.

• Shop for loans. Interest rates on installment loans vary as much as three or four percentage points. On a three- or four-year car loan, that can mean a difference of several hundred dollars. Credit unions often offer better terms than banks or savings-and-loan associations. Small local banks are often a better bet than large commercial banks. Finance companies generally charge the highest interest rates.

Before making any major purchase on credit, it's important to compare the cost of financing it through several different lenders. Don't try to figure the cost in a lender's office; go home where you can do the arithmetic without the pressure of a sales pitch.

As long as inflation continues to erode our buying power, we will continue to be concerned about our debts. That concern can be our most effective tool for making credit work and avoiding serious debt.

CHAPTER 5

Take Charge
of Family Finances

BRING YOUR BUDGET BACK TO EARTH

by JEREMY MAIN

Keep six months' pay in the bank for emergencies.
Don't spend over 25 percent of your salary on housing.
Don't borrow more than 1½ times your monthly salary.

THIS kind of advice has been passed on to generations of Americans by bankers, brokers and other sages of the family budget. Even if such folk-wisdom rules were once justified—and some students of budgeting doubt that they ever were—they are inadequate and even misleading today. True, they may keep reckless spenders out of trouble, but family economists agree that universal guidelines are no substitute for tough-minded financial planning by each family to fit its own needs.

In learning to live with today's rapid inflation, people have to think differently about spending and saving. For instance, at current real-estate prices and mortgage-loan interest rates, one married couple may sensibly decide to put 30 percent of its pretax income into a house. Another couple, determined to reach financial independence quickly, may skimp on housing to save 20 percent of its income—four times as much as the average American puts aside—while a family with a low income and several children may have no choice but to spend most of its money on food and housing.

Nevertheless, discarding the old rules does not mean surrendering to budgetary chaos. A time of inflation requires more discipline than ever. Each family needs to lay out its own plan and stick to it. This calls for rethinking of major budgetary items, category by category.

Housing

MORTGAGE lenders still go by the maxim that most people should not borrow more than 2½ times their gross income to buy a house, or that mortgage payments, property taxes and fire insurance should not exceed 25 percent of monthly pretax income. The American Bankers Association suggests also that each family take into consideration rising taxes, interest, maintenance and fuel costs in setting a limit on how much house it can afford.

Faced with this kind of squeeze, many Americans just aren't buying houses—and those who do probably spend more than conventional wisdom would allow.

Any family not obliged to move and already owning a house that it likes, or halfway likes, should probably stay put until prices and interest rates ease up. An old, low-interest mortgage can be a great comfort today.

Borrowing

THERE are rules of thumb that say borrowers should not commit themselves to spending more than 20 percent of take-home pay on consumer credit. That much debt may be fine for people whose salaries are secure and likely to rise, and who don't have other heavy commitments. But anyone with a slow-to-change income who already puts 25 percent of his salary into buying a house would take too much risk if he committed himself to paying another 20 percent on installment loans. Still, many people, particularly if they shop for low interest rates, can certainly justify consigning over ten percent of income to installment payments for important purchases.

Savings and Investments

IF judicious borrowing is more appealing during inflation than at other times, it follows that cash and savings lose appeal at such times. Too much cash is more likely to be a liability than an asset, because inflation erodes idle cash. And the exigencies that an emergency fund was meant to cover a decade ago, such as loss of income during unemployment or unexpected medical bills, are now largely covered for many wage earners by company and government benefit plans.

The American Bankers Association says that the old rule of keeping cash on hand equal to six months' salary is thus obsolete. Still, everyone needs some sort of cushion. Three months' income should do, the bankers suggest. When an emergency outside the scope of the regular budget comes along, then what a person needs is not really cash but liquidity. Money in the bank is hardly the only source of ready cash. A $1000 Treasury note, for instance, can be converted into cash in two days, or you can borrow on life-insurance policies with cash surrender values, or on stock certificates.

Some financial advisers tell people to save regularly around three to eight percent of their income after taxes, while others recommend five percent of their gross income. But such rules are no more sacred than other financial maxims. A bachelor with a secure, high-paying job and a rich father may have no reason to save anything. A man with six children, a large mortgage and an unsteady job should probably save every nickel he can.

Discouraging though it is to invest and save today, no family finance counselor would recommend that a family quit putting money aside. As inflation eases up, saving and investing will be more rewarding. Even at present, they are the only way most people can pay for certain big items in their lives—the down payment on a house, a college education, a trip to Europe, an extra measure of financial independence.

Consumption

THESE days, everybody complains about how increased food prices and other eruptions of inflation have hurt the family budget. Shoppers are less likely to remind themselves that disposable personal income, on the average, has steadily climbed faster than prices. To the extent that family budgets are bursting, it is as much the result of growing wants and fancier tastes as of inflation. How many people have said to themselves that if only they earned another $5000 or $10,000 a year, they could live the life they wanted without worrying about money? Experience indicates that this hope is pure illusion. Americans are so used to scaling their consumption upward that almost any increase in income is quickly soaked up.

Prof. Richard L. D. Morse, of the department of family economics at Kansas State University, thinks that this is a good time for people to change their attitudes on spending and buy only what really counts. It can be done. According to the Department of Agriculture, Americans spent about 2½ percent *less* in real dollars on food in 1980—when food prices *rose* 10.2 percent—than in 1979. This was accomplished partly by eating less and partly by downgrading diets—for instance, by eating more vegetables and less steak.

Heinz B. Biesdorf, professor of consumer economics

Cornell University, has similar advice. "We let huge amounts of disposable junk pass through our lives," he says. "We should buy only things that are essential to the family's well-being or employment—and take care of them once we have them." A car needn't be traded in after three years; properly maintained, it should run well for seven or eight years. Does the husband really need that 15-dollar tie? Not unless dressing well is part of his job.

Finding enough money to buy all the things a family wants is one of those problems that never do get solved in most households. Morse says it is almost inevitable that a family budget will be tight. If you are struggling with your budget, he says, "don't feel guilty because you are not doing all that other people say you should be doing." If you are not struggling, he adds, it probably means you are not really living.

BARTER:
GETTING WHAT YOU WANT
WITHOUT MONEY
by CONSTANCE STAPLETON

EIGHT YEARS AGO, newly divorced, I had to find a way to support my five children (then aged 13 to 18) and myself. I had no credit, no savings, no job and rusty work skills. How could I keep my family together? The solution turned out to be barter.

Food was our first priority. Using what money we had, I bought seeds and we planted the largest garden we could manage. Next, I took a look at our ancient station wagon; it needed work. What could I use for money? I decided to visit the repair-shop owner and find out.

"I don't have any money," I began. I paused, feeling like a fool. But it was too late to turn back, so I plunged in deeper. "Is there some other way I could pay for the work?"

"I have all the help I need," he said.

"Then what else do you need?" I persisted. At that point I would have swept floors, cleaned carburetors—anything. "What do you *hate* to do that I could do for you?"

He did a double take, grinned and said, "You want to know? I hate to collect overdue bills. I know most of my customers, and I don't like to ask them for money." He had come up with the answer. He gave me a list of names, numbers and amounts, and each call I made reduced my bill; a percentage of what I collected was also deducted. At the end of the summer, I had telephoned my way out of the bill and into credit.

In the meantime, our vegetable garden was growing. We traded off the surplus for homemade sausage, handmade pots and dandelion wine. We swapped the wine for plumbing.

That year, on a net income of $3000, we survived in style. Since then, I've worked my way out of debt and discovered the joys of barter.

Barter is meeting needs—and everyone needs something. When you're able to supply it, you can ask for almost anything in return. Besides trading goods, you can barter time, talent,

76

space, service, information and favors. If you've ever car-pooled, traded baby-sitting or swapped favors, you've already bartered. In fact, once you stop thinking "money" and start thinking "value," there's no end to what you can get.

Barter also has some unexpected side benefits. Because few deals are in writing, barterers tend to be trusting souls. Accustomed to betting on themselves, they're willing to bet on others. That first summer whenever people said, "Okay, it's a deal," they were telling me, "I believe you can do it." At the time, I wasn't sure I could. With needs pushing me into more and more barter contracts, however, an emotional-support system came into my life, one lovely thread at a time.

As the cost of living goes up and the value of the dollar goes down, more Americans are learning to barter. Here are some tips to get *you* started:

1. Add up your assets. Make lists of everything you no longer need or don't use full-time. A spare room? Trade it to a student for housekeeping or lawn care. Time? Baby-sit your way to anything you need.

List things you like to do. Did you once win an essay contest? You may have a talent for writing that you can barter. Do you sew? Sewing is a skill others will barter to get.

If you think you have no talents, think again. Are you a phone-aholic? Ask the manager of a country club if you can canvass for new members in return for a free membership, or take calls for a local business during off-hours in exchange for credit.

2. Decide what your barter is worth. Do you have more time or more talent? Talent is worth twice as much as time, but you sometimes have to put a low rate on it to get started. The more time you have to barter, the more interesting deals you can develop. Check ads in the local newspaper and make phone calls to find out the value of what you have to barter. If you're still unsure, try letting the other person set the terms—you might find them easier to meet than you thought.

3. Find your barter partner. Keep in mind one rule: no matter what a person has, there's always something else he or she needs. Sometimes the other party doesn't know he has a need until you bring it to his attention. For example, I needed housing repairs but couldn't afford the contracting fees. One builder did great work but used jarring colors that defeated his craftsmanship. I explained to him what repairs I needed, adding that I had no money but did have good taste and color sense, which could make his houses more attractive and thus more valuable. It turned out that he was color-blind. He repaired my house in exchange for my selecting roofing, paints and carpets for a number of his model homes.

4. Agree on terms in advance. Answer such questions as: What conditions are necessary to complete the barter to everyone's satisfaction? Where will the work take place? Who will pay for materials? Who delivers? Is there a time limit?

If time is not crucial, you may be able to get more favorable terms. I once wanted a furniture restorer to strip a corner cupboard. He was so good he could name his own terms, but when I offered to let him take as long as he wanted, he accepted my terms.

Instant deals seldom work as well as those you plot, plan and practice. When I craved a rocker in an antique shop, for instance, I made several visits before I figured out what the owner needed. (Remember: always deal with the person in charge.) Using construction paper and yarn, I designed price tags shaped like a "Bird in Hand" (the name of his shop). He was so eager to get them he let me take the chair home to sit in while I finished 200 tags to pay for it.

5. Keep your bargain options open. Items are worth different things to different people. If you don't like the first offer, shop around. Or see if you can get a better deal by asking for sweeteners like a trial use or, if there are working parts, a guarantee. Some people say no simply because they don't know how to bargain. If you get a no, back off and try to come up with more interesting terms. You'll eventually make a deal.

Be flexible. I once turned down a Victorian stair railing because I had a Georgian-style house. If I had taken the railing, I could have traded it for the woodwork I did need.

A baby-sitting co-op can be set up with members sitting for one another. Food co-ops are also popular. If you have an unused room, let the group use it for a supply depot in exchange for free food or a discount, or receive a discount in return for hours worked.

Accept money. A teen-ager I know sold a litter of 13 puppies for $10 each, bought a horse and saddle for the $130, traded that for a go-cart and $200, swapped that for a motor-bike, which he then traded in on a car.

6. Figure a way others can pay for what you want, If you yearn to learn the latest dances, Japanese flower arranging, or the art of self-defense—find someone who does it well and suggest he or she teach a class. Then offer to round up paying members in return for attending free. This formula also works in arranging children's lessons.

If you want a car, decide if you really have to own it. A man I know has the use of three cars: a sedan in return for baby-sitting, a convertible for letting a friend use his apartment and a truck for tending a shop on Saturdays. In addition to saving the initial investment, he has no maintenance or insurance costs.

7. Pass it on. The more people who are hooked on barter, the easier it is to arrange what you need. And the more you practice, the easier it gets. If you're hesitant to approach neighbors, start at home. Once your children learn to barter, they'll check the alternatives before asking for money. For example, my 15-year-old son talked county officials into giving him office space for his drama group in exchange for their producing plays for the summer playground.

Another son, at college, became manager of an apartment house in return for a free two-bedroom apartment. He then traded the unused bedroom to another student, who bought the food and did the cooking and cleaning.

You never know where barter will lead. But one thing is sure: it will bring new dimensions and friends into your life. The next time you want or need anything, don't reach for your wallet or checkbook. Instead, look the owner in the eye, light up your grin and say, "I like it. What will you take in barter?"

EDITORS' NOTE: The value of goods and services acquired through barter is considered taxable income by the Internal Revenue Service when the barter involves goods or services that participants deal with in their professional lives—*i.e.*, groceries that an accountant gets in return for doing the grocer's books would be considered taxable income, and vice versa. Exchanges between friends and neighbors of services such as household chores and yardwork are not taxable.

HOW TO GET YOUR FAMILY OUT OF DEBT

by ALICE LAKE

CONSUMER debt—the amount that U.S. families borrow for large purchases such as cars, refrigerators, furniture—has spiraled upward from $90 billion in 1965 to a record $311 billion in 1981. Repayment of these consumer loans—plus the money that families have borrowed to buy a house—now slices 21 cents from every dollar that a wage earner takes home.

But more and more families can no longer find that 21 cents. One in 25 homeowners is at least a month tardy in mortgage payments. The delinquency rate on installment loans reached its peak in 1980. Personal bankruptcies are running 35 percent above 1979. Money worries are showing up in frayed tempers, marital problems, edgy children.

Some couples were caught in a credit crunch even in a flourishing economy. Others who borrowed yesterday can't pay today because their working hours have been cut back or they have lost their jobs. Meanwhile, prices spiral. Part of the squeeze is also traceable to the notion held by some that flashing a credit card isn't really spending money at all.

Fortunately for the family smothered by debts, there are now non-profit organizations called consumer-credit counseling services, and from their expert experience the rest of us can learn how best to keep out of debt. The first of these community-sponsored groups—Family Debt Counselors—was formed in 1958 in Phoenix. Today there are over 200 scattered through 19 states, the District of Columbia and Canada. The largest: Credit Counseling Centers of Southfield, Mich., serving over 4000 families, with 15 branches in Michigan.

A credit counselor helps a family in debt to cut spending, devises a plan to pay off the creditors, and then convinces the creditors to accept the plan. "Our function is to help people help themselves," says Ron Kidd, Director of Client Services at the Michigan Centers. "We don't offer an easy way out. But if they make the effort, we can point them toward a less destructive life-style."

At an initial conference with husband and wife, the counselor lists the couple's income, expenses and debts. The couple hand over their credit cards, which the counselor literally cuts to ribbons—a symbol of their vow to avoid taking on further debt.

The Consumer Credit Counseling Service of Greater Denver gives this profile of its clients: Three out of four are married. Over half the couples, both husband and wife hold jobs. They are young, usually with two school-age children. Two out of five are buying their own house. Not counting the mortgage, they owe their creditors more than half of their annual salaries, and one married couple in six owe more money than they earn in a year.

"Often couples come in, each with a pile of credit cards that the other knows nothing about," said Galo Cabrera, a New York City counselor. The admissions they are obliged to make in the counselor's office sometimes set off marital explosions.

"We try to show them that the debts are not 'mine' or 'yours,' but 'ours,'" Cabrera said, "and that they have to pool their dreams and their resources to get on their feet again."

Not every couple swamped by debt is either impulsive or immature. Blend together the lure of easy credit, an urge for middle-class luxuries, sloppy budgeting and ignorance about the hidden costs of owning a house and you can get into deep trouble fast. Therefore, debt counselors offer this advice:

• *Know what you earn.* When they plan a budget, many people confuse gross salary with take-home pay or count overtime pay as regular income. Windfalls such as bonuses, profit-sharing and tax refunds are not steady income either.

• *Know what you spend.* When couples estimate their annual expenses, they're usually low by more than a thousand dollars. Many can't even account for the ten-dollar bill they had yesterday. One expert suggests that a large sheet of white cardboard be tacked up in a busy part of the house so that everyone in the family, including the children, can write down every penny spent daily.

• *Don't use more credit than you can afford.* A rule of thumb is: don't borrow more than 15 percent of your annual income, excluding the mortgage. If take-home pay is $16,000 a year, and a couple already owe $2200, they're close to their credit limit. Money problems often become acute when debt equals one fourth of income.

• *Learn how to purchase credit.* Although federal law requires that you be informed of the annual interest rate in any credit arrangement, few borrowers understand it accurately. If you're shopping for a color TV set, for instance, and the price tag reads $500, would you buy it if you knew that the final installment-payment cost would be upward of $700?

Credit costs vary greatly: from about 12 percent a year for a loan from a credit union, to 15–21 percent for a loan from a bank, to 18 percent for bank or oil-company credit cards, to 20 percent and up for installment purchases, to 25–36 percent from a finance or small-loan company. And the pay-back time is, of course, crucial. If you repay a $1000 loan in four years rather than two, you wind up shelling out doubled interest.

• *Be alert to danger signals.* Long before you're in a real bind, you should react to signals that may allow you to reverse the trend. Watch out, for example, if you find yourself paying the telephone company one month while putting aside the utility bill until the next. You make another mistake when you seek protection from the bill collectors by negotiating a consolidation loan. This means exchanging five small debts, for example, for one large one (often at higher interest).

IF YOUR debt situation has become really chaotic, your best bet is to call the local consumer-credit counseling service promptly. Steer clear of commercial outfits that offer to clear up your debts for a fee ranging upward of ten percent of the amount you owe. These commercial debt-poolers or pro-raters have been outlawed in 29 states and the District of columbia. A bank, finance company, social agency or Better Business Bureau can direct you to a reputable debt adviser. Or write to the National Foundation for Consumer Credit, 1819 H Street N.W., Washington, D.C. 20006, for a list of nonprofit services throughout the country.

Many of the non-profit services charge a small fee, generally between $2 and $12 a month, for the debt repayment program there is no charge for counseling. Apart from this, a client's only obligation is to maintain good faith. Usually a couple promise not to undertake further debt without consulting the counselor and to pay him a monthly sum to pro-rate among the creditors. Such a contract is non-binding, but couples who violate it are usually dropped from the program and their creditors are notified.

Perhaps the best advice of all is offered by a young husband who finally realized that he and his wife were spending $100 a month more than they earned. "If we're smart enough to earn money," he says, "we should be smart enough to know how to spend it."

35 WAYS TO CUT YOUR COST OF LIVING
From NORWALK SAVINGS SOCIETY BOOKLET

Loans and Interest

• Borrowing against money you have in your savings account is the cheapest bank loan you can get. The interest rate is lower than most loans and your savings continue to earn interest—which makes the *net* loan rate lower still.

• If you're considering major home improvements, the best deal you can get is an FHA Title 1 loan (available up to $10,000 through many banks).

Food Budgets, Supermarkets

• When food shopping, remember that there's nothing spooky about store brands. Often they are equal in quality to leading brands; almost always they are more economical. Figure you'll save about nine percent ($1.79) off a $20 grocery bill by buying house brands. When you include cleaning products and all the other non-food items in your shopping basket, you can save as much as 20 percent.

• Three quick tips from home economists: frozen orange juice is cheaper than bottled or fresh; peas in a can cost less than peas in a pod; dry milk is cheaper than bottled and often just as good for cooking.

• Lower-grade foods are equally as wholesome and nourishing as those of a higher grade. The difference lies in appearance (and price!). Try grade-B eggs for cooking and baking; lower-grade vegetables for casseroles and stews.

• Cents-off coupons save you money only when you can buy an item you want at a lower price than comparable brands.

• It's where you shop that counts. On a $50 weekly food budget, you'll save up to $500 a year by comparison shopping and picking the best buys among stores in your neighborhood.

• Experts suggest Wednesday or Thursday night as good times to shop—when stores are not crowded and there's a plentiful supply. Be sure to go after you've eaten, please!

• You'll spend more money for every minute over half an hour

that you're in the supermarket. Pain in the neck or not, it pays to make a list; preferably according to the layout of the store.
• Buy bulk "economy" sizes when you can use them. By law, economy sizes of non-food items must save you at least five percent over other sizes of the same brand. Often they save you anywhere from 15 percent to 20 percent.
• You can save on soap and still be clean. Just take the cakes out of their wrappers and let them dry several weeks before using. Surprising how much longer they last.

Laundry, Drugs and Fabrics

• Double up two small wash loads in your dryer. Washing machines are a bargain; they cost two cents a load in electricity to run. Dryers cost as much as 15 cents.
• For prescriptions you have refilled regularly, have your doctor prescribe the largest supply he deems advisable. Then comparison shop. Often a regular pharmacy can match or beat a discount drugstore's price when you're getting several months' supply at once.
• Some pharmacies give a discount to senior citizens. But you've got to ask to get it.
• If you sew, you can save yourself a bundle. Figure that you can duplicate any dress you see in a store—the same fabric, trim, buttons, including pattern—for half the price, if you make it yourself.

Plumbing, Telephones

• Storm windows are among the best investments you'll ever make. In as little as six years, they pay for themselves in lower heating bills; after that, it's like getting a 13-percent dividend on your investment every year. If you have air conditioning, leave storm windows on in summer. You'll keep 30 percent more of the cool air you are paying so dearly to get.
• Remember the number 60. It's the optimum thermostat setting when you're away for more than a day—high enough so pipes and plants won't freeze (and neither will you when you come home), low enough to save you some real money. (It's always a good idea for a neighbor to check the thermostat when you're away for any period of time.)
• Running the air conditioner at a steady temperature all day costs less than turning it on and off, up and down.

- You pay extra for soaking in the tub. It takes seven gallons of hot water for a five-minute shower as opposed to 12 gallons for an average bath.
- It's money down the drain if the hot-water faucet drips. A tiny leak—one drop per second—costs you $5 a year. One that fills a cup in 10 minutes (most do) costs $25 a year.
- You've saved to go on vacation; why not save while you're away? During the warm months, shut off the water heater. And turn up the refrigerator a couple of degrees.
- If you are going to be away for more than two weeks, check with your telephone business office for the vacation service available to you. In most cases, you will save money by temporarily suspending your telephone service.
- Cut your phone bill 20 percent to 80 percent—and more— by dialing your long-distance calls.

Postage, Cars, Sales

- What can you buy for five cents these days? A certificate of mailing—which is all you need if you just want legal proof that a letter was sent. Use certified mail (30 cents plus postage) or registered mail (95 cents plus postage) if you want proof that it was received. The extra charge for registered mail assures you of special handling during the delivery period.
- First-class mail is usually every bit as fast as airmail. Although airmail receives preferences in loading and in handling upon arrival, first-class mail travels on a space-available basis and more often than not arrives in the mailbox the same time as airmail. Just be sure it's mailed before 4 p.m.
- You can insure a package for any amount you want—the post office can use every cent you want to give it. But rest assured that you won't collect more than the actual value of the contents.
- Best time to trade in a car (unless it's a lemon) is early in the fourth year of ownership. Otherwise you might as well drive it through five full years.
- You can bargain better if you know the dealer's cost for a new car. You can get a rough idea by taking 23 percent off the sticker price of full-size cars, 18 percent off of intermediates and 14 percent off of compacts and sub-compacts. (This works only for domestic cars.) Figure the dealer will be happy getting $150 over cost on a new car. Depending on your stamina and bargaining skills, he might settle for less.

• If your teen-ager has completed an accredited driver-training course, you'll get on the order of 10-percent relief on the huge insurance premiums you pay to cover a young driver. A teen-ager who's a scholar is doubly smart. If he maintains a B or better average in school, many insurance companies allow you as much as another 10 percent off your car-insurance premiums.

• Ask for an insurance reduction if your son or daughter is at school at least 100 miles away and doesn't have a car there. Also if he or she is in the service.

• Tests show there's little difference in quality or performance among gasolines. Save a bundle by buying the cheapest available.

• It's penny wise and pound foolish to buy anything less than the best-quality oil for your car. The way to save is to buy top-grade oil by the gallon and put it in yourself. Unbelievably easy to do, and you'll cut your oil bills by 50 percent.

• Air is free—so check your tire pressure regularly. Under-inflated tires waste as much as six percent in fuel and accelerate tire wear.

• Regular tune-ups are a must, when you consider that they will save you as much as 15 percent in fuel.

• Learn the price-reduction lingo: "regularly" means the merchant has reduced his own price and the item is going back up in price right after the sale; "originally" means there may have been intermediate reductions in the price and there may continue to be price reductions on the item; "$X value—our price $Y" means that the merchant's sale price is lower than that in the general trade area; "comparable value" means it's similar in grade or quality to higher-priced goods; "if perfect" means it's irregular. Don't be fooled by "list price vs. our price"—most merchants in metropolitan areas sell below list price anyway. Shop around.

CONSUMERISM is "in"; it's smart to save. Ask questions. Don't be afraid you'll seem cheap. You earn nothing if you don't try; you earn money and respect when you do.

CHAPTER 6

Take Charge
of Your House

TWELVE
MONEY-SAVING TIPS ON
MAINTAINING YOUR HOME

by ROBERT O'BRIEN

EXPOSED TO sun and rain, freeze and thaw, wind, and day-to-day use, a house depreciates. Shingles blow off. Siding rots. Masonary cracks. Pipes burst. Termites feast. For a house, that's life. For you, it's expensive. But taking care of little troubles before they grow into big ones can hold costs down. Here are some helpful precepts and procedures:

• Know your own house. Try to get a complete set of blueprints and a plot plan, which is a map of your lot showing placement of water pipes, utility lines, septic tanks or sewerage outlets. If you have trouble with any of these, the repairman won't have to spend hours probing or digging up the lawn to locate them. Find out where the main water valve is (usually in the basement close to where the water supply line enters the house). Tag it, and turn it off once or twice to make sure you can shut the water off in case of a burst pipe or hot-water tank.

• Pay your electrician for an hour of his time to have him explain where the main power switch is and how to operate it, and which fuses and circuit breakers control which circuits. Have him tag them, and explain what to do if a circuit shorts out. If your lights dim when the furnace kicks on, or if your TV picture shrinks when you press down the toaster handle, it's a sign that your wiring system is inadequate, overloaded and a potential fire hazard. The cost of having it made safe and adequate is nothing to what it might cost if you don't. At least once a year have your heating and air-conditioning system and chimney checked professionally, for cleaning, adjustment or repairs.

• To save yourself costly professional help for minor repair work, you need certain aids. One is a good reference book that will tell you simply and clearly what to do, why and how. Another vital aid is a hardware-store man you can trust to give you good advice and sell you quality tools and products. Pick him almost as carefully as you would a doctor.

90

• Learn some elementary plumbing. Otherwise, you will find yourself paying substantial service charges to a plumber to replace a five-cent washer or fix a drain you could have cleared yourself in two minutes. You'll need only a few simple tools, such as a medium-sized monkey wrench, a screwdriver, a pair of pliers, a spring-steel plumber's "snake," and a "plumber's helper"—a rubber suction cup fitted to a wooden handle.

If you hear a banging or hammering in pipes whenever you turn off a faucet, don't ignore it and hope it will go away. (No problem involving home maintenance will *ever* go away, until it's fixed.) It is caused by excess vibration, and has been known to split pipes wide open. But don't call the plumber until you've checked the exposed lengths of pipe, and their metal straps and mounting brackets. If a pipe is loose, or sags, firmer support may arrest both vibration and noise.

• "Hard," mineral-laden water clogs pipes with scale deposits, coats the inside of hot-water tanks, stains toilet bowls, discolors laundry. To cut the damage it does, install a water-softener. In the long run, it will pay off.

• If yours is one of some 25 million American homes equipped with a septic-tank disposal system, you can avoid costly repairs by keeping it free of paper towels, rags, hair, string, cigarette butts and other foreign matter. Never empty cooking oils, fats or coffee grounds down the kitchen drain. Put them into cans or other containers, and throw them out with the garbage. Have the septic tank cleaned about every three years—preferably in warm weather (opening it in cold weather can disrupt its decomposition cycle).

• If your driveway is concrete or asphalt, cracks should be filled in and repaired before the onset of winter. Otherwise, water will enter them and, alternately freezing and thawing, will break up the surface. You can protect it against frost damage with a waterproof, blacktop sealer that you spread with a push broom. A five-gallon can of sealer will cover 200 to 300 square feet. It's even possible to repair sizable breaks in the driveway surface, using premixed, asphalt-patching compound. No heating is required.

• For comfortable *and* economical furnace operation, maintain an average household temperature of 68°F. instead of the nearly 75° that's customary in most homes. Government experts say that this procedure alone will cut about ten percent off your fuel bill. They recommend lowering the thermostat 10° at night. Other ways of cutting fuel costs: Shut off heat supply to unused rooms and to rooms being ventilated; keep the chimney damper closed when there is no fire in the fireplace.

Cold air can hold less moisture than warm air. For this reason, old, leaky houses are likely to be dry. To *raise* humidity, tighten up the house with weather stripping and insulation. If necessary, buy a humidifier.

New, tightly built, small houses tend to be too humid; water runs down the windows, the doors stick and, if there is no proper moisture barrier in the walls, there may be damage to the house. To *lower* humidity, try ventilation. Install ventilating fans in the kitchen and bathrooms, and give the clothes dryer an outdoor vent. If necessary, invest in a mechanical dehumidifier. But remember: neither high nor low humidity affects the health or comfort of a healthy person very much.

• Damp stains on your basement walls can be caused by seepage of water *through* the walls, or condensation *on* the walls. If it's seepage, you have the relatively complicated problem of finding out where the water is coming from and eliminating the source—faulty drainage from gutters and downspouts, or perhaps improper foundation grading. If the damp spots are caused by condensation, however, the cure is often simple—merely a matter of promoting the circulation of dry air by opening the windows, or installing an exhaust fan. How to tell whether it's seepage or condensation: Before going to bed, fasten a pocket mirror to a damp spot with chewing gum. Look at it the next morning. If the mirror is clear, it's seepage. If it's fogged over, the problem is condensation.

• In spring and fall inspect your foundation (for wood rot or termites) and all exterior door and window frames. Cracks should be calked or otherwise sealed to keep out rain, which will cause wood rot or paint peeling. Patch all holes and cracks on your exterior walls. Seal all possible means of entry against household pests. Replace damaged roof shingles; check chimney flashing, vent pipes and roof valleys to make sure they're watertight. Clean out leaves and twigs from gutters and downspouts.

Also, retouch bare spots on your exterior paint. If you decide the whole house needs fresh paint, remember that 80 percent of the cost of every house-painting job is labor. You can save this sizable amount if you do the work yourself. If you carefully prepare the surfaces as a professional painter would—scraping off flaked paint, sanding, calking, puttying—you can get excellent results. But before undertaking any sizable home painting, consult your local paint dealer. He can give you much valuable advice.

• If you are thinking about remodeling your home, determine as accurately as possible the current market value of your house—then spend no more than 30 percent of this figure before seeking a professional to see if such remodeling is in your best interest if you sell. For example, if your house will sell today for $60,000 the most you should prudently spend on remodeling before consulting an appraiser is $18,000.

ORGANIZE YOUR KITCHEN

by NANCY SCHRAFFENBERGER

BREATHES there a woman who hasn't paused midway through preparing a recipe and wished she could turn to a Grand High Poohbah Cook and ask, "How big is a medium onion, anyway?" Or, "What do I do now that my sauce has turned to molasses?"

Even the most virtuous cookbooks don't always offer first-aid hints or tell *why* you do a thing a certain way or what techniques make all the difference in food buying or preparation.

This sort of brooding led us to Dione Lucas, who was one of the most highly regarded cooks in America. Dione (pronounced dee-OH-nee) was one of the rare women in the world to hold a diploma from the famed Ecole du Cordon Bleu in Paris, and was among the first to teach cooking by television (her long-running series began in 1947). Her cookbooks—the last was *The Dione Lucas Book of French Cooking*—are perennial sellers. The restaurants she owned or supervised were meccas for conncisseurs.

Here are some of Dione Lucas' shortcuts, slick tricks and magic:

For Chopping and Molding

A chopping board is one of the most "daily" essentials. If you don't own one, put it at the top of tomorrow's shopping list. It should be a block two feet by ten inches and made like a ship's deck so there are no joints or cracks for food to lodge in. It's better to get unvarnished wood and treat it by rubbing with a little heated raw linseed oil. Let it dry overnight and it'll never stain.

A large chopping knife of excellent quality is a lifelong friend. Every chef has a certain type he or she thinks superior. (Mrs. Lucas preferred the French "Sabatier" brand.)

All stirring should be done with a wooden spoon. Metal chemically affects some foods.

In pan frying and sautéing, always get your pan hot first, then add the butter or oil. Meat—even eggs—won't stick if you use this method.

94

When dipping meat pieces into beaten egg and crumbs, use your left hand for applying the egg, you right for crumbs, to avoid getting your fingers gluey.

When unmolding hot foods, allow them to stand for five minutes before you turn them out on another dish.

When greasing pans or molds, use butter for hot dishes, oil for cold (butter stiffens and sticks when chilled, defeating your purpose).

Meat, Poultry, Seafood

Color guide to meat buying: Beef should be well marbled and very bright red with white fat; chicken should have fat as close to white as possible—if the pinfeather holes are close together the bird will be young and tender; veal should also be as white as possible; pork, pink with as little fat as possible; lamb, rosy-red and not fatty.

To keep raw meat fresh and odorless, rub it with oil or dip it into its own rendered fat or melted butter before refrigerating. Don't wrap it.

To keep raw fish fillets fresh and odorless, rinse them with fresh lemon juice and water, dry thoroughly, wrap and refrigerate.

Have meat at room temperature before cooking it, except meat that has been frozen. The latter can be cooked as soon as it is soft enough for the juices to begin to run. Wait too long and you'll lose too much of the juice.

Never pierce meat when browning; the juices will escape. Use tongs. And don't let the pieces touch each other as they cook or they'll stew instead of sauté. Better to do a few at a time than to crowd them. Brown red meats quickly, uncovered; brown poultry slowly, covered or uncovered.

Never carve any sizable piece of meat or poultry right after it comes out of the oven. Give a roast, turkey or capon at least 20 minutes and it will be much easier to slice.

Vegetables

Blanching helps to keep firmness, texture, color and flavor in such vegetables as green beans, carrots, leeks and celery. After slicing, put the pieces in a pan and cover with cold water. Bring slowly to boil, drain and then cook according to the recipe you're using.

Test boiled potatoes for doneness with a cake tester or a skewer, never a fork. Many holes make them watery.

Cut off both ends of cucumbers to avoid bitterness. To bring out their taste, slice them ahead of time, sprinkle with a little salt and refrigerate.

To chop an onion efficiently, cut it in half and place flat surfaces on your cutting board; cut in thin slices across with chef's knife. Then turn slices around, holding them together, and chop into fine pieces. This method keeps the juices in better, too. To avoid tears in the process, sprinkle fresh lemon juice on the flat surfaces after you've cut the onions in half.

Never cut salad greens with a knife—this bruises them and makes them bitter. Tear them gently into bite-size pieces by hand.

Secret of crisp salads: Dry greens thoroughly, piece by piece, till absolutely water-free. Wet salad greens won't get coated and shiny with dressing. Best way to toss them is with your own two hands.

It's perfectly safe and even desirable to wash and break up greens the day before they'll be served—just wrap them in plenty of paper towels and store in a crisper in the refrigerator. You'll save all that last-minute work and the greens will be drier.

Dairy Foods and Eggs

Heat milk slowly and stir constantly to prevent its separating and forming a skin on top. Many cooks discard this skin, but it's the richest part.

To beat cream so it stays whipped, do it with a wire whisk in a metal bowl (not aluminum) over another bowl containing ice.

To keep cheese such as Swiss, cheddar or hard Italian types, wrap in waxed paper, seal in a plastic container and freeze.

If you grate your own Parmesan cheese as needed from a bulk chunk, you'll enjoy four times more flavor than from the pre-grated kind. Dip the chunk in brandy and wrap it in plastic, then foil, to preserve its freshness; it needn't be refrigerated. Swiss cheese also stores well by using this method, but it should be refrigerated.*

---

*Brandy used for preserving and dipping can be saved and used again for these purposes.

When cooking with raw eggs, you'll get best results if the eggs have just come out of the refrigerator. They separate better and thicken mayonnaise or hollandaise sauce faster.

Egg whites are well whipped if they adhere to the bowl when you turn it upside down. Hand-beat them in a metal bowl (not aluminum) with a wire whisk to get more air, thus more volume. This is especially important for soufflés, where the whites must hold up your creation. It'll also keep the whites from getting too dry from over-beating.

Poach eggs in water flavored with tarragon vinegar for a subtle, delicate taste.

Seasonings

Garlic guides: Never cook garlic fast; never cook it alone. Chop it in a little salt and the pieces won't stick to your knife or your cutting board. Then pulverize it with the tip of the knife to make it dissolve. Don't use a garlic press—you lose the best part of the bud. Garlic should be as fresh as your salad greens. If you let it sit around too long, it becomes dry and tasteless. To sweeten garlic-scented fingers, rub them with a ripe tomato which you can use later in salad; if the scent is very powerful, rub your fingers in coffee grounds.

To keep dill, mint or tarragon fresh, wash and dry well, then strip sprigs from stalks and refrigerate in a screw-top jar.

Rub dry herbs between your fingers or rehydrate them with a little water to bring out their fragrance.

Vanilla sugar, wonderful for flavoring, can be made by putting a vanilla bean in a jar of sugar.

Sauces

Add flour to melted butter off the heat for a smoother mixture.

When adding any liquid to a sauce base, stir it in off the heat.

Add hot sauce to cold sauce two tablespoons at a time so the cold warms up gradually and doesn't curdle.

Recommended stirring technique: use a wooden spatula or a wire whisk and scrape over bottom of pan as you stir.

To beat sour cream into a hot mixture, take a dab of it on a rubber scraper, scrape it off with a wire whisk, and quickly, lightly beat it into the sauce, which must be kept under the boiling point. Continue until all the cream is added.

Secret of a good sauce: low-to-medium heat, never high.

To correct a separated sauce: if hollandaise or chocolate, beat in a tablespoon or so of cold water; use hot water for mayonnaise.

To correct a too-thick sauce: heat until simmering, then beat in, a spoonful at a time, a little cream or stock until consistency is right.

To correct a too-thin hot sauce: blend a teaspoon of flour with a teaspoon of soft butter. Beat into hot sauce off heat until smooth. Simmer.

SIGNS
OF AN AILING HOUSE
by JERRY EDGERTON

THERE'S ALWAYS something. Minor symptoms of major trouble—peeling paint, sticking doors, widening cracks, wet spots. If you own a house age 20 or over—or a newer, shoddily built house—chances are good that within a few years you will face outlays of hundreds, or perhaps thousands, of dollars just to keep it warm, dry, lighted and safe.

Fortunately, not every household symptom that causes a repairman to cluck ominously turns out to be a terminal illness. Some yield to simple, inexpensive treatments. The way to avoid being at the mercy of repairmen urging costly work is to know the symptoms of major and minor problems and normal life spans of the parts of your house.

Here are some of the most common symptoms, and some probable remedies, minor and drastic. Cost estimates are for an average four-bedroom frame house at 1976 prices. Both prices and appliance lifetimes will vary, depending on the location of your home, and will rise with continuing inflation.

Wet Basement

FOR EVERY wet basement, there are as many suggestions on what to do as there are contractors in the Yellow Pages. Wet basements are a mire of misleading claims and consumer rip-offs. "I've seen people pay thousands of dollars for a basement job when all they needed was an adjustment of rain gutters or a regrading around the foundation," says Joseph McNeill, a home-inspection-service engineer in New Jersey.

For light seepage into the basement, look for a small crack in the foundation and seal it or try waterproofing compound. If water is coming in during rainstorms, look at the gutter downspouts to see if they are broken or dumping water too close to the house. Check the ground around your foundation and see if the grade is directing water toward it. If so, try to build it up by shoveling in dirt and packing it down to reverse the flow.

Roof

A LEAK around the edges of the roof could simply mean that rain gutters are backing up and need cleaning or repairing.

99

If water is still coming in, consider installing an automatic sump pump at a natural low point. Cost: $100 to $300. If this doesn't work, you may have to have a trench dug inside the basement channeling the water to a pump. Cost: $1500.

The surest bet is to seal off the water from the outside. This is expensive, since it involves digging out around the entire foundation and applying a "membrane" of layers of tar and heavy waterproofing paper, plus drainpipes below the foundation to carry the water away. Cost: $4000 to $6000. Be skeptical of proposals to waterproof your foundation by pumping sealant into the ground around it. This can cost up to $2000 and will often fail to solve the problem.

Furnace

IF YOUR HOUSE isn't getting any heat, the problem could range from something minor, such as a blown fuse, to a need for a major replacement. Problems in the thermostat, the oil or gas burner or the circulation system can usually be repaired. But if a steam or hot-water boiler is constantly leaking, or if you smell combustion fumes, you may need a new boiler or furnace. A cast-iron boiler costs $1200 to $1500 installed, but it should last for 30 years or more. A warm-air furnace costs around $1000 and lasts 15 to 20 years.

Wiring

IF A LIGHT SWITCH makes a humming noise, emits a strange odor, is hot to touch, or if the lights flicker when you turn them on, call an electrician. These are all symptoms of a possibly dangerous situation. But the solution could be simple. Loose wires at switches or outlets often cause overheating; they may only need tightening. If you need a new switch or outlet, it should cost less than $50 installed. You might have to rewire the entire house if the insulation has burned off the old wiring. Extensive rewiring, however, is usually required only in pre-World War II houses in which modern appliances may have overloaded the old circuits. Total rewiring runs about $1500.

Roof

A LEAK around the edges of the roof could simply mean that rain gutters are backing up and need cleaning or repairing.

Another common problem is the buildup of mold on the underside of the roof. This usually results from condensation in the attic, and can be cured by installing ventilation. If you have an asphalt-shingle roof 15 to 20 years old, it may soon need replacing, at a probable cost of $1000 to $1500. If three layers of shingles are already in place, the old layers should be taken off before putting on new ones, adding perhaps $1000 to the job. A new set of wood shingles will cost about 50 percent more than asphalt, but could last up to 30 years if well maintained.

Air Conditioning

IF YOUR central air conditioning is misbehaving, you might be able to fix it by replacing a fuse or cleaning a filter. If that doesn't help, shut off the system for a few hours. The evaporator coil may have iced up because of a clogged filter, and a brief shutdown will give it a chance to thaw. If the fan blows too-warm air even after a filter change, the problem could be anything from a shortage of refrigerant or thermostat malfunction to a faulty compressor. A new compressor costs $400 to $600, and most come with only a one-year dealer's warranty. If your condenser unit is eight years old or more (suggesting that the other parts are approaching the end of their normal ten-year life span), you may want to replace the entire unit ($600 to $800) and get a new five-year warranty.

Choosing a Contractor

IF YOU'VE CHECKED the symptoms and feel certain that your house does need a major repair, be sure to get more than one diagnosis and estimate—preferably three or more. Make each contractor write out his bid in detail and explain why each item is needed. Although bids for the same job can vary as much as 100 percent, don't automatically jump for the low bid.

John L. Knott, Jr., chairman of the National Association of Home Builders' rehabilitation and remodeling committee, gives this advice for homeowners seeking a reliable contractor: "Ask your friends for recommendations; they may have had similar work well done. Ask local banks, which have to assess firms' reliability in making loans. See how long a contractor has been in business and check for affiliation with professional an asphalt-shingle roof 15 to 20 years old, it may soon need replacing, at a probable cost of $1000 to $1500. If three layers of shingles are already in place, the old layers should be taken off before putting on new ones, adding perhaps $1000 to the job. A new set of wood shingles will cost about 50 percent more than asphalt, but could last up to 30 years if well maintained.

Air Conditioning

IF YOUR central air conditioning is misbehaving, you might be able to fix it by replacing a fuse or cleaning a filter. If that doesn't help, shut off the system for a few hours. The evaporator coil may have iced up because of a clogged filter, and a brief shutdown will give it a chance to thaw. If the fan blows too-warm air even after a filter change, the problem could be anything from a shortage of refrigerant or thermostat malfunction to a faulty compressor. A new compressor costs $400 to $600, and most come with only a one-year dealer's warranty. If your condenser unit is eight years old or more (suggesting that the other parts are approaching the end of their normal ten-year life span), you may want to replace the entire unit ($600 to $800) and get a new five-year warranty.

Choosing a Contractor

IF YOU'VE CHECKED the symptoms and feel certain that your house does need a major repair, be sure to get more than one diagnosis and estimate—preferably three or more. Make each contractor write out his bid in detail and explain why each item is needed. Although bids for the same job can vary as much as 100 percent, don't automatically jump for the low bid.

John L. Knott, Jr., chairman of the National Association of Home Builders' rehabilitation and remodeling committee, gives this advice for homeowners seeking a reliable contractor: "Ask your friends for recommendations; they may have had similar work well done. Ask local banks, which have to assess firms' reliability in making loans. See how long a contractor has been in business and check for affiliation with professional associations. Check with the Better Business Bureau."

The most sensible advice of all, though, is to find out something about local repair people before you are faced with an emergency.

42 WAYS TO MAKE YOUR HOUSELIFE EASIER

by MARY ELLEN PINKHAM AND PEARL HIGGINBOTHAM

Kitchen Clues

TO KEEP LETTUCE FRESH, store it in the refrigerator in paper bags instead of cellophane.

A remedy for salty soup and stew is to add cut raw, peeled potatoes. Discard them when they have cooked and absorbed the salt.

Submerging a lemon in hot water for 15 minutes before squeezing will make it yield more juice.

Store cottage cheese upside down. It will keep longer.

You can restore crispness to soggy cereal and stale crackers by heating for a few minutes on a cooky sheet in the oven.

If brown sugar becomes as hard as a rock and you need it in a hurry, simply grate the amount called for.

To get ketchup out of a fresh bottle, insert a drinking straw and push it to the bottom. Enough air will be admitted to start an even flow.

Cleaning and Polishing

TO CLEAN COPPER POTS, dip lemon halves in salt and rub. White hard-water spots on stainless steel can be removed with white vinegar.

Sprinkle burnt pots liberally with baking soda and just enough water to moisten; let stand for several hours. Generally, the burned portion will scrape right out of the pan.

To clean varnished floors or woodwork of any kind, rub with cold tea.

To get at those hard-to-reach cobwebs, slip a sock or two over the end of a yardstick. Secure with a rubber band. This is also useful for cleaning under the refrigerator and radiators.

To clean eyeglasses without streaks, use a drop of vinegar or vodka on each lens.

Storing and Saving

TO PREVENT SCRATCHES on your fine-china plates, insert paper plates or napkins between plates as you stack them.

For sweet-smelling closets, hang an old nylon stocking filled with cedar chips. This also may help repel moths.

To preserve a news clipping, disolve a milk of magnesia tablet in a quart of club soda overnight. Pour into a pan large enough to accommodate the flattened clipping. Soak it for up to one hour, remove carefully and pat dry. Do not move until completely dry.

When postage stamps are stuck together, place them in the freezer. They will usually come apart and the glue will still be usable.

Keep clear plastic wrap in the refrigerator to prevent it from sticking together.

Carpet Cleaning

BEFORE SHAMPOOING your rug, put little plastic bags on each furniture leg to prevent rust marks from forming on the wet carpet. This also eliminates the dreadful job of moving the furniture about.

Try shaving cream as a spot remover. The foam really works. Wash up with water or club soda.

The next time red wine spills on your carpet or tablecloth, try removing it with white wine.

To remove some types of ballpoint ink marks, saturate with hair spray, allow to dry, then brush lightly with a solution of water and vinegar.

If heavy furniture has flattened the pile of your rugs, raise it with a brush and a steam iron. Hold the steaming iron over the damaged spot. Do not touch carpet with the iron. Brush briskly.

Clothing and Shoes

TO REMOVE CHEWING GUM, place garment in a plastic bag and put in freezer. Scrape off frozen gum.

A sticky zipper will slide easily if rubbed with a lead pencil.

Before wearing a new garment, touch the center of each button (front and back) with clear nail polish. This will seal the threads and buttons will stay on much longer.

If you're in a hurry and notice a stain on your white suit or sweater, cover it up by rubbing baby powder into the stain.

To dry shoes, hang them by the heels on the rungs of a chair. They will be out of the way and still receive circulation of air on both sides.

Sewing

USE DENTAL FLOSS or elastic thread to sew buttons on children's clothing. They will take a lot of wear.

When sewing on snaps, sew the snap point on first and rub chalk on it. Turn the material over, rub the spot with your finger, and you will have marked the exact place where the bottom snap should be sewed on.

If you are knitting with more than one ball of yarn, put them in a plastic bag with small holes. Thread the yarns through different holes to keep them clean and untangled.

Plants and Flowers

USE WATER at room temperature. Let water stand for a day to get rid of chlorine. Better yet, use old fizzless club soda—it has just the right chemicals to add vigor to your plants.

The next time you boil eggs use the cooled water, which is filled with minerals, to give your plants a good drink.

To add length to short-stemmed flowers, slip stems into drinking straws before placing in vase.

For flowers in winter, cut some branches of forsythia or other flowering shrubs. Put stems in a bucket of warm water. Tie pail and branches securely in a plastic bag. Soon blooms will appear on the branches.

Painting

A NEW PAINTBRUSH will last longer and be easier to clean if it soaks in a can of linseed oil for 12 hours before it is ever used.

To banish paint odor, add two tablespoons of vanilla extract per quart of paint. A large cut onion placed in a pan of cold water will also absorb paint odor.

When working on a paint job that takes a couple of days, save clean-up time by wrapping used brushes in foil overnight. Try freezing them in foil if you're using water-based paint. Let brushes defrost an hour or more before returning to the job.

Odds and Ends

IF YOUR BALL POINT becomes clogged with excessive ink and fuzz, insert it in the filter portion of a cigarette. Just a few quick turns and it's ready for use.

Candles burn more slowly and evenly with minimum dripping if you place them in the freezer for several hours before using.

Old decals can be easily removed by painting them with several coats of white vinegar. Let the vinegar soak in, then gently scrape off.

Silence floor squeaks by dusting talcum powder into the cracks.

If there's a bee—or any winged insect—in the house, reach for the hair spray. This stiffens their wings and immobilizes them immediately.

SLASH HOME HEATING BILLS

WITH energy costs up, you can control your home power use better by being aware of just where and how waste takes place. Here's up-to-date advice on cutting those costs:

Lights. When you leave a room, even for a few minutes, turn off the lights. Experiment with lower-watt bulbs (15, 25, 40 watts) wherever you can—in bedrooms, chandeliers, wall fixtures. But be sensible: don't reduce lighting at the cost of safety or health. Keep adequate light on steps and in halls.

Use fluorescent tubes instead of incandescent bulbs in kitchen, bathroom, workshop. A 40-watt fluorescent gives 25 to 85 percent more light than a 100-watt incandescent, and it costs less to operate.

When painting walls, choose light colors. They reflect more light than dark colors, and you'll need less artificial lighting.

Heat. Lost heat means lost money. Remember: warm air rises; keep it in your house with six to nine inches of fiberglass insulation—or its equivalent—on the attic floor. Seal cracks round the attic door.

Heat escapes through walls. They should have three to four inches of insulation. Another scheme: line a cold wall with inexpensive cork. Even wallpaper helps.

Heat is lost through glass: install storm windows and doors. To make do, tack, staple or tape plastic sheeting over windows. Curtain all windows. Pull down shades at night, and raise them when the sun is up. Also close draperies at night.

Warm air flows out through cracks at windows and doors. Walk around outside frames; use weather stripping inside.

Put a plastic cover over the air conditioner. When the fireplace is not being used, close the damper.

Close off rooms not in use. If you open bedroom windows at night, don't chill the whole house—close the bedroom door.

Don't enclose radiators or place furniture or draperies in front of them. Don't paint them in dark colors or with lead or flat paints. Tape sheets of aluminum foil on the wall behind radiators to reflect warm air back into the room.

Keep your thermostat at 65 to 68 degrees during the day, 60 at night. If you're going away for a few days, drop the thermostat setting to 55.

Keep your heating system clean. Drain a steam-heat boiler once a year; refill to the water level on the gauge. With a warm-air system, vacuum the filters once a month; replace them according to the manufacturer's instructions.

Hot Water. Turn down the hot-water thermostat to a setting between 135 and 140 degrees. Your hot-water heater can account for as much as 15 percent of your total energy expenses, equaling the energy cost of most of your other appliances combined. Replace washers on leaky faucets; one drop per second totals 2500 gallons per year. Don't let hot water run freely while washing dishes or shaving.

Drain a bucketful or two from the water heater every few months to carry off sediment and keep the heater efficient. Make sure your hot-water pipes are insulated, especially if they pass along outside walls.

Stove. Cook two or three meals in the oven at once, especially stews and casseroles. Don't oven-thaw foods. Don't pre-heat to broil or for long-cooking foods. For less than one-hour baking, pre-heat only ten minutes. Turn slow-cooking roasts off for the last half-hour; let stored-up heat finish the job. Cook vegetables in very little water, only until crisp-tender. Reduce boiling to a simmer—you get the same water temperature, at less cost.

If you have a pressure cooker, use it. It cooks in one-third the time needed by ordinary pots, and on lower heat.

Cleaner is cheaper. If gas flames show yellow, the burner may be clogged. Clean them with a wire pipe cleaner. Keep heat reflector pans under the burners clean.

Stove pilots, going continuously, cost about one-third of your gas-range bill. Don't turn them off, but make sure you aren't set needlessly high—a common fault.

If you have a choice, gas ranges generally cost less to run than electric models. Check both for high-efficiency features: fast-heating cooking tops, several broiler levels, automatic ignition pilots.

Refrigerator. Open the refrigerator door as infrequently possible and close it fast. Know what you'll take out befo you open the door. To put foods away, first gather them all, then open the door.

If the door won't hold a dollar bill in place, replace the door gaskets.

Frost-free refrigerators and refrigerator-freezers don't necessarily cost more to run than hand-defrost types. One reason: built-up frost that forms in manual types make it harder to cool the inside air. Be sure to defrost a manual model when the frost is a quarter-inch thick.

Best temperature in the freezer: zero degrees. Best for refrigerator: 38 to 40 degrees. When you go away for a weekend, raise the temperature slightly, since you won't be opening the door.

Dishwasher. Don't run the dishwasher until it's filled to capacity. You can select a shorter wash cycle if you rinse and scrape dishes well before putting them in the machine. To save one-third or more of the running cost, turn the machine off as soon as the wash period is done and open the door slightly to let dishes air-dry.

Clothes Washer. Much of a washer's monthly cost goes into heating the water, so never use hot water when you can use warm, or warm if cold will do. Don't wash until you have a full load, but don't overload. If the load must be small, don't use more water than you need.

If buying, choose a large-capacity machine that cuts the number of loads you must put through.

TV and Radio. Turn off the set when you leave the room. If your TV has an "instant on" feature, the cost meter ticks on as long as the set is plugged in, so disconnect when you won't be using it for a few days.

If you're buying, color uses more power than black-and-white, but solid-state sets use only half the power that comparable tube-types do.

CHAPTER 7

Control
Your Shopping

GET MORE FOR YOUR MONEY THROUGH "OFF-PEAK" BUYING

by DONALD AND DOROTHY STROETZEL

MOST CONSUMERS are aware that business costs are soaring. What you may not yet have discovered is that these business headaches can bring you real bargains on everything from electricity to phone calls, TV sets, lawn furniture and vacations. All it takes is your willingness to bend your spending habits and life-style a little to the businessman's—and your—advantage.

Called "off-peak buying," this inflation-beating technique means purchasing at the season, day or even hour when it's to the businessman's advantage to sell cheaply. By buying during his sales valleys, you can help a businessman avoid building a costly new plant, avert lay-offs, pay less overtime and incur fewer warehousing and interest charges. Your reward for helping the businessman: bargains.

Off-peak buying has always been the basis for clearance sales. But now, with inflation setting the business pace, it is spreading to sellers who never before offered consumers cut rates.

For example, in 1976, the Central Vermont Public Service Corporation, to avoid wintertime demand surges during peak morning and evening hours, experimentally offered customers a bargain. Instead of a normal round-the-clock rate of five cents per kilowatt hour, they could pay two cents per k.w.h. for electricity consumed outside the peak hours of 8-to-11 a.m. and 5-to-9 p.m. But they paid a penalty rate—11 cents per k.w.h.—for power used at peak.

David and Barbara Smith joined the experiment and cut electric bills in their Rutland home by about 28 percent. "Russian roulette," Dave called the plan at first. Soon, however, the couple and their two children were pivoting their lives around a little red light put in to signal peak hours.

During the winter of 1979 Barbara routinely pushed the heat in their three-bedroom split level to 72 degrees in midafternoon,

112

building enough two-cent warmth to stay comfortable through much of the peak-rate evening. She pre-cooked dinner casseroles and roasts in off-peak hours, using high-rate electricity only to reheat them. New timers automatically shut off the water heater, washer, dryer and freezer during peak periods. "We make a family game out of saving watts," Barbara said.

So promising is this inflation-beating approach—both for consumer and businessman—that utility companies in more than half the states are now experimenting with it (not only in winter but, in the South, to reduce summertime air-conditioning peaks).

There are similar off-peak buys on just about everything. But for your family to realize up to hundreds of dollars in annual savings requires more than knowing when and where to find bargains. You must also make psychological adjustments:

Think June in January. Buy your bathing suit in midsummer; buy your air conditioner in late winter; shop for storm windows and insulation in spring and summer. Generally speaking, the bulkier the item and the higher its price, the more dramatic the savings. Storing lawn mowers, garden tractors, summer furniture and outdoor grills through the winter not only squeezes a merchant's warehouse space but gives him a "dead money" problem: investment not bringing income.

Time Your Clothes Purchases. Real buys in fall/winter suits, outer-coats and dresses often come in October from merchants who scoop up cheaply the department-store cancellations and manufacturers' over-production. At post-Christmas and mid-summer clearances, best buys are men's suits and shirts, women's sweaters, blouses and slacks.

Shop for Discount Travel. Before planning a trip by rail or bus check with individual companies for their special discount programs. These vary greatly, and more seats are usually available in off-peak periods. But you can save a lot all year round by shopping for bargains.

Telephone Very Late or Early. Everyone knows it's cheaper to phone long distance after 5 p.m. and on weekends, but for even bigger bargains, dial direct between 11 p.m. and 8 a.m.

Look for Last Year's Models. Industry's sales stimulator— the annual model change— can work in your favor. Buying this year's model car after next year's model arrives in the showroom can be to your advantage, if you hang on to it several years. Watch, too, for appliance and TV model changes, which

A Calendar of What's on Sale and When

JANUARY
Christmas items
White goods
Shoes, clothing
Fabrics
Toys

FEBRUARY
Washington and Lincoln sales
Cars
Furniture, floor coverings
Mattresses
Major appliances

MARCH
Housewares
China, glassware
Air conditioners

APRIL
After-Easter sales
Women's dresses, coats
Men's and boys' clothing
Soaps, cleaning supplies

MAY
Memorial Day sales
Television sets
White goods

JUNE
Rug cleaning
Storm windows

JULY
Summer clearance sales
Shoes, clothing, swimsuits
White goods
Jewelry
Furniture
Refrigerators, washing
  machines
Garden supplies
Floor coverings

AUGUST
Back-to-school specials
Cars, tires
Furniture
Summer clothing
White goods
Coats, furs
Garden equipment
Painting supplies
Camping equipment
Cameras

SEPTEMBER
Labor Day specials
Back-to-school specials
Cars (end of model year)
Tires
Clothing
Housewares
China, glassware

OCTOBER
Columbus Day, fall sales
Cars (last of old models)
Coats
Lingerie
Infant needs

NOVEMBER
Furs
Sales on:
  Election Day
  Veterans Day
  Thanksgiving weekend

DECEMBER
Men's, boys' suits, coats
Christmas sales:
  gift items, decorations
  winter merchandise

Remember, though the above calendar serves as a general guide to good buys, sale months may vary regionally. A smart shopper keeps watch for bargains throughout the year, for sales can, and do, occur at any time.
—*National Retail Merchants Association (NRMA)*

occur all through the year. Even Christmas cards and wrappings change style annually. You can often save 50 percent buying them the week *after* Christmas for use next year.

Buy and Improve Houses in the Fall. Because many home buyers want to settle before school starts, September until January is the bargain time for buying a house. And home improvements such as porches and recreation rooms make most sense in the fall and winter months, too, because carpenters and other craftsmen often offer slack-season price reductions. A swimming-pool contractor admitted, "If I can spread your job over eight months, I'll *really* dicker."

THE KEY to off-peak buying is to learn how *each* business operates, pin-pointing its peak and valleys. This will help you quickly distinguish real slack-period sales from small promotional discounts. Fed by tight money, inflation and our nation's need to make better use of its resources, off-peak buying is bound to grow. Use it as much as possible—it's one of the best defenses against rising living costs.

SUPERSHOPPING: HOW TO SAVE 50% AT THE CHECKOUT

by SUSAN SAMTUR with TAD TULEJA

In 1978 I demonstrated on national television how much the shrewd shopper could save by a combination of judicious planning and couponing. As my first cart filled up and the manager wheeled over another, the TV crew began to look skeptical. They knew I had only $40 with me. When I finally wheeled two overflowing carts up to the register, the checker rang up the items, and said, "That's $130.18." I smiled and handed her my coupons. She added them, then subtracted the coupon total from the bill. The new total was $7.07. I had just saved $123.11—about 95 percent of my bill.

Since I started couponing and refunding almost seven years ago, I have gradually developed my techniques into what I call my supershopping system. With it, I am not only cutting our food bill, but I'm actually paid over $1500 per year in tax-free cash refunds by manufacturers.

It would be misleading to suggest that you will realize a 95- or even 85-percent saving every time you go to the store. On my weekly shopping trips I generally save between 40 and 60 percent of my bill.

You can use coupons for almost everything in the supermarket. Your best savings are usually on household-cleaning aids, health and beauty products, and processed foods.

If you've ever clipped a coupon to get 25¢ off on a can of coffee, or sent in two box tops and $1 to get your child some treat, you're already a novice couponer and refunder. But unless you're doing it systematically, you're losing money. The first thing to do to change this is to become an *alert* rather than a passive shopper.

Basic Techniques

HERE are four basic shopping techniques that you should use every time you go into a supermarket.

116

• *Make a list and stick to it.* I don't mean slavishly, but within reason. Buy only what you need.

• *Check the sales.* Clip and save the midweek and Sunday papers' coupons and carry them with you. Try to shop at a market that features "doubling." Doubling means that the store will give you twice the face value of your coupons.

• *Be cautious.* An item featured in a splashy display is not always a bargain. Check the prices and signs.

• *Shop with your eyes open.* Compare prices and remember that, no matter what advertising promotions are used, you have the final word.

Collecting Coupons

ONCE, in Philadelphia, I bought $65 worth of merchandise—and the store ended up owing *me* $1.67! Coupons were the key. You can find these valuable offers in:

• *Stores:* Many coupons are printed on the outside of packages. When a coupon is enclosed in a package, it will usually say so on the outside.

• *Magazines and Newspapers:* Most large-circulation magazines regularly feature coupons. Newspapers carry not only manufacturers' coupons but also retailers' coupons often good for one week only, offered by individual local stores.

• *Home mailers:* Manufacturers periodically send out advertising circulars to whole neighborhoods, and frequently these contain coupons.

Filing

ONE QUALITY distinguishes the supershopper from the casual couponer—willingness to organize. And all it takes is one large envelope.

File the coupons by type of product, alphabetically—not by brand name. Include all "rainchecks," the certificates that stores give when they are out of an advertised special. After rainchecks, alphabetically group coupons for free samples, which, like cash-offs, often come in the mail or are found in newspapers, magazines and in specially marked packages in the supermarket.

Remember that most cash-offs carry an expiration date and if you let them languish in the envelope beyond that date, you're out of luck.

Refunding

LIKE COUPONING, refunding is a promotional scheme devised by the food manufacturers to get shoppers to try, and to keep on buying, their products. Here's how it works: The manufacturers extends an offer of a refund to all customers who have bought a certain product. The shopper usually fills out a refund form, and mails it in, accompanied by whatever proof of purchase is required (labels, box panels, etc.).

The form goes to a redemption agency or clearinghouse, which processes the refund and checks whether you have sent the proper proof of purchase to qualify for the offer. Then it mails you a check in the manufacturer's name.

Refunding can be extremely profitable if used just by itself, but you'll realize the greatest savings if you use it with couponing. When you refund as often as I do, you'll find yourself on numberous mailing lists, receiving envelopes full of cashoffs, two-for-one coupons, certificates for free samples—all in addition to the regular refund checks.

Saving Qualifiers

YOU can't always tell when you buy a product which part of its packaging may eventually be required as a qualifier. So, if you want to really profit from refunding, save everything. You need not feel you're living in a paper-recycling plant if you follow a few simple guidelines:

• Make your qualifiers as small as possible: With boxes, remove the inner wrapper, peel off the thick cardboard and leave the outer covering—the part with the writing on it. Wetting the boxes and letting them sit in a plastic bag overnight makes the covering easy to peel off. Flatten the covers until they are the thickness of a couple of pieces of typing paper, and secure them in product groups with rubber bands.

• Steam or soak off can and bottle labels. File them in a shoe box.

Finding Forms

NOT ALL refund offers require forms. For many, all you do is send in the qualifier with your name, address and the name of the offer.

The offers that ask for forms are highly prized by refunders, largely because a heavy percentage of the really big rebates— $2 to $5—fall into this category. If you see a refund offer, check whether the form contains a phrase such as "with this coupon" or "this certificate required." It means that your request will probably *not* be honored without the form. These are the principal sources for forms:

• *Stores*. There are two kinds of forms available in supermarkets. One is attached to shelves in tear-off pads. The other appears either on or in the products themselves.

• *Newspapers and magazines*. These often contain forms good not only for cash refunds, but for free samples, or for coupons worth free samples at your store.

• *Home mailers*. By becoming an active refunder, you will almost certainly increase your chances of receiving forms and coupons through the mail.

• *Companies*. If your supermarket is out of forms, you can write directly to the company's customer-service department. Major firms are usually extremely helpful to the "formless" refunder.

Joining the Movement

TODAY, there are over 50 refund newsletters and bulletins serving refunders. These list current cash-rebate offers and information for swapping forms and/or qualifiers with fellow refunders. To locate one, put up a small sign in your local supermarket or coin laundry, saying that you'd like to get in touch with refunders in your area—especially with newsletter subscribers. The refunding network is nationwide now, and you should have no trouble getting responses.

Enjoying the Gravy

ONCE YOU start clipping forms and getting on mailing lists the companies will send you information about discounted and "absolutely free" samples. These premium giveaways work on the same principle as refunds. You buy a product and save the qualifiers. The manufacturer announces (in a magazine, on a package, in a mailer) that you can get a premium by sending in a specified number of qualifiers. You send them in with an order form if it's required. In a matter of weeks you are the owner of a new shirt, tote bag, cigarette lighter, toy.

People sometimes ask me if it isn't troublesome or embarrassing using all these supershopper techniques. Of course not! Why should anybody feel embarrassed about saving money?

DON'T BE TOO TIMID TO BARGAIN!

by DONALD AND DOROTHY STROETZEL

THE SALESMAN SQUINTS at the price tag. "This refrigerator will cost you $359.99," he says. You wince; the most you want to pay is $300. What do you do? Do you tell yourself that $59.99 isn't really that much and pull out your credit card? Or, do you muster your courage, look the salesman in the eye and ask, "Will you take less?"

"Those four words can save a family hundreds, even thousands, of dollars a year," claims Alan Schoonmaker, a New Jersey psychologist who coaches business negotiators for numerous corporations on all seven continents. Prices of many family purchases—actually the biggest ones—*are* negotiable. Yet most people are too timid to try it. Here, from Schoonmaker and other experts, are tips to help you bargain your way to savings:

Inform Yourself. If you are shopping for a used car, for example, visit several lots. Ask the "blue book" price—the average retail price—of the make and model you want. Pick up bits of information from friends. Do the salesmen at Honest Joe's Used Cars have a monthly sales quota? If so, shop toward the end of the month.

Work as a Team. It can make sense for husband and wife to go together—but only if you use strategy. A wife who cautions, "We can't afford it" or "Let's look around before we decide," boosts her husband's negotiating power. But one who says, "I like this car better than the one we saw yesterday," puts money in the salesman's pocket.

When you enter the lot, casually walk around the cars. Don't tell the salesman you've already located the one you want. Give him the make and model you *may* want and let him lead you to your choice. When he pitches its virtues, don't go beyond, "Well, we *might* be interested if the price is right."

Hide Your Maximum Limit. The car you want has a price tag of $3400 and you can afford only $3000. This maximum limit is the hidden card you bring to the bargaining session. *Never divulge it.*

121

What's Negotiable?

Practically everything that's for sale. Chester Karrass, director of the Center for Effective Negotiating, Los Angeles, says that, in most cases, price is simply what the seller hopes to realize or learns he can get. Remember, merchants and corporations have no inhibitions over arguing price when they buy. Chemical firms haggle to the tenth of a cent a pound, and auto makers even debate 1/100 of a cent in purchasing tiny parts for new cars.

$ Although most people work down the price when they buy a house, they often settle for a mortgage they could have bettered with a little bargaining. Mortgage interest can vary as much as one percent among rival banks in the same city. This is your invitation to play one against the other and dicker for the most favorable rate, reduce prepayment penalties or extend the number of repayment years. By opening a checking account with some mortgages, you can win a ¼-percent reduction in mortgage interest.

$ Merchandise advertised in the classifieds is fair game for really hard bargaining. Even if you are willing to pay $100 for an old buffalo head, offer $10. The seller may be under orders from his wife to "get that dirty thing out of the house."

$ When shopping for a new car, figure as much as 20-percent negotiating room between the sticker price and what the dealer paid. On occasion, the dealer may yield all his markup to a hard bargainer because he must meet the manufacturer's sales quota. And your "steal" may help him win the car maker's bonus for big-volume dealers.

$ You have bargaining room, too, on appliances, TV sets and cameras, which are usually wholesaled 40 to 50 percent below the manufacturer's suggested retail price. With furniture and clothing, the dealer customarily pays half of what he expects to realize.

Induce the Seller to Move First. Check the tires, look under the hood and frown. Comment on every bit of rust and wear. Worry aloud about the mileage. As you steadily attack the car's value, the salesman realizes he'll have to come down. "We might be able to go $3200," he ventures.

Keep Initial Offer Low. You look unimpressed, but your pulse quickens. You counter low. "I'll give you $2500," you say, watching carefully the salesman's reaction.

"No," he says, "we can't go that low." But he's still bargaining.

"Too bad," you say, starting to leave. "For the right price I might have been interested."

The salesman hesitates. "Wait a moment. Let me see what my manager will do." After huddled discussion, he returns. "You're lucky. The boss says $3000—but no lower."

He's down to your maximum limit. You're elated, but you don't show it. There may be more. "If your boss makes it $2700, he's got a deal."

Split the Difference. More huddled conversation. "I can't budge him," the salesman tells you. "But I need this sale. It'll mean shaving my commission, but let's split the difference." To allow him to save face, you agree and shake on the deal. For $2850—$550 under the dealer's asking price and $150 below what you were secretly prepared to pay—you drive away in your car.

Here are more techniques to use when negotiating for other items:

Test the Seller's Mood. Do some gentle probing. "You must get tired of showing strangers through your home," a professional negotiator remarked soothingly after touring a house he was considering buying. "After four months, I'm half crazy with people stomping through, criticizing my taste in furniture," exclaimed the owner. Handed the power of this information, the negotiator whittled $10,000 off the selling price.

Hide Behind a Third Party. When you're up against a toughie, one expert suggests you draw on a "big, bad bear in the back room." Your banker makes a fine grizzly. ("He won't loan me more than $5000 on this deal.") Or a husband. ("I love it but he'll be furious if I pay more than $50.") You avert direct ego conflict because it's not you making the demands.

Play Off the Competition. You ask three contractors to bid on a swimming pool. One proposes to spray on the concrete; another to drape a plastic liner over cinderblock walls; and the third tosses in a ceramic-tile coping. Combine the best ideas from each into new specifications and ask the contractors to bid again. Chances are, they'll bid low, not only to stay competitive but to protect the time they've already invested in seeking your business.

Alter the Payment Terms. You might, for example, get a favorable price for your home by agreeing to take the buyer's second mortgage. Or urge a merchant to give you a discount for paying with cash instead of a credit card; the merchant loses no money because he pays no credit-card service charge.

Nibble. Negotiate for extras: a couple of free ties if you buy a dozen shirts; free alterations if you go for the more expensive suit. Or, buy the refrigerator only if the dealer carts away your old one without charge.

BARGAINING may expose you to an occasional put-down, but your triumphs will more than offset the ego bruises. Once you get the hang of it, you'll wonder why you waited so long to save big money—and you'll have a lot of fun in the process.

HOW TO SHOP FOR FOOD

by SYLVIA PORTER

FOOD is one of the biggest items in today's cost of living. Because you buy food at least once a week, it is also one area where you can correct costly errors easily and get in the habit of saving substantially. Here are a few major keys to saving money on food.

1. *Plan before you go shopping.* Always have a pad at hand so you can write down food items you need as supplies run low. Consult store ads as you make your list. Weigh the cost of gasoline—and time—in choosing a supermarket. The least expensive supermarket almost surely won't be the cheapest if you have to drive twice as far to reach it.

2. *Do not shop for food on an empty stomach.* Surveys reveal that those who shop after meals invariably spend less than those who shop when hungry.

3. *Consider quality in relation to the projected use of food.* If corn on the cob is to be the heart of a meal, of course you'll want the best quality. But if you're using corn as part of another dish, you'll do just as well with a much less expensive form.

4. *Go easy on snack foods*—they can add ten percent to your weekly food bill. Rely on natural snacks with good nutritional value—*i.e.,* orange juice instead of orange pop, fresh fruit instead of candy, etc.

5. *Every food chain and many independent stores sell their own private-label products at prices running as much as 20-percent lower than those of nationally advertised brands, and the quality is generally comparable.*

6. *Always check seasonal specials.* Many fruits and vegetables that come to market in abundance in summer cost up to 50 percent less than in winter. But don't buy the *first* of a crop; prices will go down as the supply increases. Also time your buying of canned and frozen fruits and vegetables to take advantage of lower-priced end-of-summer surpluses.

7. *Compare package sizes in relation to how quickly you will consume the contents.* The "family economy size" is no bargain if you end up throwing out leftovers. But buy bulk

items that you use often, such as flour and sugar, in bags rather than in boxes. You're likely to save at least 20 percent.

8. *Determine whether an item is cheaper to buy fresh, canned, frozen or dried.* Per-serving costs of condensed soup, for example, can run as little as one-third the cost of water-added varieties.

9. *When you shop for low-calorie foods, stick to ordinary foods (if you're not on a special diet)*—fresh celery, carrots, radishes, fruits, consommé, low-fat milk—and avoid higher-priced items on the diet shelf.

10. *Stretch your food dollar by learning about food standards and the rules for food labels.* Under a 1974 federal law, ingredients on every package or can of food must be listed in descending order of volume (if beef stew shows beef way down on the list and potatoes way up, this is a clue that you are buying mostly potatoes). It must be stated on the label if the food is an imitation. Be aware that common label terms often have precise meanings: beans with frankfurters in sauce means at least 20-percent franks; beef with gravy means at least 50-percent beef; spaghetti with meatballs means at least 12-percent meat.

11. *Realize that the date on a package of perishable or semi-perishable foods is frequently the last permissible day of sale.* If you see an item on sale after that date, it should be offered at a greatly reduced price. If you discover that you have bought an out-of-date item at a non-sale price, demand a refund.

12. *Use the unit prices which many stores now feature.* Look for a label (on the edge of the shelf under an article that you are considering buying) which tells the cost *per measure* (pound, pint, number, etc.). That's the unit price. This breaks down the cost of the particular item into a simple standard so you can choose between brands and sizes on the basis of price.

For instance, say you are buying tomato juice. If a 46-ounce can of brand A is priced 93 cents, the unit price is 65 cents a quart; if a six-pack of 5½-ounce cans of brand B sells at 99 cents, the unit price is 96 cents a quart. With prices thus given per quart, it's easy to find the best buy.

13. *Buy meat by season.* As a rule, beef prices are lower in winter and higher in late summer. Steak prices tend to be highest during the summer "cookout" months, and roasts cost more in the late-fall and early-winter "oven-cooking" months. In contrast, veal prices tend to be lowest in the spring and

summer and highest in the winter. Your No. 1 way to save on meat is to shop regularly for such meat specials and stock your freezer. You can save a considerable amount on your meat bills simply by buying meat at special times and prices.

14. *Shift your family to less-expensive cuts of meat.* The nutrient content of these cuts is at least as great as that of the more expensive cuts, while the fat content is in most cases significantly lower. These cuts may be less tender, but they are also leaner, and you can tenderize by grinding, cubing, pounding, using commercial tenderizers, marinating, or pot roasting.

15. *You will save an impressive amount of money if you roast meats at no more than 300 degrees to 325 degrees F.* They will shrink less, be tenderer and easier to carve.

16. *Buy bulk "family packs of hamburger, chops, chicken.* Meat in large quantities almost invariably costs less than in small packages.

When you buy ground beef, try the least expensive forms first. In a major study, Consumers Union found that the price difference in hamburger meat from ground beef to ground round was as much as 40 cents a pound in the same store, although analysis showed that the differences in amounts of fat, water and protein were "indistinguishable."

17. *Canned-meat meals—ham, beef roast, corned beef, luncheon loaves—are money-savers for small families.* although they are initially expensive, there will be no waste.

18. *Whole chickens and turkeys generally cost less per pound than cut-up chickens and turkeys.*

REMEMBER: real food savings *are* possible. All you need do is *plan.*

PART THREE:
ORGANIZE YOUR LIFE

CHAPTER 8
Make a Life Plan

SEVEN STEPS TO GREATER PERSONAL FREEDOM
by VANCE PACKARD

AMERICANS are a free people, perhaps the freest in the world—but some are more free than others. How about yourself? Are you free enough to live the way you wish? Or do you often feel hemmed in, manipulated, frustrated? Do you have to spend an unreasonably large part of your life doing things you don't want to do? Do you yearn to be a more vivid and effective individual than you feel you are?

If so, you are not alone. Most of us feel a crowding in on our lives, as we dwell in ever larger communities and work for ever larger organizations. In the course of researching five books I wrote on the pressures that threaten personal freedom today, I found that we are increasingly pressed to conform in order to climb business pyramids and achieve social status; that we are increasingly subjected to attempts to manipulate our opinions and pry into our personal lives. Many readers have asked me: What can we do to preserve freedom in our society?

We as individuals can be truly free only as we are sufficiently independent, powerful and influential in our own right to become persons to reckon with. This is also the path to individual satisfaction in life, for freedom, with responsibility, is the only sound basis for personal happiness.

What then can each of us do to strengthen personal freedom? Here are seven lines of action which you might consider:

1. *Save Money.* Too many of us think of savings as security for old age. A more important function is to strengthen our independence right now. Yet I have seen a statement that the average family is living three months from bankruptcy, and our consumer installment indebtedness has risen many fold since World War II. Obviously, a man who cannot afford to be out of work for a few months cannot afford to quit a job that leaves him feeling stifled or guilty.

This stifling, guilty feeling afflicted the sales manager of a printing business. He was well-paid. But he suffered from agonizing headaches because he got most of his orders from purchasing agents who expected kickbacks, which his firm provided in disguised form, and this troubled him deeply. His wife, who managed his income, urged him to quit. He protested, "But what can I do?" She told him that she had enough saved in government bonds and a bank account to give them a year to make a fresh start.

They moved to the Northwest, and he settled in a job as his own boss, selling household equipment. When I met him he was exuberant. "You know," he said, "thanks to my wife's thrift, I haven't had a headache in ten years."

By contrast, an advertising executive once told me that he and his family could not live on his $50,000 salary. He contended that his employers expected him to maintain a certain style of life. The truth is that any family above the poverty line can build up its savings—and independence—if it is frugal and relatively nonmaterialistic in what it considers to be the good life.

I knew a financially pinched family in which the husband smoked two packs of cigarettes a day, his wife and teen-age son a pack each. One night when the husband was groaning about his money troubles, I mentioned that a lot of his income seemed to be going up in smoke. Put in a bank annually to gather interest, this sum would in 15 years amount to thousands of dollars more than their mortgage, which had 12 years to go! The family stopped smoking.

2. *Build Your Education and Skills.* Personal freedom can be expanded by education and skills because they open up a wider range of professional opportunities. Knowledge is a tangible asset, quite often the most important tool in our work. The more marketable knowledge you possess the freer you are, for it can't be taken away from you—it's a tool you carry around in your head.

This competence cannot, in fact, be taken away from us except by obsolescence. In today's world many of us can feel competent, and free, only as we keep abreast of new developments in our field. We are going to hear a great deal, in coming years, about the importance of continuing education. For example, a friend of mine who is a successful electrical engineer goes to college several nights every week. He keeps himself up-to-date in his fast-changing field by repeating ten percent of his college courses every year!

3. *Keep Your Honor Clean.* To maintain freedom, we

should reduce personal frailties, for these make us vulnerable. It is still true that an upright man is more likely to dare to speak the truth.

In today's world, our dubious or foolish acts of the past are more likely to haunt us than they would have in yesteryears. With the growth of vast record-keeping organizations, electronic memory banks and far-flung investigative bodies in both government and business, there is less chance that past foolishness or indiscretion will be overlooked.

Recently a young man in Connecticut was being questioned by police late at night after an accident. He was offended by the routine questions and, instead of responding matter-of-factly, he taunted the police to arrest him or let him go. Rather reluctantly they put him in jail. The lad didn't realize it, but the fact that he has served time in jail will have to be recorded if he applies for a job with the government or with many business firms. This can limit his chances of getting a job, and thus his freedom, too.

4. *Keep Your Private Life Private*. Privacy is at the heart of our concept of freedom. It is the first thing to disappear when freedom disappears. And privacy is in danger today.

What can we do about it? We can at least preserve the privacy that remains to us, instead of, as so many do, *giving* it away. Emerson said, "The private life of each person should be a more illustrious monarchy than any kingdom." The genuine individualist needs a private life as well as a public one—in order to be himself. Young people need privacy to dream and plan and to discover what they stand for. In his biography of President John F. Kennedy, Arthur Schlesinger, Jr., noted Kennedy's firm determination while he was in the White House to defend his periods of privacy because they permitted his inner self "to ripen into free and confident maturity—and to renew and replenish the public self."

5. *Don't Give Your Life to One Organization—Unless It Can Be Given Wholeheartedly*. Today, most of us work within vast organizations that we do not personally control, and one of the sad spectacles of our time is the large number of people who feel that they have been swallowed up or "absorbed" by such organizations. The many layers of authority surrounding them may leave them feeling insignificant.

Fortunately, many "organization men" are starting to show a new sense of freedom. It has become increasingly easy for a person of talent to change jobs: a host of "search" firms have sprung up that are glad to serve as intermediaries. But the problem of the Big Organization is also a problem of individual planning and choice. Many people make no plans; they just drift, then make the best of whatever job they get. But life is a matter of choices, and freedom consists in making them for yourself. All of us should assess the potential for freedom in any important action. Ideally, we should only work for things we believe in.

A man in my town was offended recently by a long personality test his company required him to take. He resigned,. stating that he did not wish to work for a company that probed into his family life, sex habits, etc. He quickly obtained a job with another company, where, today, he is happy. In my view, his choice made his future a freer one.

6. *Build Your Web of Influence*. I have to travel more than I like and have difficulty in keeping posted on the problems of my hometown in Connecticut. Fortunately there is a businessman in my neighborhood who is my guide when it comes to such issues as changing the zoning laws or revising the high-school curriculum. There are men and women like this in many neighborhoods. Political scientist James MacGregor Burns found that a "web of leadership" stretches through society. He includes in this web the "man next door who seems to know the score," the grandfather who still influences his whole clan, the well-informed man who shares his views with the people who ride to work with him. All are leaders. They are all the more effective because they are trusted and have nothing special to "sell."

The democratic process rests largely on these millions of opinion leaders. Political scientist Hannah Arendt observed that tyrants are effective only over people who have been isolated against one another; one of the tyrant's first concerns is to bring about such isolation so that people feel impotent and unable to act in concert. Where webs of influence exist, no man is an isolated cipher. And those of us who, by keeping informed and making responsible decisions, become opinion leaders, develop freedom power thereby. People think twice before pushing an opinion leader around.

How can you build a web of influence? By reaching out and sharing your concerns with others. And by making certain that they are well-informed and well-balanced concerns! If you keep informed and cultivate a sense of good judgment, your views are bound to influence others. And as others come to respect your views, you gather strength.

7. *Develop a Passion for Personal Responsibility.* The sovereign way to personal freedom is to help determine the forces that determine you. Be active! Take on responsibility! This means not merely voting, but working for the things you believe in. If you do not, you are surrendering your fate to others who do act. What groups are you active in that help make ours a better land? Or are you leaving it to the government? If so, you might be interested in what the noted historian of Greece, Edith Hamilton, wrote of the decline of Athens: "When the freedom they wished for most was freedom from responsibility, then Athens ceased to be free and was never free again."

Individuals can work effectively through volunteer groups to correct conditions that offend them, but a strong-willed individual working alone can sometimes generate action. Many years ago, in a southern state where other colleges were involved in bitter disputes over whether to enroll their first black student, the president of a community college quietly enrolled more than 40 such students, with good support from the community and student body. I asked one of his associates for an explanation of the president's remarkable success. He replied: "Wasn't it Thomas Jefferson who said that a majority is one man with courage?"

The truth is that there is a great deal that most of us can individually do to increase our freedom. We can combat the forces that would make us tame. We can fortify ourselves with the qualities and conditions that promote individual freedom. In doing so, we will be helping to create a better environment of freedom for all.

HOW TO BE MORE SUCCESSFUL

by EDWIN DIAMOND

Is IT possible to predict whether or not an individual will succeed in any given occupation? In business colleges, psychology research centers and large corporations today, there is increasing recognition that the factor of motivation may be more important than many others in making such predictions. Common sense has always suspected this; now there is impressive confirmation in scientific studies.

Under the leadership of Harvard Psychologist David McClelland, behavioral scientists isolated the kind of motivation that seems correlated with success. They call it "achievement motivation"—and believe that they can test it in any individual and then predict his performance. More remarkably, they believe that they can *increase* motivation, a factor that used to be thought of as relatively unalterable. Let's look in on one of the tests:

In 1973, in a downtown Baltimore office building, about 15 people milled about rather uncertainly. They had been invited to play the "ring toss game." A spike was set out at one end of the room, and each person was given a handful of rope rings to pitch onto the spike. It was like a game many of us have played as children; but this was no kid stuff. It was part of an experimental course underwritten by the U.S. Small Business Administration—one of a number of tests to see how much achievement motivation the students—people with plans to operate small businesses—already had.

The way it was set up, there was no fixed line to toss from. Some people stood quite close, easily ringing the spike—and quickly lost interest. Others stood relatively far away, failed to make any ringers and became discouraged. But a few stood just far enough away to make the toss challenging, yet not so far away as to make success impossible. That was one sign that they had a high degree of achievement motivation. For the class taught that highly motivated people always set goals high enough that they present challenges, but within reach so that at least some of them can be realized quickly. These people

135

are hooked on what McClelland calls "accomplishment feed-back"—a continuous sense of satisfaction in their ability to meet short-run goals.

After tests like this, the people were subjected to intensive training that actually increased their motivation. More than 200 participated in this demonstration project in eight major cities; six months later, a check of their business accomplishments revealed that most had made substantial advances. Similar training had aided iron-foundry owners and truckers in India, farmers in Tunisia, hard-core unemployed in Boston, Mass., and junior-high school math students in St. Louis, Mo., and San Mateo County, Calif.

McClelland's whole approach consists of changing motivation by changing the ways people think about themselves and their surroundings. Change how a man habitually *thinks* about his performance, McClelland and his associates believe, and you can change his actual performance.

Motives, McClelland asserts, can be located mentally just below the level of full awareness, in the "preconscious mind"— the borderland between the conscious and the unconscious. This is the area of reverie, of daydreams, where people talk to themselves without quite being aware of it. But the pattern of these reveries can be tested, and a person can be taught to change his motivation by changing his reveries; the individual can program his fantasies so that they constantly urge him on instead of blocking him.

On one level, McClelland's ideas sound like nothing more than just good common sense. But he stresses that they are based on more than 25 years of "hard-line" research and have therefore supplemented popular intuitions with precise scientific verification.

Indeed, by the mid-1960s McClelland and his associates in the Harvard-M.I.T. community believed that they had enough concrete knowledge to test anyone for achievement motivation and improve his subsequent performance. So they organized the firm of McBer and Co. (McClelland is now board chairman) and have since conducted testing and training programs for such clients as Mattel, Inc., Monsanto, Baxter Laboratories, Inc., General Electric and Coca-Cola.

The firm employs a battery of tests to measure motivation. Once this has been done, how do you *change* your motivation? McClelland and his associates hit upon a novel approach: Teach the subject how to score higher on the tests that measure his imagination. If motivation was rooted in his thinking, and the tests measured its quality, training him to do better on the test might actually change his thinking and hence his motivation. Evidence soon accumulated that this unusual approach worked. So "motivational training" courses—exercises in imagination—were developed, in which students are taught how to outwit the exams.

Men and women train for ten hours a day during a period of three to five days. In a typical test, for instance, they are shown a picture of a man working with a slide rule at a desk and asked to write a "brief but imaginative story" about what is happening in the picture. The "best" answers (those showing strongest motivation) cluster around the theme of problem-solving, of devising new ways of doing a job better. This principle is explained to the trainees after they have taken the test, and they then keep writing scenarios until they can produce, easily and spontaneously, stories that will rate high.

McClelland sees in these motivation studies distinct self-help possibilities. Here are some suggestions:

1. Arrange for some "accomplishment feedback." This is the art of designing tasks so that you succeed bit by bit, reaping a reward each time, and thus strengthening your desire to achieve more. This has worked for me. I was bogged down in an extremely complex book project, when I decided to try to publish parts of each chapter as separate magazine articles. The sense of accomplishment from each step kept me going.

2. Seek models of achievement. According to David Kolb, associate professor of management at M.I.T., "If I see people around me succeeding, it will stimulate my desire to succeed." The process works in other ways as well. Harry Truman came from a modest home, but he attributed the eminence he attained to the heroes he modeled himself after—the famous statesmen he had read about in books.

3. Modify your self-image. People with high achievement motivation seek personal challenges and responsibilities, require continual feedback of success. These are experiences that they desire so much that they may be said to *need* them. McClelland believes that it is possible to develop such wants by reconceptualizing oneself as someone who requires these things. As a first step imagine yourself as a person who *must* have success, responsibility, challenge, variety.

4. Control your reveries. Just beyond the border of awareness, most of us are constantly talking to ourselves. Some of us give ourselves assurance; others do quite the contrary. Great athletes—Billie Jean King, for one—talk to themselves during matches, repeating words of encouragement. Conversely, negative ideas that linger in reverie can be discouraged by simply saying, "Stop!" whenever they are detected at the border of consciousness. There is plenty of evidence from new studies of behavior that this works.

People who have developed this kind of motivation are largely responsible for the economic growth of their communities, McClelland believes. He describes some of the human transformations his courses bring about. A small radio-shop owner in Hyderabad, India, is motivated, after a course, to start a large paint and varnish factory; it succeeds, and jobs are created. A banker decides he has been too conservative about the security he demands for commercial loans; he starts to gamble purposefully, and his bank flourishes

McClelland's point is that *you* can be one of the do-ers, if you change your motivation. "People can be different if they *want* to be," he says. We can all "re-invent ourselves" by consciously changing the motives which, more than anything else, determine how we will act and the kind of person we will therefore become.

PLAN FOR A LONGER LIFE
by BLAKE CLARK

"How CAN I feel better and live longer?"

For the answer to this question, some 255,000 people a year come to the famed Mayo Clinic. Since the turn of the century, when brothers William and Charles Mayo started the clinic in the small town of Rochester, Minn., this medical mecca has been sought out by more than three and a half million persons—kings, plumbers, presidents, famous artists, farmers, corporate executives.

Though they come with every malady known to medical science, what they really want to know is, "How can I feel better and live longer?"

"What do you tell them?" I asked ten present and former members of the Mayo staff (average experience at the clinic: 28 years). Their answers are based on observations of thousands of individuals, many of whom they see year after year, and are colored by their distress that such a large number of people could have prevented their own illness or early death. Indeed, many need not have come at all.

Here are the steps that these doctors recommend for longer, healthier days on earth.

1. Realize that a longer life is chiefly up to you. "To a greater extent than ever before," says Dr. Bruce E. Douglass, chairman of the division of Preventive Medicine and Internal Medicine, "barring acidents, many of which are preventible, longevity is up to the individual." The enormous gain in life expectancy in America—73.3 years in 1978, an increase of 24.8 years since 1900—is a gift of modern medicine, research and public-health measures. The top killers at the beginning of the century were infectious diseases—pneumonia, influenza, tuberculosis, diarrhea and diphtheria. They accounted for one third of all fatalities. Now, thanks to hygienic and medical advances, all are far down on the danger list.

Today's major killers, says Dr. Douglass, are the diseases of the middle and later years. Arteriosclerosis and cancer account for 70 percent of all non-accidental deaths among adults. Yet the alert individual can do *more* than the doctor to protect himself from getting these disorders. Knowing this gives us the

139

incentive to be less fatalistic—and to take better care of ourselves.

2. *Have a periodic medical checkup*. This is your first investment in future health, says Dr. Albert Hagedorn, senior consultant in hematology and internal medicine. Chest X rays may reveal an early lesion, a prostate exam a tumor, the cardiogram an indication of ateriosclerosis, blood-pressure tests a susceptibility to hypertension. If so, you can take preventive action at once.

It is especially in the crucial age group from 40 to 50 that today's killers creep in. "We find that if you weather this dangerous decade," says Dr. Douglass, "and continue to take care of yourself, there can be many years of smooth sailing to the 70s and beyond."

3. *Don't ignore symptoms*. "I think of a young lady from Wisconsin who had ignored a vaginal discharge," says gynecologist Dr. Mary Elizabeth Mussey. Her cervical cancer was discovered too late. A woman may greatly diminish her chances of dying of this type of cancer, adds Dr. Mussey, if she goes once a year for the painless, inexpensive "Pap" test, which detects malignant cells in time for successful treatment.

"Just this morning," senior consultant in the Division of Medical Oncology Dr. Harry Bisel said in dismay, "a woman in her early 30s admitted she'd watched the lump in her breast grow until it was the size of a baseball. Breast cancer is the No. 1 tumor we see, and we can cure at least three out of four if we treat them early." If they have had time to spread to the lymph nodes in the armpit, the chances for cure go down to one in four.

"People have a great ability to ignore symptoms," observed Dr. Kenneth G. Berge, consultant, in the Division of Community Internal Medicine and professor of Internal Medicine. "All of us here have seen men who have endured repeated chest pains without telling anyone. They say, 'I was afraid it was my heart and hoped it would go away.'" But an early visit to the doctor frequently means the difference between living in fear of a disease that does not exist and taking proper care of one that does.

4. *Reduce your weight steadily each year*. "Most patients," Dr. Douglass told me, "come here believing that it's normal to gain as they grow older—a dangerous misconception. As we age, we gain fat at the expense of muscle. If at 30 you

weigh 170 and keep the same weight at 60, you may be carrying a disadvantageous excess."

"I saw a well-muscled, 30-year-old mechanic this morning whose stomach bulged with fat," said Dr. Clifford F. Gastineau, consultant in the Division of Endocrinology, Metabolism and Internal Medicine. I told him he has two jobs—first to get his weight down to normal, and then to continue to lose weight slowly. At 60 he will be 5 to 10 pounds lighter and have the same relation of fat to muscle he had as a well-proportioned 30-year-old.

5. Stop smoking. The doctors who know tobacco best hate it most. Dr. Daniel C. Connolly, consultant in the Division of Cardiovascular Diseases and Internal Medicine, used to smoke 40 cigarettes a day. But, seeing the tragic effects on patients, he stopped. "Patients are highly motivated to quit *after* a heart attack," he said. "We'd like them to get the motivation first."

"My specialty is peripheral vascular diseases," said Dr. John L. Juergens. "I sometimes tell my friends who are artery surgeons that I can do almost as much for a patient's legs by getting him or her to quit smoking as they can by operating." Dr. Juergens has followed closely the progress of 159 cigarette smokers suffering from advanced arteriosclerosis of the extremities. Of 71 who stopped smoking, none required amputation. But of the 88 who continued to smoke, ten had to lose a limb. "Nicotine," says Dr. Juergens, "is a potent constrictor of arteries. Smoking accelerates hardening of the arteries through some as yet unknown mechanism. I have told patients, 'It's your cigarettes or your leg.'"

Dr. David T. Carr, who left the Mayo Clinic in 1979 and is presently co-chairman of the Thoracic Oncology Unit at M. D. Anderson Hospital and Tumor Institute in Houston, has treated thousands of persons with lung cancer, hates cigarettes with a passion. He considers them the No. 1 health hazard in diseases of the chest. Stopping smoking, he says, is one thing millions of individuals can do to protect their health and prolong their lives. Tobacco is not going to be outlawed, he tells patients. You alone can save yourself from its lethal effects.

6. Watch out for alcohol. Dr. Gastineau says that the average person does not realize how quickly alcohol creeps in for the kill. Liquor carries a lot of calories, he points out. "A two-ounce martini before lunch and a couple before dinner and you're taking in nearly 400 calories a day. A man's total requirements may be only 1800 to 2000." At this rate, he may feel he's not much of a drinker. But, says Gastineau, he is "grossly distorting the pattern of his body's fuel supply. Eventually, in a certain number of cases, fat accumulates in the liver and leads to cirrhosis—a *preventable* cause of early death." The drinker may not realize that the liver can be damaged over a period of time without causing pain.

7. *Exercise regularly.* "Once considered an indulgence for a few, exercise is now a must for all," declared Dr. Douglass. Fit, responsive muscles squeeze the veins and force the blood back toward the heart, helping it pump the blood through the circulatory system.

How much exercise? Dr. Donald Erickson, member of the Mayo emeritus staff, retired, has a rule-of-thumb. "Excercise until you're somewhat short of breath. Like any other muscle, the heart needs deep swings of demand—maximum work, maximum rest." For the normal person, he recommends twenty minutes of activity, such as brisk walking, jogging, swimming or bicycling. "The pulse rate must increase, the breath get short." By exercising at least three times a week, he says, the individual can do more and more all the time, greatly benefiting his cardiovascular system, physical vigor and mental alertness.

8. *Be optimistic.* Physiologically, happiness is healthy. A man depressed suffers a slowing down of all his metabolic processes. A merry heart does good like medicine, runs the proverb, but a broken spirit dries the bones. "You can will yourself to be ill," warns Dr. Hagedorn. "A case of nerves is not just 'in your head,' but is as real as a heart attack." The nervous system has a job, like the heart, and its functioning is affected by stress, such as extra responsibility and futile worry.

"Our patients have similar problems," says Dr. Hagedorn. "Yet we see certain of them die young because they lack a positive attitude." A physician friend of his had a myocardial infarction and literally died of fright. "Yet Presidents Eisenhower and Johnson had similar attacks," observes Hagedorn, "and took the attitude that they could handle them, and did."

9. *Take a vacation.* Relief from everyday strains restores the joy of living. "Many patients look you straight in the eye and say they can't take a vacation," says Dr. Juergens. "This is ridiculous. The poorest farmer in Minnesota can find someone to do the chores while he goes fishing for a week."

Your vacation must be sensibly planned, cautions Dr.

Berge. "To some, a week camping with the family in Yellowstone is not a rest but a nightmare." Golf and bridge are also no good if their competitive aspect leaves you biting your nails. Just get away from your work routine and do something you enjoy. Happiness may be as close as your own garden.

THESE ARE the recommendations of some of the world's most highly regarded medical men. Following them might easily extend your own life-span by 10 to 30 years.

For the first time in history—it's up to *you*.

better. "To some, a week camping with the family in Yellowstone is not a rest but a nightmare." Golf and bridge are also
no good if their competitive aspect leaves you biting your nails.
Just get away from your work routine and do something you
enjoy. Happiness may be as close as your own garden.

THESE ARE the recommendations of some of the world's most
highly regarded medical men. Following them might easily
extend your own life-span by 10 to 30 years.
For the first time in history—it's up to you.

CHAPTER 9
The Big Money Decisions

This year, the homeowners' and auto-insurance policies of hundreds of thousands of Americans will not be renewed, or will be abruptly canceled. A far larger group—as many as 10 million people—will be penalized with auto-insurance premium hikes 35 to 50 percent over normal rates. And at least half of U.S. homeowners, according to one study, will be under-insured against fire and storm damage, some so badly that they court financial ruin.

What about you? Do you have the right policies? Do you review them every year? Or do you, like most Americans, pay more attention to selecting a new brand of toothpaste? If that's true, better change your ways, fast. With premiums for auto and home policies now sopping up five to ten percent of many families' take-home pay, there's real incentive to handle your insurance carefully. If you know what you're doing, you can buy more and better coverage for less money. Here are some points to bear in mind:

The "high-deductible" sidestep. Jack Crawford's homeowner policy might have been renewed had he increased his $100-deductible policy to a $250-deductible. Why? Because the first $250 of any loss would have been his burden, not the company's. Thus he would not have applied for, or collected such trivial claims as $28.70 for the replacement of a stolen bike that had originally cost $128.70, or $42.89 for a throw rug ruined by a dropped cigar. But his costs for homeowner insurance, year after year, would have been ten percent lower—or 20-percent lower if he chose $500 deductible, or 25-percent if he opted for $1000.

HOW TO BE INSURANCE-WISE

by DONALD AND DOROTHY STROETZEL

JACK AND MARY CRAWFORD stared in shocked disbelief at the computer-typed letter. "We regret to inform you," it began, "that we will not renew your homeowner's insurance...." Forced to shop frantically for another company willing to give them insurance protection, the Crawfords had involuntarily joined a large army of Americans who are bewildered and not infrequently outraged by problems with their home and auto insurance—problems that are frequently of their own making, and which could have been avoided.

This year, the homeowner- and auto-insurance policies of hundreds of thousands of Americans will not be renewed, or will be abruptly canceled. A far larger group—as many as 16 million people—will be penalized with auto-insurance premium hikes 35 to 50 percent over normal rates. And at least *half* of U.S. homeowners, according to one study, will be under-insured against fire and storm damage, some so badly that they court financial ruin.

What about *you?* Do you have the right policies? Do you review them every year? Or do you, like most Americans, pay more attention to selecting a new brand of toothpaste? If that's true, better change your ways, fast. With premiums for auto and home policies now sopping up five to ten percent of many families' take-home pay, there's real incentive to handle your insurance carefully. If you know what you're doing, you can buy more and better coverage for *less* money. Here are some points to bear in mind:

• The *"high-deductible" sidestep.* Jack Crawford's homeowner policy might have been renewed had he increased his $100-deductible policy to a $250-deductible. Why? Because the first $250 of any loss would have been his burden, not the company's. Thus he would not have applied for or collected such trivial claims as $28.70 for the replacement of a stolen bike that had originally cost $128.70, or $42.89 for a throw rug ruined by a dropped cigar. But his costs for homeowner insurance, year after year, would have been ten-percent lower—or 20-percent lower if he chose $500 deductible, or 25-percent if he opted for $1000.

On automobile-collision insurance, the savings from a high-deductible policy can be even greater. But the principle, say the experts, is the same: insure only against possible *disaster*, not against mere financial inconvenience. Says Arkansas Insurance Commissioner William Woodyard III, "Insurance money is more cost-effective when spent to protect oneself against a $75,000 negligence lawsuit than to cover a $50 car battery or $200 bumper." (Such losses are better handled as casualty-loss deductions on federal and, where possible, state income taxes.)

• *New deal for old houses.* Suppose a fire destroys only two or three rooms of your home, which is old. In such a partial loss, the insurance has traditionally paid only a portion of the restoration cost unless you're insured for at least 80 percent of the dwelling's *replacement cost* (what it takes to rebuild it, just as it was, if totally destroyed). But that much insurance becomes expensive and hard to get for a rambling Victorian house worth perhaps $50,000 on the real-estate market but likely to cost $150,000 to replace.

The solution? A new type of policy that permits owners of solidly built older homes to collect the full cost of repairing partial damage if they are insured for 80 percent of *market value* and if the restoration is made with contemporary building materials (plaster board, for example, instead of hand-applied plaster).

Generally speaking, insurance on a new house is ten-percent cheaper than on an old one (though this discount is gradually reduced as the house ages). If your dream house is within 1000 feet of a fire hydrant, that can save you another five percent over an identical dwelling farther from such protection. With some companies, you can knock off five percent by putting dead bolts on your doors, having a fire extinguisher and installing a smoke alarm; ten percent if you have an electronic burglar alarm; 15 percent if the alarm automatically alerts security police.

• *Beware of hidden surprises.* Read any policy carefully before you buy it, looking especially for so-called exclusions—losses *not* covered, or limited in coverage. Don't fret over exclusions on CB radios and tape-deck stereos. While their theft is infuriating, it's bearable.

But when a policy limits reimbursement to $500 to $1000 on jewelry, furs, silver and hobby collections such as stamps and antique guns, you may be flirting with disaster. You can protect such valuables only by having them appraised, then insuring each item with a "floater policy" rider on your homeowner's insurance, at a cost ranging from about 20 cents per $100 of appraised valuation for silverware to about $2.50 for jewelry and furs.

• *Know the law.* Knowing your state insurance laws can warn you in advance of threatened policy cancellation, since states carefully limit the circumstances under which a company can legally unload you: generally only for giving the insurer false information, filing a fraudulent claim, failing to pay premiums on time or, in the case of auto insurance, if your driver's license is revoked. Companies can also refuse to renew policies if the number of claims is excessive. Don't hesitate to seek advice from your state insurance commission.

• *Guard against high jury awards.* If your liability coverage for personal injury and property damage is only the minimum your state law requires, watch out! You could be inviting financial ruin—forced to sell your home and all your possessions, even your business, to settle a big award against you. In 1963, there was only one million-dollar liability award granted in the United States; in 1979, there were more than 50.

If you're well-off—and thus a prime target for soft-hearted juries—consider a so-called umbrella liability policy. For less than $100 a year, it puts a one-million-dollar umbrella of personal-injury and property-damage liability coverage over both your auto and homeowner policies. Among other things, such high coverage guarantees that the insurance company will have an astute lawyer by your side in any damage suit.

• *Beware of inflation.* Find out what it costs today per square foot to build a house like your own in your area; then multiply the figure times the number of square feet in your house. That's how much homeowner's insurance you should carry. And plan to hike your coverage each year as the cost of building materials and labor rises. Many companies will now make these inflation adjustments automatically, if you wish. And it's not as expensive as you think: cost per $1000 declines sharply as you increase coverage.

How can you know all the things that affect your insurance policies? You probably can't. But you *can* avoid most pitfalls with a few precautions:

1. Shop before you buy. In most states, rates are set by free competition among companies, not by regulation. In one Delaware survey, auto-premium levels varied as much as 91 percent for *identical* coverage. In Kansas City, Mo., a family shopping for homeowner's insurance got offers ranging from $122 to $286 for the same $100-deductible policy.

2. Get a good agent. Look for the striver trying to build a volume business. And *test* him. Does he, for example, call you back promptly when you phone his office? Does he, unasked, update your policies yearly?

3. Ask questions. Ask your agent, for example, about special circumstances you may have. "Can I get a break on auto insurance for being over 65?" (Yes. Senior citizens drive fewer miles and more slowly, often earning a ten-percent discount.) "Are students eligible for reduced auto-insurance premiums?" (Yes. As much as 25 percent for males, and 15 percent for females, who achieve a "B" average or better.) "Can I get a discount for car pooling?" (Yes. Ten percent at some companies.)

4. Control your own insurance destiny. When your fender is dented, think twice before requesting insurance reimbursement; it could push up your premium cost shortly thereafter. (But *always* tell your company when there's even a remote chance of personal injury.) Want the best settlement from a claim adjuster in the case of theft or damage to household effects? Then put into your safe-deposit box an inventory of your possessions. Photos of your things—especially items of contestable value, like antiques—can help.

HOW TO SURVIVE —
OR AVOID—A TAX AUDIT
by LINDA SMALL

EVERY YEAR the IRS sends out approximately two million letters announcing: "We are examining your federal income-tax return for the above year(s) and find we need additional information to verify your correct tax. . . ."

The language is not particularly threatening, yet many taxpayers are terrified of being audited. "It's like getting a heart attack in the mail" is the way one taxpayer puts it.

One professional tax preparer says, "There is a fear that if anything comes up at an audit you are going to go directly to jail." But the possibility of jail arises only when fraud is involved. (Fraud is deceit, misrepresentation and subterfuge in an attempt to evade taxes due the U.S. government. An honest mistake, or even exaggeration, does not constitute fraud.) Otherwise, if it's determined that you owe additional tax, and you agree, you simply have to pay that tax, plus an interest charge. In 1978, moreover, about 25 percent of those audited escaped untouched—and seven percent got some money back.

Over the last couple of years, the IRS has audited a scant two percent of the individual returns filed. Can you avoid being part of that percentage? Yes and no. Anyone can be audited, but there are ways of increasing or decreasing your chances.

"Think of the tax form as a conversation with the IRS about your taxes," says tax consultant Susan Lee. "It then makes sense that the IRS would question any 'silences,' or unexplained areas."

Since the IRS cannot possibly audit every return, it has a policy of selecting the ones that seem to have the highest probability of error. Returns are screened through a highly complex computer program—the Discriminant Function System, called DIF. The system is fed a composite of average taxpayers based on previous returns. It is likely to "spit out" returns that show deductions above the IRS norm for such items as medical expenses, charitable contributions, business travel and entertainment, relative to your income, family size and other variables. Each return is scored, and as your score goes up, so does the chance of your return's being flagged for review. (Even the auditors do not know the exact, top-secret figures that are used as norms, but every few years the IRS does publish a report of average deductions. See box, page 152.)

Other factors may call attention to your tax return, such as the type of income derived from your occupation—especially that received from fees, gratuities, self-employment, or payments made by contract. In addition, the restrictions have been severely tightened on certain kinds of deductions. If, for example, you take a deduction for an office at home, but you have a regular place of employment as well, up goes the flag.

If you pass DIF's muster, you still increase your chances of "automatic review" if you earn over a certain amount, or if you use a tax-form preparer considered by the IRS to be fly-by-night or unscrupulous. You might also be the victim of a "tip" to the IRS by an angry lover, employer, neighbor or "bounty hunter." The IRS receives thousands of such tips each year; some of them result in additional tax for the IRS and a financial reward for the tipster.

To avoid being audited, some taxpayers fail to take legitimate deductions—a practice frowned upon by the IRS and most tax preparers. If you have a doubt as to whether to take a deduction, most accountants agree that you should take it. If you have a deduction you think may be suspicious, attach an explanation to the return. For example, if your house is blown away by a tornado, you'll have a tremendous casualty loss. The computer may think it's out of line. But if you attach an explanation, it may well be accepted.

IRS auditor Andrea Goldberg cautions, however, that "the explanation itself could trigger an audit. If we see a very thick set of records, we may automatically send it on to audit because it's too much to look at."

Finally, no matter what you do or earn or attach to your tax return, it may still be flagged as part of the IRS's Taxpayer Compliance Measurement Program. About 50,000 taxpayers are selected at random, and their returns are used to compute the top-secret formulas for DIF.

What can you expect if you are selected for an audit? There are three different kinds, and they all normally begin with the IRS sending you a letter. The letter indicates whether you are being asked for additional information to be mailed in for a correspondence audit; whether you are being called in for an office audit; or whether you will be visited for a field audit.

Average Deductions

FOLLOWING is the latest table of national average deductions based on the tax returns filed in 1978 for the previous year. This is *not* an official IRS table. These figures are averages compiled and published by the Research Institute of America, Inc., and are simply meant to enable you to see how your own deductions compare with those of other taxpayers in your income bracket. (The averages for individual states can vary substantially from the national average and from each other because of different tax structures, interest-rate ceilings, etc.)

National average deductions claimed based on adjusted gross income
(Adjusted gross income in thousands of dollars)

	8–12	12–20	20–25	25–30	30–50	50–100	100 up
Medical expenses	$ 977	$ 679	$ 505	$ 520	$ 551	$ 748	$ 1063
Taxes	1165	1508	1945	2300	3124	5488	13,839
Contributions	526	516	563	676	893	1965	9673
Interest	1556	1880	2085	2271	2637	4230	9354

For the *correspondence audit* you simply mail in copies of missing information. If the IRS accepts your explanation, that is the end of it. If not, you may receive a bill. In 1978, nearly ten percent of all audits were handled through the mails.

A letter requesting that you come in for an *office audit* will state the areas on your return that are being questioned, as well as the date and time of your appointment. Goldberg suggests that "if you have any questions about what to take with you, call. And if you can't make the date, call and explain the problem." The best attitude to adopt for the audit is "neutral," she advises. "Don't prejudge what it's going to be like." Be calm and coöperative. In general, it's not a good idea to be too talkative. Keep in mind that you do *not* have to volunteer any information.

A *field audit* is generally restricted to businesses, to self-employed persons and to complex individual returns—situations in which the necessary records are too voluminous to bring to an office.

If you're going to be audited, the first question to answer is: Should you call for help from a qualified tax preparer or accountant? If you think your return is relatively ordinary, you might decide to represent yourself. Susan Lee uses this rule: "Figure out how much you stand to lose if every deduction being checked is disallowed—it may still come to less than the cost of hiring a professional. You might prepare yourself for the audit by having a consultation with a tax professional beforehand. But if you stand to lose too much, or if you are unsure of what is and is not legal, having someone with you who knows the tax law can be useful." (*Note:* If the person who prepares your tax return will not sign it, as tax regulations provide, with his or her name and identification number, find another tax preparer!)

The second consideration if you are representing yourself is what to take with you. *You must be able to justify your deductions and prove you spent the amount claimed.* Have all of your verification or documentation assembled. Do *not* go to an audit with all of last year's canceled checks in a shoe box and expect your auditor to sort them out.

Sharon Hutton, a lawyer, suggests, "Keep a 'paper trail.' Keep canceled checks, receipts for tax-deductible items, documents relative to property, and copies of all materials and documents, including the 1040 form itself which you sent to the IRS at the time you filed your return."

How long should you hold on to records that support an item of income or a deduction? Until the statute of limitations expires—usually three years from the date the return was due (or two years from the date the tax was paid, whichever occurs later). In certain cases, such as income averaging, records may have to be retained longer. And some records, such as those concerning the purchase of or improvements to a house, should be kept indefinitely, so that, if you sell the house, you can prove how much you paid for it, and how much you spent on improvements.

When the audit is over, if you are satisfied with the results, fine. If you do not come to terms about how much is due, you can ask to see a supervisor, which is often arranged on the spot. If the supervisor agrees with the auditor, you still have several levels of appeal. You *could* take your case from the agency's appellate division to tax court, all the way up to the U.S. Supreme Court.

There is no way to eliminate totally for "I-for-Intimidation" from the IRS. But most agents will meet you at least halfway. "We do try," says IRS agent Lillian Sohnen, "although there is no nice way to put your hand in somebody else's pocket and come up with money."

WORKING WIVES: THE SUPERWOMAN SQUEEZE

I can put the wash on the line, feed the kids,/Get dressed, pass out the kisses,/And get to work by 5 of 9—/'Cause I'm a woman. —TV jingle for Enjoli, "the 8-hour perfume for the 24-hour woman"

UNLIKE the tireless temptress in that fragrance ad, Sue Greenwell is only an 18-hour woman. From midnight to sunrise every weekday, she actually goes to sleep—before struggling through yet another working-mother marathon. Once she bolts from bed at 5:45 a.m., the 37-year-old science teacher is shackled to a split-second schedule. While husband Jim dashes downstairs with dirty laundry, Sue slaps together sandwiches for school lunch boxes and spreads a cold-cereal breakfast for the couple's four young children. Then, after a swipe at tidying their Victorian home in Evanston, Ill., Sue sprints out at 7:30 to make her eighth-grade class.

In the afternoon, the marathon runs in reverse. If Sue has to work late, her mother will check up on the kids; in a pinch, Sue's 83-year-old aunt will baby-sit. By 5 p.m., the brood is usually reassembled, and Sue starts to cook; at 6 p.m. or so, Jim Greenwell returns from his job as co-owner of a metal-finishing plant to sit down to a family meal. Increasingly, he helps clean up or puts the kids to bed. But for the most part, Jim reads in the living room while Sue does late-night grocery shopping, grades papers from 9 p.m. to 11 p.m.—and collapses.

Sue Greenwell's go-it-alone grind has become achingly familiar to millions of American women. They are trapped in the superwoman squeeze, the constant pressure to juggle home, family and job. Prodded by inflation, cheered by feminists and abetted by a boom in white-collar jobs, women poured into the labor market during the last decade in a revolutionary tide. Today, a record 51.7 percent of American women work outside

155

the home. As far as support systems go, however, their revolution remains largely unrecognized—by government, business, unions and husbands.

No one toils harder at living two lives than the 5.1 million married working mothers of children under six, the fastest-growing segment of the work force. Overall, 45 percent of married mothers with children under six now work outside their homes. While they earn needed paychecks, these mothers have 6.2 million small children to worry about—and there are precious few places to put them. Counting public, private and commercial facilities, the United States has about 1.6 million licensed day-care slots available. That leaves some 4.6 million kids to be parceled out among baby-sitters and nursery schools—or left alone. "We are one of the few developed nations in the world that do not have serious child-care programs," says feminist Betty Friedan. "We force women to make agonizing choices."

Although Congress has discussed day care endlessly—between 15 and 20 bills relating to the subject have been introduced in every session since 1970—only a few significant measures have passed. Since 1976, parents have been permitted a tax credit of up to $400 for annual child-care costs per child, not to exceed $800 per family. (The actual annual cost per child averages $2500.) And in 1971 Congress approved a $2.1-billion child-development program aimed at making child care available to all, according to ability to pay. But it was vetoed by President Richard Nixon, who declared that such government interference would threaten family life. That sentiment, which still prevails among conservatives, has helped defeat every comprehensive day-care bill for the past ten years.

But things are changing. The women's movement has vowed to make day care and other family issues top political priorities in the '80s. "These are workers' issues, not only women's issues," says feminist Gloria Steinem. "We made the 'revolutionary' discovery in the '70s—that kids have *two* parents. But most people can't share parenthood yet because the system won't let them."

The issues are hardly simple. Many women are uneasy about sending their kids to day care, believing it their personal responsibility to raise them. Compounding the problem is the lack of definitive research on what child care does to kids. Most child experts seem to agree with Cornell University psychologist Urie Bronfenbrenner that "there is no hard evidence that day care has a negative effect." But opinions vary. Psychologist Lee Salk warns, "If parents anticipate not providing enough time for one-to-one contact in the first three years, they should consider not having the child at all."

Some women take Salk's advice. Others quit their jobs, however reluctantly, when they have children. For the majority of working mothers, however, the course is painfully clear: to forage for whatever day care they can find.

According to a 1978 survey of 10,000 working women by *Family Circle* magazine, most mothers want federally subsidized, not federally controlled, day care, where the parents can pick the facility that suits their needs. They would also prefer day-care centers with well-trained staffs to any other arrangements—including family. But one expert estimates that only 20 percent of those who seek day-care centers find openings they can afford. Instead, mothers deposit their kids in neighbors' homes, with relatives or with sitters. (The cost of this make-do care ranges anywhere from $1.50 an hour for a sitter to $150 or more a week for a housekeeper.) And an estimated two to five million "latch-key" children between 7 and 13 simply come home to empty houses.

As many as 200 employers ventured into day care during the "Great Society" '60s, but most started dropping out in the '70s for a number of reasons, including high costs. Today, 41 percent of all available day-care center facilities are operated for profit. Granddaddy among them is Kinder-Care Learning Centers, Inc., of Montgomery, Ala., which operates 700-plus centers throughout the nation.

For many employed mothers—and a growing number of fathers—the most welcome change would be less rigid workdays. An estimated 11.9 percent of all U.S. workers and 24.9 percent of all government employees are now trying "flexitime," which enables workers to pick their own starting and quitting times, as long as they work a required number of hours and are present during a certain "core" period. A mother might come in at 7 a.m., for example, leaving a child in the father's care, and go home when school lets out at 3 p.m.

Part-time jobs are also flourishing. An estimated 17.1 million Americans work less than a five-day, 35-hour week, and 66.1 percent of these are women. And some women now share full-time jobs. "I wanted to raise my own children, but I also wanted to keep working," says Sheila Fritzler, 35, whose share of one probation officer's job in San Jose, Calif., is two ten-hour days a week. At first, Fritzler was treated as an oddity. But now, she says, "even the men are asking about it."

Male interest is crucial if institutions are to adjust. "We will never bring about these changes unless fathers demand them, too," says Betty Friedan. But most men won't buck the traditional male role—and most companies refuse to accommodate those who try. Since passage of the Pregnancy Discrimination Act of 1978, some companies have offered paternal as well as maternal leave. But there have been almost no takers.

"The smart company that wants to tap the best people is going to have to be more flexible," says Felice Schwartz, president of Catalyst, a career-development organization. Control Data, the Minneapolis-based computer and financial-services firm, is one company that got smart. One-tenth of Control Data's 48,000 U.S. employees—including all the workers in a plant primarily staffed by working mothers—now work part time with vacation and sick leave. Control Data also helps sponsor a day-care center, provides an employment service for temporary and part time workers, and offers a liberal leave policy.

Some unions are belatedly beginning to push family-related issues in contract demands. "The national need for day care is critical," says Muriel Tuteur, director of the Chicago day-care center run by the Amalgamated Clothing and Textile Workers Union, one of the few unions thus far to sponsor centers. In its recent contract negotiations with AT&T, the Communications Workers of America, which is 51-percent female, pushed hard for company-subsidized day care and more flexible scheduling for its 625,000 members.

Rep. Cardiss Collins (D., Ill.) has introduced a bill that would include some form of federal funding as well as permit for tax incentives to subsidize child care. But officials are wary of any comprehensive legislation because of its potentially prohibitive cost—and even day-care stalwarts admit glumly that a national system may be a decade away.

By the beginning of that decade, however, working mothers with young children will be nearly 14 million strong—and powerful enough at last to demand the forced retirement of Superwoman and an end to this decade's dictum that working mothers must struggle to live two lives.

WHEN
SHOULD *YOU* RETIRE?
by THOMAS R. BROOKS

Some Americans take retirement early, some late, some never. Others "retire," then start second careers. In these inflationary days, who fares best? Which is right for you? To find out, try this quiz.

1. Retirement under Social Security may be taken at age 62, and some private pension plans make it feasible at 55 or earlier. Yet federal law says almost nobody *has* to retire before 70, and some not even then. With such latitude, what is the trend? Are Americans retiring (a) earlier, (b) later?

2. Suppose you retire at 62. About how many more years can you expect to live? I. (male) (a) 7, (b) 15, (c) 17, (d) 20. II. (female) (a) 9, (b) 21, (c) 23, (d) 26.

3. To maintain a reasonable standard of living in retirement, you need how much of your present income? (a) 50 percent, (b) 75 percent, (c) up to 100 percent, (d) it varies with different income levels.

4. Inflation averaged about 2 percent a year in the '50s, nearly 5 percent in the late '60s, 7 percent or more in the '70s, and as of June 1980 was running at an annual rate of 12.4 percent. With inflation at, say, 12 percent, about how many years will it take to cut the value of your money by half? (a) 25, (b) 20, (c) 15, (d) 12, (e) 6, (f) 5.

5. Americans' retirement income in recent years (a) rose dramatically, (b) rose moderately, (c) remained the same, (d) declined.

6. Which group suffers most from inflation? (a) low-income, (b) middle-income, (c) the wealthy.

7. Most persons who retire at 62 or younger take post-retirement jobs. True or False?

8. What proportion of your retirement income will Social Security provide? (a) all, (b) three-quarters, (c) one-half, (d) depends on pre-retirement income covered by Social Security.

9. Where you live affects your retirement cost of living. True or False?

10. Taxes are no concern once you retire. True or False?

Answers

1. (a) Early retirements became increasingly attractive in the 1970s—they rose from 51 percent of all retirees receiving Social Security benefits in 1962 to 66 percent in 1976. A survey of 100 major employers in the first half of last year found 70 percent of retirees were under 65. Twenty years ago only 8 percent of those 55 to 59 had retired; in 1979, 18 percent had. For the 60-to-64 group, the rate climbed in those 20 years from 19 to 38 percent. But inflation could change this. A 1978 Harris poll found that 51 percent of employees surveyed wanted to work past retirement age, either full- or part-time. Right now, however, the average age of retirement for those receiving Social Security benefits is 63.7 years.

2. I: (b), II: (b). Life expectancy at birth today is 73.2. But you cannot simply subtract your retirement age to estimate how far your retirement income must stretch. Life expectancy varies with age. The average at 55 is 20.6 years for men, 26.2 for women. At 65 it is 13.9 and 18.3 years, respectively; at 70, 11.1 and 14.7.

3. (d) It varies with income. If you earn $15,000 or more, some experts say about 65 percent will do for your *first year* of retirement. But if double-digit inflation continues to erode buying power—especially if you retire early—you may need as much as 100 percent of your current income to maintain your living standard in five or ten years.

4. (e) Six years. To determine how fast income is halved, divide the annual rate of inflation into 72. With 12-percent inflation, buying power is halved every six years (12 goes into 72 six times).

5. (a) It rose dramatically. Social Security in 1950 covered only one-quarter of older citizens. Today, 93 percent are eligible. Private pension plans now cover around half of all workers in private employment, up from less than 40 percent a decade earlier, and many have become more generous. However, only one retired person in seven receives a private pension and, although that will soon change to one in four, other assets—including savings—will continue to be important.

6. (b) Middle-income people suffer most, according to many experts. Social Security provides most retirement income for low-income people; as it is indexed to inflation, their income is not fixed. Wealthy retirees can invest in stocks and real estate. Middle-income taxpayers are relatively more fixed. So-

cial Security is a smaller percentage of their income, and they rely more on private pensions. (Only four percent of private plans are indexed.) Many companies have voluntarily increased retirees' checks, but increases are generally small and occur only every two or three years.

7. True—but many do not plan it that way. With 12-percent inflation halving income every six years, those who retire at 60 have only one-quarter as much buying power at 72. Thus, many are forced into part-time jobs that often become full-time; others, desperate, take any menial and low-paying tasks available.

8. (d) It depends on covered income. Social Security assures only that benefits will replace a stable percentage of pre-retirement income, based on your career earnings, family status and a host of other factors. If you earn the 1980 Social Security taxable maximum of $25,900, some experts say, you will need at least 65 percent ($16,835) to maintain a reasonable standard of living. Social Security, however, will "secure" only approximately 50 percent of that amount ($8600). Couples qualifying for benefits based on the federal minimum of $3.10 an hour (about $6500 a year) will receive slightly over 100 percent of pre-retirement earnings. Those receiving benefits based on career earnings of $12,500 will get about 80 percent. Single workers earning the taxable maximum are most vulnerable; their Social Security benefits are only about a third of pre-retirement earnings covered under Social Security.

9. True. Using the Department of Labor's average budget for retired couples ($7846 a year) indexed at 100, it costs more to live in the Northeast and parts of the Midwest—a 118 rating for Boston, 115 for the New York-New Jersey area, 104 for Cleveland, 99 for Chicago. San Francisco-Oakland is rated 106, Los Angeles-Long Beach 97, San Diego 95.

10. False. Social Security benefits are not taxable, but most other income is. Moreover, if you earn over $5000 a year, and are between the ages of 65 and 72, your Social Security benefits are reduced by $1 for every $2 earned. Real-estate evaluations, too, are rising, so you may pay more property tax. Income deferred under Individual Retirement Accounts and Keogh plans becomes taxable when drawn upon in retirement. Sales taxes continue to bite.

Conclusion: Americans should face the facts about inflation *before* retirement; then, if necessary, plan for satisfying second careers in low-stress or part-time jobs. With retired people growing in numbers, job competition will become fierce. More planning and retraining will be needed to help avoid the crunch that drives older people into menial or unpleasant minimum-wage jobs.

You have the best chance for a comfortable retirement if you have at least two-thirds to 100 percent of your present income freed up, much of it not fixed, and you're headed toward some kind of post-retirement employment. And if you retire early, it should be to seek a challenging second career.

DO-IT-YOURSELF PROBATE—IT'S HERE

by MURRAY TEIGH BLOOM

JOANNE CASEY, a 42-year-old Greendale, Wis., housewife, is a minor neighborhood heroine. In 1974, with no legal help, she probated the $50,000 estate of her father—and saved her mother, the sole heir, more than $1000 in lawyer fees. Moreover, she accomplished the whole business in less than six months; with lawyers, it generally takes about 14 months. "I have only a high-school education. If I can do it, anyone can," she told me.

Wisconsin became the first state to allow do-it-yourself probate, in 1973. When Gov. Patrick J. Lucey signed the historic law, he said, "Wisconsin's probate-reform act represents a great victory for the individual citizen. No longer does the law assume that the average man or woman cannot handle his or her own personal affairs. No longer is the citizen required, in effect, to pay a legal tax, amounting to hundreds or thousands of dollars for a service he wants to perform for himself."

Getting the reform wasn't easy. There was intense opposition from probate judges and lawyers. "Probate has always been one of the lawyer's easiest dollars," explained one non-lawyer legislator. "No business wants to lose a high-profit item."

A statewide petition, carrying 350,000 signatures, helped persuade many legislators. In the legislature, 28-year-old State Rep. (now a State Senator) David Berger of Milwaukee spearheaded the probate-reform movement.

"At first, my lawyer-legislator colleagues tried to talk me out of it," Berger, a non-lawyer, recalls. "They told me how technical probate was; how ordinary people wouldn't be able to handle it; how they'd end up in expensive litigation with estates tied up for years. They tried to defend the minimum-fee percentages they were getting on probate work by stressing the great responsibility they had to assume. When I'd point out that nearly all the probate paper work was actually done by their secretaries and friendly court clerks, they'd say I was just anti-lawyer.

163

"In short," Berger concludes, "the Bar Association had to be dragged, kicking and screaming, into the 20th century by the average citizen fed up with the fees and the filings and the folderol."

The heart of the Wisconsin law is "informal administration" of the estate. *Any size* estate can be probated without constant court supervision as long as all the heirs agree. It helps if the will names someone in the family to be personal representative. If the will doesn't, the heirs can agree on who should take on the job—which consists of distributing the estate, paying the debts of the deceased, filing tax returns and giving each heir an inventory of the estate.

Occasionally there may be a family dispute, and the law provides for taking the issue into court. "In effect," says Berger, "we established that the court's role should be strictly limited to settling disputes—not interfering in the basic, ordinary administration of estates."

Wisconsin has also stopped several forms of probate patronage. Many couples hold their house and their savings and checking accounts jointly. Under the old system, lawyers used to get five percent of the total value of the dead person's share of the property just for ending these joint tenancies. Now the transfer is made by merely filling out a simple affidavit and paying a $10 fee.

Appraisers often got large fees for merely checking the prices of the stocks the deceased held. Not any more. In every case where a minor was mentioned in a will, a guardian *ad litem* had to be appointed in the past—usually a lawyer who received handsome pay for minimal work. Now guardianship is not mandatory; if needed, the guardian can be the child's parent. Finally, the legislation did away with "public administrators," usually lawyers appointed by the local probate judge to collect state inheritance taxes.

Many Wisconsin residents have taken advantage of do-it-yourself probate. In Dane County (Madison), Robert R. Pekowsky, Circuit Court Judge with probate jurisdiction, set up a free consultation program to help do-it-yourselfers. "I explain what's involved, what papers are necessary, how it all works," says Pekowsky, an attorney. "The do-it-yourselfer can purchase, for $2, a copy of our booklet 'The Layman's Guide to Probate.'" (A similar booklet, "Probating an Estate in Wisconsin—Without an Attorney," written by Senator Berger and a legislative assistant has sold more than 40,000 copies, at $1.25 apiece.)

Here is a fairly typical Wisconsin case. Adele Conway* conferred with Pekowsky after her husband, Arthur, died of a heart attack. His will had appointed her as his personal representative to serve without bond. He had left his son and daughter $5000 each, and the rest of his estate to Adele. He and Adele had jointly owned their home, worth about $35,000, a 1972 car, a savings account containing $2600 and a checking account containing $900. He also had in his own name a mutual fund worth about $14,000. His $20,000 life-insurance policy named Adele as beneficiary.

Here's what Adele Conway had to do after opting for do-it-yourself probate:

1. She purchased the necessary legal forms for $1.50 at a local stationery store.

2. She filled out the simple forms to transfer the jointly held home, bank accounts and car into her name.

3. She sent a copy of her husband's death certificate to his life-insurance company so that the $20,000 would be paid to her.

4. She and her daughter made an inventory of the property held by Arthur Conway. They filled out a petition for informal administration (including the signed approval of the three heirs to Adele's appointment as personal representative) and a notice to possible "interested persons" to come forward. They also prepared a simple form to be used in legal-notice ads for creditors to present their claims.

5. After inspecting the will and the other signed forms, Pekowsky issued "domiciliary letters" formally giving Adele full permission to administer her husband's estate. She signed and had notarized a form accepting the role of administrator.

6. She opened a special checking account for the Estate of Arthur Conway and paid all outstanding medical and funeral bills. She obtained her husband's mutual-fund money by sending the company a copy of the domiciliary letters. She gave each of her children a $5000 check.

7. She hired an accountant to fill out the income-tax, state inheritance-tax and federal estate-tax forms.

8. After waiting the required three months for creditors to

---

*This is a composite case; the names are fictitious.

come forward (none did), she made a list of the estate's expenses, subtracted the total from the final inventory value. She got a letter from the Wisconsin Department of Revenue that all taxes had been paid. She filled out, had notarized and signed the final form, "Personal Representative's Statement to Close Estate." Elapsed time: 4½ months. Actual time spent: about 30 hours. Cost to Adele: about $45.

I talked to a dozen do-it-yourselfers all over the state. They had finished or were processing estates ranging in value from $10,000 to $100,000. All of them found the procedure a worthwhile investment of their time; none found any major difficulties. In fact, none of the 400-odd estates probated without a lawyer has resulted in litigation.

As simple as it is, not everyone who comes to Pekowsky opts for do-it-yourself probate. For those who want a lawyer, Pekowsky advises on how to shop around and find one willing to work on an hourly basis. "I have rarely seen legal fees on an informally administered estate go over $600," he says. "And young lawyers—who never used to get a crack at probate work—are anxious to get these cases even on a non-percentage basis."

There are also instances—rare—where do-it-yourself may not be advisable because litigation may follow. For example: when an illegitimate child is deliberately cut out of a will; when an estate is left to a widow whose marriage was considered illegal by others in the family; when there is a large estate—in excess of, say, $250,000. In such cases, a good lawyer might effect tax savings that would earn his fee several times over.

Other state legislatures have been watching Wisconsin's example with intense interest.* In 1975, a do-it-yourself probate law was passed by the Minnesota legislature, thanks to the six-year effort of Neil Haugerud, a farmer and former county sheriff and state representative.

"We've had the same problem Wisconsin had," Haugerud said. "A lot of lawyers and most probate judges were against the reforms." Recalling his battles on behalf of probate reform, he concluded, "It shouldn't take so long to get a basic reform that people want—simple, inexpensive probate."

---

*Thirteen states have adopted the Uniform Program Code and seven more have probate laws which are similar.

CHAPTER 10
Organizing a Life-Style

THE CASE
FOR A SIMPLER
LIFE-STYLE
by LAURANCE S. ROCKEFELLER

THE growing national concern for a better environment and a simpler life-style is already improving America's physical surroundings. It may be a major new moral and spiritual resource as well.

The last twenty years have been as traumatic and divisive as any in our history. Assassinations, a tragic war, and political and economic upheaval have divided and dismayed this country.

In order to face problems like these, a democracy needs themes and common goals which bring unity and commitment. The emerging ecological ethic and the changes in life-style which accompany it may be such a force.

Some may think it ironic that one who has been blessed with a large measure of material resources should be advocating a simpler life-style. Actually, it is, in my view, entirely consistent. The tradition of the value of work runs deep in our family's heritage. My father and grandfather always taught us that waste was a sin no matter how great one's resources.

More and more people are coming to understand that man must live in harmony with nature and not as its adversary. The concept that we have boundless resources of materials, manpower and spirit, and therefore can afford waste, clearly no longer is true. Individually, people are finding that a simpler life-style provides greater satisfaction than relentless pursuit of materialism.

A simpler life-style is a relative term which means different things in different lives. Basically, it involves reducing waste, and employing physical as well as mental and spiritual capacities to the fullest. It does not necessarily involve radical change. For most, it does not mean renouncing modern conveniences and returning completely to nature.

It does mean opening up some form of communication with nature. It does mean reducing reliance on mechanical things and discovering the joy of self-reliance and the satisfaction of physical work. For instance, out of my own experience I know that chopping and splitting firewood can bring not only complete physical involvement but also spiritual and mental relaxation and reward.

An environmental ethic holds that man must live as part of the natural world. He must treat the land, water and air as links in a vital chain upon which life depends. Man already prevails, but will he survive? He must go beyond the concern necessary for his own survival to that required for all other living creatures. Thus, ecology and ethics merge, interact and reinforce each other in what Albert Schweitzer called "reverence for life."

Put another way, the science of ecology tells us pragmatically that we cannot continue to waste, and the ethics of our Judeo-Christian tradition tell us that morally we should not.

Americans in growing numbers are finding that satisfaction of material wants does not necessarily bring a sense of lasting well-being. Many long for something which will give a greater sense of purpose and meaning to their lives.

Myths and misconceptions about a simpler life-style, usually based on the drug-centered behavior of alienated "pseudo-practitioners," have turned some people off. Such behavior does not truly represent this philosophy. An environmental ethic is not an aberrant departure from, but a natural evolution of, a maturing American society. Let's look at the factors which make it part of the mainstream of American thought:

1. Far from spelling deprivation and hardship, a simpler life-style can well mean a more pleasant and even a more comfortable life. Some may choose dramatically austere or esthetic life-styles as their way, but for most a more simple way will need to involve only modest shifts. Exchanging time in front of a television set or in a car for time in a physical activity closer to nature is not sacrifice; it's enrichment. Writes the perceptive bacteriologist René Dubos:

"We shall not go back to the Stone Age nor give up the priceless contributions of technology. But as we worry about shortages of resources and energy, we can derive comfort from the fact that many groups of people at all stages of history have been at least as healthy and as happy as we are, and have achieved great feats of civilization, with techniques and materials that are extremely primitive according to our criteria."

2. Over a century ago such classically American thinkers as Henry David Thoreau and Ralph Waldo Emerson were preaching the values of self-reliance and living in harmony with nature. They understood that man was chosen as a steward for other living things and the earth, not as an exploiter.

Here is Thoreau preaching the doctrine a century ago:

"If a man walks in the woods for love of them, half of each day, he is in danger of being regarded as a loafer; but if he spends his whole day as a speculator shearing off those woods and making earth bald before her time, he is esteemed as an industrious and enterprising citizen."

3. A simpler way of life can be practiced in the cities as well as the country. Many economies and sensible practices are equally applicable in towns, suburbs and rural areas. Wise planning, and the intelligent use and control of our air, water and land are equally important to the quality of life in both the city and the country. It is the sense of being part of nature and not its enemy that is important.

4. The return to more simple and less-wasteful living is entirely consistent with economic growth. For example, the energy crisis creates markets as well as problems. To use less energy, we need more solar-heating units, more insulation, more mass-transit cars and tracks. Major changes in manufacturing processes to save energy call for investment and jobs, the very stuff of which growth is made.

We often hear that environmental-control measures cause industries to close and jobs to be lost. On balance, this need not be the case. Minimizing water and air pollution and cleaning up our cities is creating thousands and thousands of new jobs in this country.

5. The new approach to life fits right in with our concern for the disadvantaged. Too many people still do not have enough of the basic elements required for even a modestly rewarding existence. Complex problems of distribution are involved here, but that part of the gross national product which is used to provide food, housing and the basic necessities for the poor must grow. The same is true for that part of the world which is still poor. More simple, less demanding, less wasteful

living by the advantaged is not inconsistent with this form of growth. If advantaged Americans make fewer demands on limited resources, there will, in the long run, be more for those who now have access to very little, both in this country and throughout the world.

6. Science and technology can be our greatest allies in reducing waste in the production of energy and in industry. Today, we obtain only about four percent of our total energy supply from renewable sources. We must now shift from our reliance upon such non-renewable resources as hydrocarbons and metals to such renewable ones as wood, water power, solar energy, wind, waves and tides and the heat of the earth. Finding ways to use these plentiful, clean and *renewable* sources of energy efficiently is a high-priority challenge. Finding less-expensive and cleaner ways to use coal, of which we have a vast, untapped supply, could drastically reduce our reliance on imported fuels.

Recycling and re-use of non-renewable resources play a large role in eliminating waste. Municipal garbage alone could supply an appreciable part of municipal energy needs if we applied scientific and technological skills to solve the problem.

But what about individual people? What can they do to put a simpler approach to life into practice? Examples readily come to mind.

• More and more people are walking to work or riding bicycles. In the process, they're saving fuel and money, and they're finding that they also feel better. Many people who are now buying cars are looking for smaller ones. and rediscovering the economy of the four-cylinder engine.

• There is a general movement toward participating in all manner of sports, a beneficial change from being passive spectators. People are hiking, camping, cross-country skiing, jogging, swimming and in general enjoying outdoor living in vastly increasing numbers.

• Simple old-fashioned habits of thrift and self-reliance are reappearing in many forms. Some of these are quite ordinary. For instance, many of us have discovered that leaving lights on unnecessarily is a habit that cannot be justified by either convenience or necessity. The great surge of interest in handcrafts illustrates an inward longing for self-sufficiency as well as self-expression. People are starting to save food by refusing to take more on their plate than they really want or need.

• Finally, there is a growing awareness of the importance of family planning. We are coming to understand the crucial relationship between the number of people living on this globe and the continued availability of our limited natural resources.

In total, this all adds up to a new pattern of living—one that is essential to the well-being of individuals and of the nation. If we do not follow it voluntarily and democratically, it may be forced upon us. Some economists and analysts argue that, if we continue consuming resources as we are now, the only way to bring about a balance between demand and supply will be through authoritarian controls. Robert Heilbroner, the distinguished economist, is particularly pessimistic about the capacity of a democratic and capitalist state to impose the discipline necessary to survive in a world of scarcity.

In summary, a simpler life-style and a national commitment to an environmental ethic can help America overcome its material and spiritual crises. Although we think of ourselves as pragmatic and unphilosophical, Americans have always been heavily influenced by what is morally right. The really large events in our history have centered on spiritual values.

The Revolution of 1776, the Civil War, World Wars I and II were all fought for reasons other than conquest or material gain. After each conflict, America exerted itself to make secure what had been at issue in the fighting. We did build a new nation and a new form of government after 1776. Although movement has been too slow, we have been spreading the right to human dignity since the Civil War. After World War II, we have made the greatest efforts in history to help other nations.

During the tragedies of the past, we used our institutions to correct mistakes. We changed a war policy, and we changed a President. It was difficult and divisive but we did it, not for material gain, but to express our moral values.

Now we are faced with the *moral* challenge of simplifying our overly complicated, overly wasteful lives and forging a national commitment to an environmental ethic. We must do this to protect the limited resources on which all life depends. If we do it well, this personal and national commitment *can* enhance the spiritual life of every one of us.

Further, we shall be forging a basis of common commitment and shared goals which will lend basic strength to this nation. It is from such common efforts that democracies draw the strength and develop the moral fiber and self-discipline they need to renew themselves and meet the political, social and economic challenges that now confront them.

HOW TO GET MORE OUT OF YOUR VACATION
by WILBUR CROSS

ONE SUMMER, I spent two weeks in a rented cottage at the shore with my wife and four daughters—our first family vacation in five years. Though we kept saying, *"Tomorrow* we'll get organized and do something that's fun," the days slipped by unrewardingly, with nothing worth remembering to look back on. Later, my wife presented me with an album labeled, "Your Vacation." Its snapshots showed Father listlessly reading a business magazine, yawning on a sagging hammock, washing muddy socks in a tidal pool. To accompany these and other dismal exhibits, she had penned in an old Zen proverb: "No day comes back again; an inch of time is worth a foot of jade."

By contrast, when I arrived back in my office, I heard a glowing account of an associate's vacation. Like me, he had selected a cottage at the shore. But, unlike me, he had put his time to constructive use. For one thing, he had tried "house swapping," turning over his Westchester County home to a Maine couple who wanted a vacation near New York City. In return for compiling a personal notebook of things to see and do in New York City and arranging with friends to include his guests in their activities, he received similar attention from his new shore-community neighbors, who otherwise would have been strangers.

As a result, he and his family crewed in sailing races, enjoyed clambakes, toured historic buildings not open to the public, and returned home with a prized collection of rewarding snapshots. Listening to him, I realized how much more constructive an investment I could have made in my vacation time if I had possessed his perspective when we made our plans. Yet I've discovered that Americans have, by tradition, found it difficult to make good use of their precious leisure time.

Various studies have made this regrettable point. The Southern California Research Council went on to say, "We cannot happily contemplate a future society in which leisure is vacuous or merely filled with hectic amusement. We need to develop new forms of leisure which stretch our minds."

There is no magic formula for planning a fulfilling vacation. But here are some guidelines, with specific examples, for achieving more rewarding, refreshing vacations:

Plan ahead. One family we know sets aside a "Vacation Sunday," usually in mid-January, when they gather around the kitchen table and spread out travel folders, newspaper clippings, letters from friends telling about their vacations, scribbled notes, all collected over past months. On a calendar they mark off all holidays, long weekends, and the most feasible dates for a full-length vacation.

"Everyone has a chance to make suggestions," the father explains, "and we mark them all down, no matter how wild or unrealistic they may seem. Then we circle as objectives those ideas that appeal to the most people. It's remarkable how many of the ideas eventually become realities."

Many people justifiably ask, "How do we know that what seems in advance like a great vacation scheme won't turn into a bust?" The answer: *pre-test* the idea.

The Robert Deanes, for instance, became interested in folklore, and decided that it would be fun to "go on location," rather than merely read about colorful characters and events in books. But they were not sure whether their three children— 12 to 15 years old—could take it. So they pre-tested the notion, using long weekends to explore nearby regions known for legendary heroes and happenings. They were delighted to find that, far from being bored, the children became absorbed in ferreting out little-known information on their own. So, jointly, they all planned their whole two-week vacation around the theme, "Folklore Fiesta."

Become absorbed in a new interest. Good planning combines looking ahead on a long-range basis and seizing unexpected opportunities. Consider, for example, the interesting pursuit of Pennsylvania physician Maurice Seltzer. One day, hiking across an abandoned coalfield, he paused to crack open a piece of limestone waste. "With great wonder," he relates, "I beheld a fern fossil that had been buried in mud for 300 million years. All its harmonious details were etched in yellow pigment."

That chance moment of curiosity so stimulated Dr. Seltzer's interest that he began to read books on minerals and the earth sciences. His wife, too, became intrigued, and together they began planning vacation trips where they could find unusual geological formations. Over the years, their rovings have ranged from the Delaware Water Gap and the Mississippi River delta to the U.S. and Canadian Rockies.

History can provide a useful focal point for a vacation of enduring interest. Texans Marion and Frank Davidson learned that the state highway department had charted and tested ten "Travel Trails" from border to border. Then, the Davidsons, with their 10- and 12-year-old sons, took a vacation trip along "Independence Trail," visiting places like the San Jacinto battleground, San Luis Pass (renowned for its rugged stagecoach run) and the headquarters of pirate Jean Lafitte. "For the first time we had a point of view," says Marion. "Everything we saw and did related to it." The experience was so stimulating that they now plan to cover all the rest of the recommended Travel Trails.

Plan vacation pursuits that you can continue all year. We have a neighbor who used to complain regularly that evenings were "so boring," because her husband was frequently out of town on business. Last year a remarkable change occurred: she took up oil painting, and was soon doing well enough to enter her canvases in local exhibits.

"It all started," she explains, "because of our marvelous vacation. We signed up for an art course on Cape Cod. I never knew that art could be such fun. And, of course, you don't have to put your enjoyment in mothballs once the vacation is over."

Millions upon millions of Americans belong to associations which give them a common bond with strangers and thus can serve as the key to rewarding vacation planning. For example, I have heard about the International Kitefliers Association, whose members transcend language barriers in exchanging visits; about bell enthusiasts who find bells old and new almost anywhere in the world, along with local fans who willingly act as guides and hosts; and antique-car or airplane buffs who welcome one another like brothers.

Consider vacations that can help mold careers. A teacher I met used to devote part of his vacations regularly to helping his three sons and one daughter look into career possibilities. Once they devoted two summer weeks to a broad sweep of transportation facilities (a field in which his son had expressed interest): railroad terminals, airports, shipping offices. On another occasion, they went to a dozen state capitals, as well as to Washington, D.C., for a close-up look at life in government and politics.

And I'm astonished to learn how many people have become so deeply absorbed in new interests during vacations that they have actually *changed* careers. Jerry Wood, of Annapolis, Md., an executive in the toy business, had always wanted to try his hand at sailing. Finally, he bought an old boat and began fixing it up. When a man on the beach asked where he could rent a sailboat for the day, Jerry offered his. That was the beginning of a part-time rental service that gradually made it possible for the Woods to acquire a small fleet.

"As the rental business grew," Jerry told me, "I started giving sailing lessons—mostly in self-defense to protect our investment from misuse." Now Jerry devotes the major part of his time to boats, and has created "Sailing Vacations" and "Sailing Weekends," which enable novices to learn and have fun at the same time.

Use vacations to help others. A working widow in a New York suburb spends half of her vacation time taking underprivileged city children to country fairs, farms and other places and events she would never have gone to alone. "It takes me out of my shell," she says, "and keeps me active and relaxed—instead of sitting on a porch and straining mentally to relive the fun I used to have before my husband died and my daughters moved away."

A creative vacation—whatever sort best suits one's own needs—has many rewards. It infuses something into living that becomes a continuing source of refreshment, and even inspiration, long after the vacation itself has ended. As author and educator Sebastian de Grazia, who made an exhaustive study of man and his free time, has written, "Work may make a man stoop-shouldered or rich. It may even ennoble him. Leisure perfects him. In this lies its future."

TO GET MORE OUT OF YOUR READING

by JOHN KORD LAGEMANN

I NOTICED one evening that my 19-year-old son, Kord, an avid reader, was having trouble getting started in one of my favorite Faulkner novels, *The Sound and the Fury*. How well I knew why! The opening chapter describes a golf game from the point of view of an idiot boy—and it *is* hard to follow.

I remembered a stratagem that I learned years ago when I bogged down in the opening pages of Dostoyevsky's *The Brothers Karamazov*. "Skip the first chapter," I said to Kord. "Get into the story farther on. Later, you can come back to the beginning."

After that, he could hardly put the book aside for meals.

There are other little tricks that seasoned readers use, often quite unconsciously. I once watched Edward Barrett, publisher of *The Columbia Journalism Review*, go through a shelf of newly arrived books. Pulling out a volume, he glanced through its preface, scanned the table of contents, ran through the index and bibliography, looked up a few key references in the text, and consulted the notes about the author. In 15 minutes he evaluated about ten books in this manner, and picked three for further reading.

"Skimming a book is like prospecting for oil," he remarked. "After you learn the signs, you get fewer dry holes."

Most people believe that the way to read a book is to start on page one and read straight through. William G. Perry, Jr., retired director of the Bureau of Study Council at Harvard, agrees that , sometimes, with a great author, this is the *only* way to real understanding. "But it consumes a prodigious amount of time and energy, and not all books are worth it," he says. "Ultimately a busy reader must ask of a book, 'What is this author driving at?' and get directly to the point."

Often when I approach a difficult work of nonfiction I start with the conclusions. Scientists read technical books and articles this way. Almost invariably they start with the summary at the end, then turn back to check the basic findings.

177

There are times when you can't get going, no matter how you start. "Don't try to take a book by storm," my college philosophy professor, James Bissett Pratt, used to advise us. "When you try to read and nothing happens, put the book aside for a time, then come back to it. Eventually it will yield."

Eugene Ehrlich, in charge of Reading Improvement at Columbia University's School of General Studies, recommends getting several books on the same subject and switching from one to another. "Three or four difficult texts are easier than one," he says, "for one book illuminates another."

It is easy to underestimate our capacity to read good books. A popular error, according to Joseph Wood Krutch, the critic and essayist, is to assume that only trivial or foolish or badly written books are "fun" to read. "Nothing is harder to read than that which is not worth reading," he says. "Mediocrity is never entertaining, and nothing is heavier in the hand than too light a volume." Once the reading *habit* is acquired, it is surprising to note how enjoyable serious reading becomes.

In the hands of a seasoned reader, a pencil is a probe that digs the meaning out of a book. "I underline key passages, number them in the margin and index them by subject on the flyleaf," the late Dr. John C. Thirlwall, former professor of English at New York's City College, once told me. "Whenever I need a quotation or an idea of what an author said about love, death or taxes, my index tells me the page number. With the help of the markings I can go back to a book I haven't read for years and quickly make it my own again. If the book I'm reading doesn't belong to me, I jot the page numbers of key passages on a piece of paper."

Summarizing a book, chapter by chapter, is a highly effective way of comprehending and retaining what one reads. Farnsworth Fowle, formerly a writer for the New York *Times*, has a trick he uses to crystallize the gist of what he has read: he pretends he is cabling a summary to his office at $1 a word.

But doesn't this business of marking books slow one's reading? "That is one of the reasons for doing it," says Dr. Mortimer J. Adler, one of our nation's most knowledgeable counselors on reading. "Most of us have been taken in by the false notion that speed of reading is a measure of our intelligence. Some books should be read quickly, others slowly, even laboriously. Intelligence in reading is the ability to read different things differently according to their worth. With good books, the point is not to see how many you can get through, but rather how many can get through you!"

In an apparently shoreless sea of books, it is easy to lose direction, to wonder if one is really getting anywhere. Stuart Chase solved this problem by making a list of "Some Things Worth Knowing"—the title of a book he eventually wrote on the results of his exploratory "voyages." He simply asked himself, "What do I want to know more about?" He started with the universe, got down to earth via the solar system, followed events from the beginning of life to the appearance of man and then investigated man's various activities through reading in economics, psychology, anthropology and religion. A large order—but the kind that can lead to large accomplishment.

Symphony conductor Guy Harrison has been keeping a reading "diary" for years. "I jot down the title and author of each book I read," he told me, "along with a line, sometimes a paragraph, summarizing it—and my reaction to it. I think about what I'm going to say as I read, and this helps me get to the point of a book. Jotting it down fixes it in my mind. Looking back over my notes, I find that even the briefest entries bring back a great deal of the spirit and substance of books I might have lost track of completely."

Reading enhances the other pleasures of life. Recently when I bought a record album of Beethoven sonatas I also picked up a book of Beethoven's letters. I enjoyed the music more because the book made the composer real. As an amateur gardener I depend heavily for counsel on books—and now I probably do fully as much reading as digging, planting and weeding!

For months before taking his family on one of their summer trips—to Canada, Mexico, England, France, Greece—a friend of ours makes a practice of bringing home books on the about-to-be-visited region and holding living-room seminars. When they finally stand on the heights of ancient Chapultepec or watch the changing of the guard at Buckingham Palace, the family's enjoyment is twofold because of the imaginative preview.

Books have a way of bringing people together. A friend told me of a recent experience reading James Agee's *A Death in the Family* in the dining car of a Chicago-bound train. "I read on without stopping, hardly tasting the food, oblivious of everything. Midway in the book I felt tears rolling down my cheeks. I was wiping them away, hoping nobody had noticed, when the stranger across from me said quietly, 'The same thing happened to me when I read it.' I felt as if I had known him all my life! We spent an enjoyable evening together and have been friends ever since."

But, "I have so little time to read," you may say. One winter, while helping my 17-year-old son, Jay, unpack after a ski trip, I pulled a soggy wad of paper from one of his boots and found it to be the first 100 pages of Virgil's *Aeneid*. The other boot yielded a sizable portion of Palgrave's *Golden Treasury*.

"Going up in the chair lift six times a day gave me three hours of reading," Jay explained. "The books wouldn't fit in my parka, so I tore out what I needed."

This was a little rough on the books, of course. But they were expendable paperbacks, and I was delighted that Jay had learned the trick of reading on the run.

My wife has been known to complain about the clutter of books in our house. Admittedly, they are everywhere—on coffee tables, bedside tables, windowsills, even in bathroom and kitchen (she's responsible for that!). But I suspect their availability may have had something to do with developing our son's habit of reading wherever he finds himself.

A visitor to the White House reported that President Kennedy frequently buried himself in a magazine during the few moments it took one visitor to walk out and another to walk in. "Roosevelt got most of his ideas from talking with people," President Kennedy said. "I get most of mine from reading."

So perhaps the best suggestion of all for reading better and getting more out of it is the simple one: *Never pass up a chance.*

HOW TO GET MORE OUT OF WEEKENDS
by FARRELL CROSS

AN ATTRACTIVE secretary awes the crowd by performing stunts on the wings of a speeding biplane. A life-insurance agent wades for hours with his two sons in icy streams, panning for gold. A surgeon splints and prunes trees for his neighbors. And a lady author conducts strangers on guided tours of the landmarks in her hometown.

What do these people have in common?

The answer is that they are all part of the growing clan of ingenious weekenders who approach their two- or three-day respites from routine jobs with imagination, flair and, in some cases, daring. Each weekend, these people lift themselves from a workaday world into one that is so different that two or three days in it are as re-invigorating as a whole month of typical vacation indolence.

"Weekend specials" are now offered by a growing list of colleges, treating just about everything from art and photography to geology, psychology, religion, Chinese and Hindi. In the process, the colleges not only are increasing their income by getting additional use out of their facilities, but are providing stimulating, yet relaxing, weekends in place of the typical evening hours and fatigue setting of standard adult education.

"Weekends are potential 'pocket vacations,'" says writer Janet Graham, who sometimes transforms her own family into weekend archeologists. "The average employe has about five times as much weekend time each year as he has for his entire vacation." Add it up: it's at least 104 days, not counting holidays.

Weekends offer definite advantages over full-length vacations. The cost does not make as big a dent in the budget. Planning is simpler. Also, it's easier to leave children behind with relatives for just a few days than for several weeks. But the most important advantage is variety: you can do 52 different things on the weekends in one year.

The increase in three- and even four-day weekends has made the weekend more significant than ever. Many employers are now giving Friday or Monday off when a national holiday falls on Thursday or Tuesday. Why not use this additional leisure time creatively?

Says Dr. Harry Johnson, president of the Life Extension Institute, "It is definitely better for a person to get frequent short breaks in the routine than one long, continuous vacation. But *change* is the important factor. People need to enjoy activities that are refreshing and different, and they should get as much *physical* activity, within reason, as possible." Backing up this viewpoint is the concrete action of a West Coast doctor who states, "We often prescribe the long weekend as a medical treatment. It gives people a chance to recharge their batteries."

A dramatic example of the physical weekend is provided by a doctor who lives near the California-Nevada border. He gets his action as a weekend rodeo star, roping and riding in several events every year. Although few people would consider this a "relaxing" avocation, he finds that the sport relieves him of tensions and sends him back to his hospital duties with a fresh outlook.

Another doctor felt so refreshed and relaxed after chopping trees and sawing logs that he didn't want to stop when he ran out of timber on his own small plot. He began cutting trees for his neighbors—with the stipulation that in return he could keep as many logs as he wanted for his own fireplace. As his skills in forestry developed, he also learned how to prune and brace branches and even to graft them. "I enjoy it so much," he says, "that I'm tempted to retire at 55 and take up forestry as a full-time job. But then I'd have to find something *else* to do weekends."

Like so many families, mine used to look forward to weekends, only to sleep late, bumble our way through the Saturday and Sunday "chores," and finally end up Sunday night exhausted from doing practically nothing meaningful. Then we learned that weekends can become real vacations if they are planned and scheduled weeks or months in advance.

The best plan, we've found, is an *annual* plan; it enables one to book well ahead for major three- and four-day weekends, helps ensure a well-balanced program that includes amusement, education, physical activity and other important values well distributed for all members of the family. Such planning also increases flexibility: you can have alternative programs worked out so that if, for instance, bad weather cancels a field trip, you have an indoor substitute ready to take its place.

The focal point should be a special calendar and, if possible, a "leisure-time library." Start collecting travel books, magazine articles on weekend and short vacation trips, transportation schedules, maps, postcards from friends, and other information. Ask to be placed on mailing lists of travel agents, clubs, universities, state historical spots, nature organizations and museums. Schedule visits to famous or popular places on an off-season basis, to avoid crowds and peak-of-season prices.

The Curtis Bancrofts of Cleveland, Ohio, have developed their own uniquely imaginative approach to creative weekend-ing. They own a houseboat, with accommodations for ten, on the upper Mississippi River. On several weekends a year, they select subjects about which they know absolutely nothing—astronomy, botany, Greek literature; then, through their college alumni associations and professional societies, they locate professors and others in specialized fields who might like a week-end boat trip. The Bancrofts supply the craft and the piloting, while their guests furnish—in a relaxed, informal setting—expert discussions in their fields of study. Curtis refers to these sojourns as his "seagoing seminars."

Or take a violinist who, when not appearing in weekend concerts, takes his wife and three children "touring on paper." It all started when the oldest son asked his father where the local stream had its source. Not knowing, but curious, the father suggested that they spend Saturday finding out. So they all trooped upstream and found that the water emerged from a mysterious underground brook near a rocky hill.

This experience led to further explorations, and soon they began to make crude maps of their findings. When they could find no names for geographical features, they made up their own—immortalizing first their own names, then those of neighbors, their dog, a hamster. "It made us all a great deal more observant," says his wife, "and aware that there are many natural 'wonders' within hiking distance of our own backyard."

Another family explores the local scene in a somewhat different manner. It's members become weekend journalists, interviewing people with unusual careers, writing up community activities, compiling material from libraries, historical societies and other sources about points of local interest. Once a month they publish a limited-edition newsletter, circulated by the children to friends and neighbors. Now and then the children get an extra thrill when one of their stories is reprinted in the town newspaper.

Quite a few families find a fascination and a broader outlook on life in spending a Sunday or two a month visiting church services of denominations other than their own. Two families we know use their spare time to trace their family trees. They do not simply pore through old records and genealogy books; they go and visit scenes that play a part in ancestral history— the church where a great aunt and uncle were married; the lake where Grandfather was canoeing when he proposed to Grandmother; the trails where the first settlers of the clan hunted deer.

At least half of the fun and satisfaction of creative weekending comes before and after the weekend itself, discussing plans and keeping records. One of our neighbors maintains a checklist of all the things of import that members of the family have done or are interested in doing. When the question, "What'll we do *this* weekend?" comes up, one of the children is sure to scurry delightedly to the drawer where the dog-eared list is kept, and start rattling off ideas. This immediately stimulates discussion, and the family invariably ends up doing something interesting—frequently an activity not even mentioned on the list.

The creative weekend is the answer to the frustrations expressed by author Max Gunther in his book *The Weekenders*. "The weekend in America," he wrote, "is its moment of hope. Every Friday night a national metamorphosis begins to take place. . . . But do weekenders find what they seek? Leaden with fatigue, almost all of them are filled instead with the desolate post-weekend feeling that they have lost something. The rich, full life they dreamed about last Friday has eluded them again."

This kind of depression is not likely to set in with people who think, discuss, plan—and then *create* their weekend fun.

A MATTER OF
LIFE OR DEATH
by ARLENE SILBERMAN

IN 1980, AMERICANS spent $243.4 billion on health care. We also smoked nearly 630 billion cigarettes—and smokers risked minutes of their lives with every cigarette. We supported over 7000 hospitals wth more than 1.5 million beds. We graduated 14,000 new doctors. We also drank 51 billion bottles of beer and 934 million gallons of wine and alcohol—and paid the price in human life again. Almost two-thirds of all murders and drownings and nearly one-third of all suicides involve alcohol abuse, as do roughly half of all fire deaths and fatal car accidents.

In sum, we have chosen a life-style that sacrifices health. Yet we then try to *buy* health back. Unfortunately, as we're discovering, health is not always for sale.

Today's doctors, of course, do perform remarkable feats. But as medical economist Victor R. Fuchs wrote in *Who Shall Live?*, "At present, there is little that medical care can do for a lung that has been overinflated by smoking, or for a liver that has been scarred by too much alcohol."

Our national health record over the past 25 years bears him out. Deaths from lung cancer have more than tripled—and over 75 percent of them are attributed to smoking. Alcohol-related deaths have remained at a constant rate over the last 20 years. We're spending twelve times more on medical care now than we did in 1956 but even if we tripled the current amount those twin killers would hardly be affected.

More money isn't much help, either, to doctors and hospitals confronted with bodies that have been mangled in car wrecks. Motorvehicle accidents are the leading killer of people between the ages of 5 and 35. In fact, our national driving recklessness annually accounts for more deaths than the worst year of the polio epidemics.

What *is* the answer? Clearly, we need to take a hard look at what we can reasonably expect our doctors to do for us— *and what we must do for ourselves.*

Life-expectancy tables make it strikingly clear that doctors alone cannot determine our life-span. If they could, New York State, endowed as it is with 265 doctors per 100,000 people, would be the healthiest state in the nation, not 31st from the top. South Dakota, on the other hand, with only 106 doctors per 100,000 people, should be 50th in life expectancy. Instead, it ranks 11th.

The states where people can anticipate living longest—including Hawaii, Iowa, Kansas, Minnesota, Nebraska, North Dakota and Utah—all have something in common: a tranquil, generally agrarian life-style. Nostalgia for agrarian America cannot, of course, transform large, metropolitan areas into small-town U.S.A.; commerce and industry have shaped us, for the most part, into a nation of city dwellers and suburbanites, and we have to find ways of living and working there without killing ourselves. This isn't always easy. For example, no matter how much individual responsibility a person is prepared to exercise, he cannot, single-handedly, prevent environmental health hazards. No one *chooses* polluted air and water; yet, along with a growing number of other environmental dangers, we are often forced to live with them. Thus "What can *I* do—I'm only one person?" is a legitimate question.

In certain instances, however, surprisingly successful answers have been found. To conserve gasoline during the 1973 energy crisis, for example, speed limits were reduced by law. As intended, we saved gasoline; we also saved lives—more than 9000 of them. Traffic deaths dropped from an estimated 54,600 in 1973 to 45,500 in 1975, a 17-percent decline. The most able doctors and the best equipped medical centers could not have done, even at considerable cost, what "we the people" and our lawmakers did without cost.

What might happen if we drove our human machine with greater care? The neighboring states of Utah and Nevada that Victor Fuchs pointed to in *Who Shall Live?* suggest a promising answer. The two states share a similar climate, roughly the same degree of urbanization, and nearly comparable income levels. But comparability ends there. Life expectancy is 72.90 years in Utah, third from the top; it is only 69.03 years in Nevada, sixth from the bottom. Why?

Fuchs found a startling excess of deaths in Nevada, compared with Utah, from cirrhosis of the liver and lung cancer—indications of too much drinking and smoking. Note that Utah's largely Mormon population is forbidden by the Mormon church from drinking alcohol, tea, coffee, and sodas that contain caf-

"Your-Fault" Insurance?

*By Keith Reemtsma, M.D., chairman, department
of surgery,
Columbia University College of Physicians
and Surgeons*

IN THE UNITED STATES today, with the infectious diseases of the past under control, health is largely a matter of personal choice. But how do you persuade 227 million Americans to take better care of themselves?

In an ideal world, education might be the answer. In our real world, however, where the hazards of smoking and excessive drinking have been known for years, there is scant evidence that education has had any significant impact on health habits.

A more rational approach would be a reward/punishment system based on individual choice. Under this concept—call it "your-fault" insurance—persons with good health habits would be rewarded with lower taxes, while persons who choose to smoke cigarettes, drink whiskey, drive cars at excessive speeds and own firearms would be taxed to cover the medical consequences of these choices. Taxes for medical care would be added on to the price of tobacco products, alcohol, high-powered automobiles and firearms. And industries that produced pollutants would be taxed for the medical consequences of pollution.

There is a fundamental question here: which medical costs should be borne by society as a whole, and which paid for by those who choose to place themselves and others at risk? Clearly, the costs of medical problems over which the individual has no control—of keeping waters pure, or immunization, or the treatment of diseases of unknown cause—should be borne by all of us.

But when health hazards have been identified, and some individuals and industries choose to ignore society's warnings, it seems reasonable to ask that those individuals and industries, and not society as a whole, pay for the medical consequences of their choices.

—*New York Times*

feine. Neither do they smoke any form of tobacco. And since the Mormons view the human body as God's temple, physical fitness is ordained. There aren't many fat Mormons.

Of course, you don't have to be a Mormon to live a long, healthy life, as Hawaiians and Minnesotans clearly demonstrate. (Good health, however, can be a difficult dream for millions of poor Americans. No nation spends more on health than the United States; yet many of our poor still lack adequate medical care.)

But if longevity is a state the overwhelming majority of Americans can afford to choose, the question becomes: how best to do it? The Human Population Laboratory of California State Department of Health, in Berkeley, has spent more than 15 years studying the life patterns and resulting health of 7000 adults in Alameda County. During the study, seven health habits were identified that provide at least the foundation of an answer. For example, a 45-year-old man who practices six of these habits, the laboratory finds, can expect to live 11 years longer than a man of the same age who observes fewer than three—78 years to 67. Even more dramatic, a man 55 to 64 years old who has observed all seven habits will have the same physical condition as a man 25 to 34 years old who has observed zero to two. There is no magic elixir in all this, no exotic prescription. Only these seven habits:

1. *Meals at regular times; no snacking.*
2. *Breakfast regularly.*
3. *Moderate to brisk exercise two to three times a week.*
4. *Adequate sleep—seven or eight hours a night.*
5. *No cigarette smoking.*
6. *Moderate weight.*
7. *Alcohol only in moderation, if at all.*

AS THE FREEST, most independent people on earth, we Americans will doubtless continue to live as we choose. But it is time each of us faced up to the cost of each choice that we make. How many hours of life are you willing to forfeit for your next carton of cigarettes? How many sunrises will you forgo for your midnight raids on the refrigerator? Consider the sound of children's laughter, the sun's warmth against your face, the joy of a family gathering.

Then make your choice.

PART FOUR:

ORGANIZE
YOURSELF

CHAPTER 11

Self Control

A STRATEGY
FOR DAILY LIVING
by ARI KIEV, M.D.

IN MY practice as a psychiatrist, I have found that helping people to develop personal goals has proved to be the most effective way to help them to cope with problems. Observing the lives of people who have mastered adversity, I have noted that they have established goals and sought with all their effort to achieve them. From the moment they decided to concentrate all their energies on a specific objective, they began to surmount the most difficult odds.

The English author Edward G. Bulwer-Lytton wrote: "The man who succeeds above his fellows is the one who early in life clearly discerns his object and toward that object habitually directs his powers. Even genius itself is but fine observation strengthened by fixity of purpose. Every man who observes vigilantly and resolves steadfastly grows unconsciously into genius."

The establishment of a goal is the key to successful living. And the most important step toward achieving an objective is first to define it. I am sure you have at least 30 minutes a day in which to list your thoughts about possible goals. Set aside such a period each day for a month. At the end of that time, choose from the possible objectives you have listed the one that seems the most important, and record it separately on a single card. Carry this card with you at all times. Think about this objective every day. Create concrete mental images of the goal, as if you've already accomplished it.

Don't be afraid of failure. As Herodotus wrote: "It is better by noble boldness to run the risk of being subject to half of the evils we anticipate than to remain in cowardly listlessness for fear of what may happen."

You can determine your special talents or strengths in a number of ways, ranging from psychological tests to an analysis of the unexpressed wishes in your dreams. No one method works for everyone. You might start, for example, by clipping and pasting newspaper articles that interest you. After 30 days, see if there isn't some trend suggestive of a deep-seated interest

190

or natural inclination. Keep alert to the slightest indications of any special skills or talents, even when they seem silly or unimportant.

From this exercise, you should be able to get some sense of potential strengths. Whenever you discover a strength or talent, think of five possible ways to develop it. Write these down on a card as well, and check them periodically to keep them fresh in your mind.

Focus on one objective at a time. Like a servomechanism, the brain, set on a target, will call into play those mental processes that will bring your efforts to fruition. Your actions will conform to your expectations, thereby bringing about the event. If you believe that you will reach your objective, you will continue to work at a task until you have accomplished it.

Always have the next goal in the back of your mind, since the most satisfaction comes from pursuing a goal, not simply from achieving it. Above all, don't be impatient about reaching your objectives. It may be that at first you can devote only one hour a day to the activity that really matters to you. But even one hour a day can mean seven hours a week, 3650 hours in ten years. You can accomplish much in that period of time—take a course, write a book, paint a portrait.

Five Enemies of Peace. The more you break tasks down to their elementary components, the more readily you will be able to accomplish the more difficult and complicated tasks. The belief that you can't do something is merely a rationalization for unwillingness to take a risk.

According to Ernest Newman, the English music critic, "The great composer does not set to work because he is inspired, but becomes inspired because he is working. Beethoven, Wagner, Bach, Mozart settled down day after day to the job at hand with as much regularity as an accountant settles down each day to his figures. They didn't waste time waiting for inspiration." An overriding goal governed the activities of these composers, and others, enabling them to overcome the most extreme handicaps. Activity itself generates the impetus for further activity.

Be aware of situations that generate the five great enemies of peace: avarice, ambition, envy, anger and pride. Petrarch said: "If those enemies were to be banished, we should infallibly enjoy perpetual peace."

Avarice comes from believing that you need certain things

when you probably don't, and from the feeling that what you depend on will be taken from you.

Ambition arises from dissatisfaction with yourself and your activities. It's fine to set up challenges and to want to succeed. But excessive ambition can lead you to set unattainable goals. Pursue your objectives at a pace suited to your temperament. Concentrate on your efforts, not on the results.

Envy comes from an irrational comparison of what others have achieved and what you have achieved. Lack of what others possess does not cause frustration, but failure to develop your assets does.

Anger can envelop you and destroy your incentive. Whenever you become angry, review what has happened. Has somebody ignored or criticized you? Should that bother you? Must you depend on others' opinions? Have you allowed others to impose their expectations on you or to control your behavior?

Pride develops from a need to impress yourself and others with qualities you lack. The mature individual acknowledges his limitations, acts humbly, and tolerates differences with others. Your distress will vanish when you admit your fallibility.

Self-reliance comes from two separate acts: a positive orientation toward goals, and a reduction of unnecessary and inhibiting dependency patterns. Trying to meet the expectations of others in order to be accepted by them creates a compulsion to act in certain ways which limit your own ability to fully express yourself. This is dependency.

Many people become oversensitive to the non-verbal—and often unconscious—attitudes of criticism, hostility or rejection of others. If you find yourself reacting to real or imagined slights, don't argue with people over your impressions. Accusing others of ambivalent feelings or lack of interest in you may frustrate you, foster conflict, and may provoke the very response that you anticipate. Avoid any inclination to respond to sarcasm or innuendo. Acknowledge that everyone has a right to think for himself and close the discussion. Maintaining a positive attitude will, in the long run, draw positive responses from others.

Focus on your attitudes toward other people. Are you too concerned about what they think of you? Does your perfectionism mask an underlying depression? Are you afraid of criticism? If these patterns sound familiar, you should take stock and define goals more compatible with your interests, needs and skills.

Ask yourself, "What factors in my life are draining me? To what extent am I neglecting my own needs?" Are you known as someone with strong shoulders, willing to assume all kinds of burdens? Are you too easy to approach, so that friends, relatives and others feel no hesitancy about imposing on your time? Positive gratification from this must be weighed against the negative price you pay in giving up free choice.

Don't worry about refusing requests that seem to be demanding of yourself. It is better over the long haul for family and friends to know that what you do for them you do willingly, because you want to, and not because you hadn't enough courage to say no.

The ability to withdraw into solitude will increase your faith in your capacity to achieve objectives. It will also give you strength to endure frustrations and uncertainty. Learn to listen to your own thoughts. This will help you to learn more about your inner self and your real goals. Spend some time alone each day, familiarizing yourself with your thoughts. You can do this while walking outdoors or relaxing at home, in a church or synagogue, or even in the public library. Solitude will provide you with an opportunity to become comfortable with your feelings and thoughts, and to assess the strategies for reaching your objectives.

Confucius wrote: "He who wishes to secure the good of others has already secured his own." There is a direct link between service to others and rewards in life.

Whom can you serve? Where can you make a contribution? Look at the people around you, your family, friends, co-workers, customers, others whom you meet in daily life. To the degree to which you contribute to their welfare you will be rewarded.

If you wish others to respect you, you must show respect for them. To achieve this, you may want to try a special program. For a month, approach everyone you meet as if he or she were the most important person in the world. Everyone wants to feel that he is important to someone; invariably, people will give their love, respect and attention to the person who fills that need. Remember that there is something to be learned from everybody. Each of us has a story to tell and a unique perspective. The way to try to understand the world is to see it from as many different viewpoints as possible.

According to lawyer John Foster, "One of the strongest characteristics of genius is the power of lighting its own fire."

Those who accomplish much have a unifying purpose to their life and express themselves in whatever manner is necessary to achieve their purpose. Call it simplicity, humility or self-sufficiency. You may believe that a Stravinsky, an Einstein or a Picasso has, by his genius, earned the right to be eccentric, idiosyncratic, self-willed. I contend that it was the decision to become master of their own fate that gave them the courage to try new things.

The willingness to think the unthinkable requires courage to spend time alone, to run the risk of ridicule. Not everyone is a Picasso, but everyone can consciously distinguish himself from the world around him. Swift said: "Although men are accused of not knowing their own weakness, yet perhaps few know their own strength. It is in men as in soils, where sometimes there is a vein of gold which the owner knows not of." The time you are wasting thinking about your inadequacy could be spent searching for that vein of gold in your activities and yourself.

Light your own fire. Pursue your own objectives without fear of failure, censure or criticism. This will free that unique combination of factors that lie buried beneath your social self. Your mental activity is as much a part of you as your heartbeat, your respiratory rhythm. You will find peace of mind when you determine and act in terms of your own nature and your own goals.

CONTROL YOUR MOODS

by DAVID S. VISCOTT, M.D.

NEGATIVE feelings require action. When you're in a bad mood, try to characterize it. Sit down in a quiet room, close your eyes, and let your mind go blank for a few minutes. Then concentrate on your feelings. Ask yourself, "What is it that I am feeling? Am I snippy, short-tempered, weepy, dissatisfied with myself?" Write down the adjectives that best describe the way you feel, and try to group them under one general mood, such as angry, hurt, anxious. Now probe. What is going on inside you? Have you felt like this before? What caused similar bad feelings? What could you do now that would make you feel better? What would you change if you could change anything you wanted? If you can't change, why can't you?

No matter what we call them, most of our bad moods are merely manifestations of certain basic feelings—hurt, anger, guilt, etc. What follows is a "road map" into those feelings, to help you see how they work and where they come from:

Hurt. People feel hurt when they lose something—friendship, a loved one, self-esteem. When you feel hurt, try to understand what it is that you have lost. What did the loss mean to you? What needs did it fill? Where can you now have those needs taken care of?

What should you do when you feel hurt and *know* who hurt you? If possible, approach the person face-to-face and tell him that he hurt you, how he hurt you, and exactly why you feel this way.

Why tell him? Because, like it or not, your feelings will demand to be expressed in one way or another. If they are not directed at the person who caused them—as they should be—they will find expression wherever they can. Often this happens in the wrong place at the wrong time, as when a wife breaks dishes in the kitchen instead of telling her her husband what she really thinks at the dinner table. It is best to express feelings when they first occur and toward the person who caused them.

Anxiety. People get anxious (worried, frightened, uptight) when they are afraid of being hurt or of losing something. When her mother was hospitalized for tests and minor surgery, 17-year-old Joan was told nothing specific about her mother's condition; the family did not want to worry her. Thinking the worst, Joan began to interpret every phone call as a potential message of doom. She became so anxious she was barely able to function in school or at home. When she was finally told the truth, she was still upset. But now she was better able to withstand it, because she understood what was happening and had more control over her situation.

If you feel anxious, try to pinpoint what it is you are afraid of losing—whether it is the love or attention of other people, your control over a situation or yourself, or your self-esteem and worth as a person. See what help you can get to prevent the loss or to prepare for it. Don't push it aside because it is too frightening to think about; avoiding things you fear only makes them more entrenched and difficult to manage.

Anger. People generally get angry when they are hurt. When you are angry, ask yourself, "Who hurt me? How? What did I say to the person? What did I want to say? Why didn't I say it?"

If someone makes you angry, tell him so right away. Most people will be apologetic and will want to remain friends. If anger is long submerged, it is difficult to express appropriately, because its sources have been buried for so long they are all but impossible to recognize.

Guilt. When anger is not expressed appropriately, it often becomes directed at the person who feels it. When a person feels anger toward himself, he feels guilty and generally to blame for everything that's wrong. For example, he may think he has disappointed others by falling short of their expectations. He may even be secretly angry at others for expecting so much of him, even if he feels too worthless to speak out on his own behalf.

Mrs. Little spent her life as the devoted servant of her husband and three sons, always burying her own needs and sacrificing herself on the altar of their egos. But secretly she felt her life was empty, that she had done nothing to make herself happy, nothing to be proud of. Eventually, her anger and resentment began to interfere with her ability to serve the men in her life. She became sloppy and unhelpful. Her behavior was really her guilt speaking out—a voice that should have been raised years ago.

But it was difficult for Mrs. Little to be angry with her family. She had always believed that expressing anger meant you didn't love someone. It *is* unfortunate that we get angry at each other, but feeling angry is just as natural as feeling affectionate. There is no need to characterize our feelings as "good" or "bad." We have only to characterize them as pleasant or unpleasant and to understand and resolve them so we can live our lives constructively.

How do you deal with guilt? If you remember that most guilt comes from suppressed anger and that anger comes from being hurt, the solution should be found in understanding the hurt and what caused it, and permitting the anger to be directed where it should have been in the first place.

ALL feelings, especially unpleasant ones, have to run their natural course. This takes emotional energy—something we do not have an unlimited supply of. When a child loses a pet, for example, we don't expect him to perform well in school—for a while. This child must grieve and loosen his ties to the lost pet; when this is accomplished, his energies will once again be free to invest in work and play.

It's the same with adults. If we use our emotional energy to push away unpleasant feelings, we will have little energy left for life itself.

CONTROL YOUR HANG-UPS
by NORMAN VINCENT PEALE, D.D.

DAY AFTER DAY the mailman challenges me with a small avalanche of letters. Even before I open them, I know what's there. Problems. It's almost as if the great Arranger of things felt that problems were essential to human growth and development—otherwise He would never have allowed so many to plague and baffle us.

I'm convinced that the Creator also planted in each of us the capacity to deal with our problems. What, then, prevents so many thousands of troubled correspondents from reaching their own solutions? It's not lack of intelligence, as a rule, or lack of education. Almost always, I conclude, it's because they have certain roadblocks in their minds, psychic obstacles that limit or paralyze their problem-solving abilities. Whatever their problem, real or imaginary, they're convinced they can't cope with it. And so, of course, they can't. As Emerson said, "Life consists in what a man is thinking of all day." If you think success, you create a climate in which success is probable. If you think failure, you set the stage for it.

Since these mind-shackles have no tangible existence, they must be dealt with on a spiritual level. When I offer suggestions, therefore, I find them in religious principles that have been used successfully by suffering people for centuries. This is the message that I've been trying to get across for more than 40 years: religion *isn't* a musty set of rules and beliefs handed down from the dim, forgotten past. It's a reservoir of mind-changing concepts which can give anyone enormous leverage in dealing with problems, great or small.

I believe that there are four major hang-ups, and that almost always one or another is casting its shadow over the problem-ridden person.

Control Self-Doubt. Some years ago, I remember, a man came to see me full of apprehension. A self-made businessman, he had just been named ambassador to a European country. Most people would have been pleased, but self-doubt had convinced him that he would never be able to master the social graces of diplomacy, or learn a foreign language. He thought that he should back out of the whole thing.

"Stop running yourself down," I told him. "Concentrate on the talents God *did* give you. You haven't been picked for your linguistic ability or your social graces. You've been picked because you're a tough, honest, plain-spoken, patriotic American. That's what we need overseas. So tell yourself you can do a good job, ask God to help you and go on over there and do it!"

And that, as it turned out, is precisely what he did.

Sometimes I suggest to my despondent correspondents that they are displaying more strength and courage than they think. They have come this far in a difficult life-situation and are still functioning. I may urge them to choose one episode in their lives where they excelled, then relive it as vividly as they can until the image of themselves as a victorious person burns bright again.

I remind them that the best way to forget their own problems is to help someone else solve his. Finally I tell them where they can find triumphant passages in the Bible. The blazing call to courage in Joshua 1:9, for example: "Be strong and of a good courage; be not afraid, neither be thou dismayed, for the Lord thy God is with thee whithersoever thou goest." Or the opening words of the 27th Psalm: "The Lord is my light and my salvation; whom shall I fear?"

I urge them to memorize such passages, let them sink deep into the twilight regions of the mind where, slowly but surely, they will drive out the demon of self-doubt. It's never easy. Changing patterns of thought is the hardest thing in the world. But it can be done. I know, because I have seen so many people do it.

Control Resentment. Every batch of mail I receive brings letters from people convinced that their difficulty is the result of some failing on the part of *somebody else*. Quite often they themselves deny any feeling of ill will. It's always the other fellow who has shown the ill will, said the spiteful word, done the hateful thing. Even so, their own suppressed anger often surges behind every word.

Such unresolved resentment is far more damaging to the person who harbors it than to the object of it. Carrying a load of anger around with you wastes your energy. It blocks communication. Christ told us that it was useless to pray with resentment in our hearts. "Go first and be reconciled with your brother," He said—and said nothing about who might be in the right or in the wrong. Another of His commandments, t

pray for those who despitefully use you," is specifically designed to neutralize resentment.

Believe me, it's a difficult thing to do. A few years ago,
I found myself the target of quite a barrage of criticism from
some of my fellow ministers. They said that I made Christianity
sound too easy. Well, there's nothing easy about a religion that
requires you to pray for people who have hurt you. But I made
myself do it, because I knew it was the best and quickest way
to get the resentment out of my system.

The only permanent answer to resentment, of course, is
forgiveness. Sometimes this takes time. When the disciples
asked the Lord if they should forgive up to seven times, He
answered, "Seventy times seven." He knew that in some cases
it might t   parate efforts before the grudge could be
eliminated

Control Guilt. Religion has always known that lasting guilt
can be a deadly poison. Buried or repressed guilt feelings don't
just fade away. They stay there, festering. Religion teaches
that the only way to deal with a guilt problem is to regret the
offense, resolve not to repeat it, make amends if possible, seek
forgiveness of the person you have wronged—and then forget
it. If you do these things, the wound in your psyche will heal
cleanly and leave no scar.

But many people will not follow this blueprint. The other
day a lawyer told me about difficulties he was having in his
job: he couldn't concentrate; he was irritable; he didn't sleep
well. What should he do?

"Answer a question truthfully," I said. "Is there any area
in your life that would cause you great dismay if you saw it
reported in tomorrow's headlines?"

He stared at me. "Well," he said finally, "I guess so. Everyone has a few skeletons in his closet, doesn't he?"

"Not if he's intelligent," I said. "Until you give those skeletons a decent burial and clean up your life you're going to go
right on being poisoned by guilt feelings."

The man, executor of his father's estate, had been cheating
his brothers and sisters of their rightful share of the inheritance.
He had persuaded himself in his conscious mind that it didn't
matter, that they need never know, that they already had enough
money. But such rationalizations did not appease the unconscious guilt. It was only when he made amends and sought
forgiveness that he began to climb back out of the pit.

"Blessed is he," says the Bible, "whose transgression is

forgiven." It's a message that should be pondered by every person who keeps trying to forge ahead with the dead hand of guilt holding him back.

Control Worry. This fourth hang-up is the most common of all. Worry, a wise man once said, is a thin stream of fear trickling through the mind. "If encouraged," he added, "it cuts a channel into which all other thoughts are drained."

Over the years, I've had letters foretelling everything from religion's doom to atomic war. Dozens of people worry about their health: just today I read a letter from a woman convinced that she was destined to have cancer because her grandmother died of it. All these things are conceivable, but far from inevitable. The truth is that the vast majority of feared disasters will probably never take place. In any case, merely worrying about them does nothing to prevent them.

One remedy for excessive worry is a clear understanding of how much emotional and physical damage it can do. "Worry," said the great Dr. Charles Mayo, "affects the circulation, the heart, the glands, the whole nervous system. I have never known a man who died from overwork, but many who died from doubt."

Another remedy is deliberately to distract yourself. Play a game. Go for a walk. See a movie. Chop wood. Dig in the garden. Paint a fence. Do anything except sit and brood. If you change your setting, you can usually change your mood.

But the greatest remedy of all is faith in God, belief that He is, that He cares, and that He stands ready to help. "If God be for us," said St. Paul, "who can be against us?" Worries shrivel in the face of such conviction. *Trust God, and live one day at a time.* That's the best antidote for worry I know. If you can do that, the fourth hang-up will never haunt you.

Problems! The world will continue full of them. But we shouldn't complain or despair. Challenge and response—that's what life is. That's where its greatest triumphs and fulfillments lie. Sweep away self-doubt, resentment, guilt, worry—and you'll be amazed at how the strength and joy come flooding in.

HOW TO CONTROL FRUSTRATION
by STUART CHASE

IN 1948, Seattle authorities feared that a race riot would break out in a run-down housing area. A thousand families—300 of them black—were jammed into temporary barracks built for war workers. Tension was in the air, rumors rife, a stabbing reported. The University of Washington, called on for advice, rushed 25 trained interviewers to the scene.

The interviewers went from door to door, trying to discover the extent of racial hatred. They were surprised to find very little. Ninety percent of the whites and blacks interviewed said that they felt "about the same" or "more friendly" toward the other group since moving into the area. What, then, was eating them?

These families were angry about the ramshackle buildings, the back-firing kitchen stoves and the terrible roads inside the property. Many were worried about a strike at Boeing Airplane Co. In short, a series of frustrations from other causes had infected the whole community, and could have resulted in a race riot.

Fast work by the authorities staved off this disaster. Once the true causes were discovered, buildings were repaired, new equipment installed, the roads improved. The crisis passed.

This case is a dramatic application of a challenging theory about human behavior exhaustively demonstrated by a group of Yale scientists in an old book, *Frustration and Aggression,** which has become a classic. Since reading it some years ago, I have met many of my personal problems with better understanding, and gained fresh insight into some big public questions as well.

A common result of being frustrated, the Yale investigators have shown, is an act of aggression, sometimes violent. To be alive is to have a goal and pursue it—anything from cleaning the house, or planning a vacation, to saving money for retire-

*By John Dollard, Leonard W. Doob, Neal E. Miller, O. H. Mowrer and Robert R. Sears, Yale University Press, 1939.

202

ment. If somebody or something blocks the goal, we begin to feel pent up and thwarted. Then we get mad. (1) The blocked goal, (2) the sense of frustration, (3) aggressive action—this is the normal human sequence. If we are aware of what is going on inside us, however, we can save ourselves a good deal of needless pain and trouble.

Everyone has encountered frustration on the highways. You are driving along a two-lane road behind a big trailer-truck. You're in a hurry, while the truck driver seems to be enjoying the scenery. After miles of increasing frustration you grow to hate him. Finally you step on the gas and pass him defiantly, regardless of the chance you may be taking. This kind of frustration must cause thousands of accidents a year. Yet, if you realized what was going on in your nervous system, you could curb such dangerous impulses.

The aggressive act that frustration produces may take a number of forms. It may be turned inward against oneself, with suicide as the extreme example. It may hit back directly at the person or thing causing the frustration. Or it may be transferred to another object—what psychologists call displacement. Displacement can be directed against the dog, the parlor furniture, the family or even total strangers.

A man rushed out of his front door in Brooklyn one fine spring morning and punched a passer-by on the nose. In court he testified that he had had a quarrel with his wife. Instead of punching her he had the bad luck to punch a police detective.

Aggression is not always sudden and violent; it may be devious and calculated. The spreading of rumors, malicious gossip, a deliberate plot to discredit, are some of the roundabout forms. In some cases frustration leads to the opposite of aggression, a complete retreat from life.

The classic pattern of frustration and aggression is nowhere better demonstrated than in military life. GIs studied by the noted American sociologist Samuel A. Stouffer in the last war were found to be full of frustrations due to their sudden loss of civilian liberty. They took it out verbally on the brass, often most unjustly. But in combat, soldiers felt far more friendly toward their officers. Why? Because they could "discharge their aggression directly against the enemy."

Dr. Karl Menninger, of the famous Menninger Foundation at Topeka, pointed out that children in all societies are necessarily frustrated, practically from birth, as they are broken in to the customs of the tribe. A baby's first major decision is "whether to holler or swaller"—when it discovers that the two acts cannot be done simultaneously. Children have to be taught habits of cleanliness, toilet behavior, regular feeding, punctuality; habits that too often are hammered in.

Grownups with low boiling points, said Dr. Menninger, probably got that way because of excessive frustrations in childhood. We can make growing up a less difficult period by giving children more love and understanding. Parents in less "civilized" societies, Menninger observes, often do this. He quotes a Mohave Indian, discussing his small son: "Why should I strike him? He is small, I am big. He cannot hurt me."

When we do experience frustration, there are several things we can do to channel off aggression. First, we can try to remove the cause which is blocking our goal. An individual may be able to change his foreman, even his job or his residence, if the frustration is a continuing one.

If this cannot be done, then we can seek harmless displacements. Physical outlets are the most immediately helpful. Go out in the garden and dig like fury. Or take a long walk, punch a bag in the gym, make the pins fly in a bowling alley, cut down a tree. The late Richard C. Tolman, a great physicist, once told me that he continued tennis into his 60s because he found it so helpful in working off aggressions.

As a writer I receive pan letters as well as fan letters, and some of them leave me baffled and furious. (Some, I must admit, are justified.) Instead of taking it out on the family, I write the critic the nastiest reply I can contrive. That makes me feel a lot better. Next morning I read it over with renewed satisfaction. Then I tear it up and throw it in the wastebasket. Agression gone, nobody hurt.

But perhaps the best way of all to displace aggressive feelings is by hard, useful work. If both body and mind can be engaged, so much the better.

The world is filled today with a great surplus of anger and conflict. We are far from knowing all about the sources of these destructive feelings, but scientists have learned enough to clear up quite a load of misery. Their findings can help us reduce that load and even utilize its energy, through a better understanding of ourselves and our neighbors.

WE EACH HAVE A FORT TO HOLD

by I. A. R. WYLIE

THE DELIVERY MAN stopped his truck in our lane to take an amused look at me.

"Painting quite a bit of the countryside, ma'am," he said.

An exaggeration. Still, the grass around the picket fence I was painting *was* spattered white. Some of the paint, I knew, was on my nose. My overalls were stiff with it.

Ours is no ordinary fence. It is a pampered parasite demanding constant care. And there are, it seems to me as I straighten my aching back, miles of it. In the spring I set out with paint, brushes and brisk determination. But no sooner do I get one section immaculate than I realize with exasperation that the sections I painted last fall have a forlorn, reproachful look.

It is like our house. No sooner do we get one room spick and span than another clamors for fresh curtains or a new carpet. Or the roof leaks, staining the bedroom wallpaper. Or the electric pump suddenly needs a new motor.

For that matter, I reflect grimly, it's like myself. There's always something about me that has to be put to rights. Physically, mentally and spiritually there are constant repair jobs required. Yet, sooner or later, I'll be an old woman and someone else will have to paint that fence. So why not stop right now and let everything in me and about me slide comfortably downhill?

Somehow I don't, or I can't. Something more important than the fence itself is involved.

I think with sympathy of my young friend Jane with her small, crowded house, her husband and three children. Every morning she gets breakfast for her hungry people who in a few hours will be hungry all over again; she washes dishes that will have to be washed tomorrow and tomorrow. Sometimes, she confessed once, she has an almost irresistible urge to slam the door on it all and escape, at least for a day, into freedom.

But she knows that those plates, congealed in grease, would be waiting inexorably for her return. So she keeps right on.

Like most of us. Like her husband, who comes home to weed the garden, knowing well the weeds will grow again overnight. Or out he goes with the lawn mower, to cut the grass that he mowed only a few days ago.

Everywhere the fight to "keep things up" goes on—monotonous, repetitious tasks that sometimes seem so meaningless and fruitless. But, to humanity's everlasting credit, most of us keep right on cleaning, repairing, patching up walls that would, if left untended, fall, leaving the fort wide open to the enemy.

It is not merely a matter of self-preservation. "There's Mrs. Frazer next door," Jane said once. "She gets overwhelmed with things and, in despair, lets them go altogether. Then when she comes over to weep on my shoulder and finds everything here all bright and shining she gets mad with both of us. But she sees it can be done, and goes and does it. Maybe if she found that I'd given up she'd give up too. And the thing would spread all around us, like a sort of domestic measles."

She looked at me wistfully. "Or am I being self-important?" I didn't think she was. . . .

"Well, you're doing a good job, ma'am," my delivery man assured me. "You're sprucing up the neighborhood!"

I hadn't consciously thought of it in that way. But perhaps subconsciously I *had* felt when I set out with paint and brush that I owed something to my neighbors, an obligation to keep things up on our road. And if our road and its inhabitants keep up, the whole community gets a lift. It's like a stone thrown in a pool—the ripples spread out in ever-widening circles.

Basically, civilizations don't fall because of lost battles or material misfortunes. They crumble from within—because the average citizen has fallen down on his job, sold his integrity for ephemeral gain, and by neglect and indifference allowed his civic and private virtues to fall into decay. Others, infected by his example, follow suit until the whole structure of his world, built up by the patient labors of his forefathers, rots and tumbles about his ears and the barbarian invader takes over.

In this respect we have no private lives. We are not just responsible to and for ourselves. Small fry though we be, we are vital links in a vital chain. When the links, untended, rust, the chain breaks.

A friend of mine, now an old, heartbroken woman, was once happily married. She had two daughters and then a son, Peter. Because he came late in their lives, and because he was a handsome, clever, lovable youngster, Peter was the darling of his parents' hearts. What in their daughters would have been danger signals became in him merely symptoms of boyish high spirits.

When Peter was caught stealing from his mother's purse and lied about it, he was only lightly reprimanded. ("It was just a childish prank. All children pilfer like magpies.") When Peter neglected his homework, his father helped him out—though his aid amounted to cheating. It was easier for the parents to let a little dust gather on their principles than to subject themselves and their darling son to a vigorous house-cleaning.

Years later, Peter became vice-president of the local bank. In this responsible position he made disastrous speculations, then falsified accounts. He finally landed himself in prison and part of his community in ruin.

"Nobody else understands how it could have happened," his mother said to me. "But *I* understand. He began to default as a child when he stole from me. His father and I glossed over his weaknesses. We were slack and careless. We let him down."

It's fatally easy to let down—to turn a blind eye on dusty corners in our households and in ourselves. This neglect works like a mysterious alchemy which turns our best into our worst. As in Sam, for example—the brilliant engineer whose cleverness turned to cutting corners in his contracts for a bigger profit. Or Jim, who set out as a politician with a high purpose, but found it easier to buy votes—and eventually sold out the voters. These people are sentinels who betrayed their citadel. Yet if early in their careers they had sensed the danger of neglecting daily self-discipline, they might have ended up as trusted captains. Instead they went down, dragging others with them.

Every time we yield to the temptation to let down our standards we are letting down a civilization which has been built up with immeasurable pain and effort. It is the patient labor of ordinary men and women repeating their daily, monotonous tasks, always a little better, a little more intelligently, which has made our world—not perfect, but livable and a few steps above that of the savage. Laboriously, stone by stone, they built the fort. It is up to us to hold it.

CHAPTER 12
Getting Yourself Together

WHY YOU MAKE MISTAKES
by DONALD A. NORMAN

"In a hotel restaurant, when the check came, I signed my name to it but couldn't remember my room number. So I looked at my watch."

This example illustrates a typical slip of action among more than 200 that I have collected in two years. Slips are amusing and happen to all of us; except when they lead to embarrassment, they usually seem like harmless oddities.

But slips that occur in the conduct of certain tasks can be dangerous. An air-traffic controller once told a plane to taxi to the left runway when he meant the right. Such a left/right slip is the most common of verbal confusions, but in this case it could have led to tragedy (fortunately, it didn't). Forgetting to turn on headlights when driving a car at night is also common. The slip is usually caught before an accident occurs, but not always. Today, human error is one of the largest causes of accidents.

The founder of psychoanalysis, Sigmund Freud, analyzed errors primarily to discover a person's true beliefs or intentions. One case he examined involved the president of the lower house of the Austrian parliament, who opened a meeting by shouting, "I declare this meeting closed!" That act does seem to reveal hidden motives; as Freud noted, "The president secretly wished he was already in a position to close the sitting, from which little good was to be expected."

But I believe that the human mind is an exceedingly complex computer, and that slips can also occur when stray information throws off human information-processing systems. During Freud's era, the science of computation, information processing and control was primitive, and Freud was not led to think about the nature of a human processing system that could contribute to errors. I interpret Freud in modern terms as saying that slips result from competition and intermixing among underlying mental-processing mechanisms, often working parallel to one another.

What about the pilot who lands a plane with the wheels still up—does he have a hidden wish to kill himself? It's possible, but simpler explanations are possible, too.

Most actions, I propose, are carried out by subconscious mechanisms. We will an action. The intention, once specified, releases control processes, or "schemas," that lead to the exquisitely timed, complex motor actions involved in manipulation of mind and body. When I drive home from work, the appropriate schemas are activated by previous actions. I need not plan the details; I simply decide and act.

Do I wish to detour to the fish store? I must have "fish store" actively in mind at the time I pass the critical choice point between work and home. Let it lapse from my memory at that critical junction, and I am apt to find myself at home shortly thereafter, fishless.

In different slips, different parts of the information-processing sequence go awry. For purposes of convenience, I categorize them according to which part of the human machinery is involved. As an example of a **description error**, consider the following:

A chartered airliner flying from Houston to Montreal crashed exactly on the border between the United States and Canada. A major political issue developed over the following question: In which country should the survivors be buried?

Most people puzzle over the choice of country. In fact, the story was made up to trap the unwary: it is the *dead* who should be buried, not the survivors. The story sets us up to be lazy mentally—to except the critical leftovers to be the dead ones—so we don't process the word "survivors" deeply enough.

In day-to-day activities, **selection errors** are similarly common. For instance:

In getting ready for a party, one person carefully prepared a cake and a salad, then put the cake in the refrigerator and the salad in the oven.

Such inadvertent ambiguity can also lead to eating your friend's sandwich from a plate that looks like yours, or to putting the top of the sugar bowl on top of a coffee mug of the same size. One of my graduate students returned to his home after a track workout, pulled off his sweaty T-shirt, and tossed it into the toilet. It was not an aiming error—the laundry basket, his intended target, was in another room.

Activation & Triggering Errors. Once an intention is selected, executing it can easily misfire. We can, for example, forget the initial intention while some of the schemas it ordered run their course. One colleague reported that before starting work at his desk at home he headed for his bedroom, only to realize after getting there that he'd forgotten why he had gone. "I kept going," he reported, "hoping that something in the bedroom would remind me." Nothing did. He finally went back to his desk, realized that his glasses were dirty and, with a great sense of relief, returned to the bedroom for the handkerchief he needed to wipe them.

Yet another category was analyzed by William James in his classic textbook on psychology; he reported that "very absent-minded persons in going to their bedrooms to dress for dinner have been known to take off one garment after another and finally to get into bed, merely because that was the habitual issue of the first few movements when performed at a later hour."

Such errors, called **capture errors**, constitute one of the most fascinating categories in the field of error. They involve a simple principle: pass too near a well-formed habit and it will capture your behavior. A colleague in England who studies errors reports that someone told him this story:

"I meant to get my car out, but as I passed through the back porch on my way to the garage I stopped to put on my Wellington boots and gardening jacket, as if to work in the garden.

Our errors are easy to detect, of course, when they have such obvious consequences. Sometimes the consequence materializes several minutes after the event: for example, when you plug in the coffeepot in the morning and forget the coffee, you learn of your slip only when you start to pour.

The likelihood of human error increases when there is stress. Consider a situation in which innocent errors can have serious consequences—as, say, in nuclear-power plants. The total length of all the control panels in these complex systems may be more than 100 feet, with some 700 instruments and controls that require testing or servicing from time to time.

The difficulty of controlling reactors is simply poor systems design. Indeed, modern systems of all sorts are inconsiderate of human beings. In my research laboratory, we are attempting to understand the basic properties of human information processing, with emphasis on how skilled people select and guide their actions—and make their slips. Although the basic thrust of the research is theoretical, we share an important subgoal: to give designers the guidelines for designing systems that work *with* people, not against them. We hope not only to eliminate any disastrous effects of error, but also to make human interaction with machines pleasurable, efficient and creative.

Think of what a salesperson must do in a department store. Even for a simple purchase, a huge array of numbers must be entered into the computer cash register. The numbers are supposed to make the accounting system work, but the priorities are backward. Instead of forcing people to act like machines for the benefit of machines, why not make it the other way around? Machines can be made to do the translation into whatever hidden, laborious codes they require. The cash register should "know" automatically in which department it is located. The sales person would simply punch a button for "shirt"; if the computer needs to know more, it could be programmed to ask for specifics, which the salesperson could then provide by punching other buttons.

In industrial, aircraft and nuclear accidents, my analyses indicate that the system is most often at fault, not the operator. People make errors as a fundamental byproduct of the same information-processing mechanisms that produce their great creativity and flexibility. Yet today's systems seem sometimes designed to cause the very errors they should be set up to prevent.

SHOULD YOU SEE
A CAREER DOCTOR?
by LESTER VELIE

IF YOU had two bright teen-age daughters but could afford to send only one to college, what would you do? To John McKenzie, an electrician, the answer seemed obvious. Send the one most likely to succeed. Daughter Alice was not only near the top of her high-school senior class but a favorite with teachers and students alike. Her twin sister Betty, shy and retiring, would go to secretarial school.

But the McKenzies (this is not their real name) had nagging doubts. Although overshadowed by her sister, Betty nevertheless was in the top quarter of her class and was excellent college material, too.

The McKenzies took their dilemma to a career doctor. He is one of a swiftly growing breed of professionals who hold a graduate degree in psychology or guidance counseling and are trained to diagnose mental ability, aptitudes and potential for acheivement in school or job. They also keep track of the swiftly changing world of work, know where the opportunities are and help their "clients" choose the jobs that fit.

The McKenzies found their career counselor at the Vocational Service Center of the New York City YMCA, now the YMCA Counseling and Testing Service. And his tests revealed some surprises.

Separate interviews showed that star student Alice didn't much care whether she went to college or secretarial school. But, to please her family, she had said nothing. Betty, however, was eager to widen her horizons, to explore mathematics and the sciences. She had said nothing to her family, either, because she thought it would be unfair to her apparently abler sister.

The counselor tested the girls' intelligence, their reasoning power, their reading comprehension, their interests. As expected, Alice scored in the superior range, or top ten percent, of 17-year-olds. But, unexpectedly, Betty scored in the top *two* percent. Moreover, in a test that predicts likely performance in college, Betty again outstripped her sister.

"But how could this be?" the girls' mother wanted to know.

214

School grades clearly showed Alice to be superior.

A "personality inventory" of the girls held the probable explanation, the career doctor said. Alice was confident and assertive. So, he suggested, Alice's teachers responded unconsciously to her positive self-appraisal and marked her higher than the self-doubting Betty. Perhaps, too, Betty shrank from competing with her outwardly superior sister. Subsequent interviews helped all the McKenzies to realize that Betty had her own special talents and interests to be recognized and encouraged.

Buoyed by these findings, Betty made such high grades in the final months of her senior year that she almost overtook her sister. Both graduated among the top six of their class.

"Instead of sending one to college for four years," the career doctor counseled, "why not send both girls for two years, and see what happens?"

Both girls won scholastic honors and money-saving scholarships. Both stayed for four years, graduated as mathematicians, then took jobs as computer programmers in the same company. Betty's earnings soon were almost double what they would have been had she taken a secretarial job to help out her family.

Here, a career doctor not only helped solve a family problem but achieved the career doctor's chief aim. He helped a client, Betty McKenzie, face up to herself and answer such questions as: Who am I? What mental and emotional gear do I pack? What talents, interests and energy?

Facing up to oneself is the first step toward choosing a job or career. It may determine for some 45 years whether you like or dislike your work; whether you're good or bad in it.

The second step requires knowing the opportunities as well as the pitfalls in the changing world of work. New technology and knowledge have created some 6000 new kinds of occupations and professions since 1949, while some older occupations have become obsolete. It takes a specialist to keep track of job information.

So, our public schools have more than doubled their guidance-counseling forces since 1958. University counseling centers have sprung up to offer career-doctor services to students and outsiders alike. The YMCA, the Jewish Vocational Service, church groups and other voluntary agencies regard career counseling as an important part of their community service. The nearest office of your state employment service offers employment counseling free; a growing army of private practitioners provide it on a fee basis.

When should you see a career doctor?

Once, counseling was largely limited to high-school pupils. Now it reaches down to elementary-school level and upward into adult groups. Dr. Albert S. Thompson of Columbia University cites three stages of personal development at which professional counseling can help.

Growth. Bobby, 12, was in the first or "growth" stage when his mother took him to a career doctor because—as she explained tearfully—Bobby was "retarded." Indeed, Bobby acted the part. He was impassive and fearful. He said he disliked school and preferred to play with children several years younger than himself.

The career doctor learned that Bobby's grades had been satisfactory until fifth grade. Then a fellow pupil read Bobby's I.Q. score in the school office and taunted him with the news that he was "stupid." Bobby became listless, did less homework, was put in a class for slow learners, where he barely made passing grades. Bobby's father, a salesman, began to call him stupid, too.

From Bobby's school, the career doctor found that the boy had scored 78 or "borderline" in a group I.Q. test which depended entirely on written answers. The career doctor put Bobby through a "junior intelligence scale" test, which is administered individually and includes oral as well as written responses. Bobby scored 110, high-average for his age. A reading-comprehension test provided the clue to the boy's poor showing in the school I.Q. test. He had a severe reading disability.

Aptitude and interest tests revealed that in manual dexterity, numerical ability, spare-time activities (Bobby tinkered with electrical equipment) and interests Bobby had an aptitude and interest "profile" similar to those employed at electrical and mechanical work.

On learning his true capacity, Bobby brightened up. He is now doing well both in his studies and in his laboratory work.

Exploratory. At 20, Frank, a college senior, was in the "exploratory" stage—groping toward a career—when he went to a university-center counselor with his problem. He had tried a pre-med course, with mediocre results. Then, when a teacher told him he could write, Frank took journalism courses. But, with graduation approaching, he wasn't sure he was on the right track.

In a general-intelligence test, Frank scored in the top four percent of his age group. But in areas in which a potential writer should excel—in reading comprehension, vocabulary, sentence construction and grammatical ability—he was only average. He was not good in sciences either.

So, in choosing medicine or journalism, Frank was accentuating the negative—his weaknesses. He was also neglecting the positive. Tests showed that he was in the top one percent of college seniors in mathematical aptitude. And he scored in the superior range in commercial and business understanding. A test of his supervisory judgment showed that, despite his lack of experience in such a job, his score was as good as the top third of those actually employed as department or section managers.

Frank, it turned out, had talents for accounting, for personnel work and for management—fields he hadn't considered. Now Frank has shifted gears toward a business career.

Establishment. Although most of those who get counseling help are in the "growth" and "exploratory" stages, many need help during the early adult or "establishment" stage, when one has already chosen an occupation.

Alan, 28, had done well in engineering school, but couldn't hold an engineering job. He was anxious and depressed when he came to see a career doctor in a voluntary agency. He was ashamed of being a failure, he said, and despaired of the future.

Alan scored high in intelligence, but in "spatial perception," the ability to visualize a true-life figure from a drawing, and in other yardsticks of engineering aptitude, he didn't measure up. His interests were not those of an engineer, either, but of a salesman. And he had the verbal skills and outgoing personality to go with this interest. The career doctor's suggestion for Alan: "Combine your technical training with your aptitude for selling and try a new career as technical salesman."

Soon, Alan had a job as a sales engineer. He had enough technical background to explain equipment to customers. Before long, he was earning more than at the engineering job he had lost.

What kind of career doctor can help you or your child most? The answer may depend on your ability to pay a fee, and on the availability of the service. Probably within a bus ride of your home is one of the 2000-odd state employment-service offices run as a neighborhood facility by your state and financed by the federal payroll tax. Recent legislation has begun to turn these offices into a network of counseling as well as job-finding agencies. The service is free and widely available.

Many universities and colleges have testing and counseling centers which serve outsiders for fees up to $200. For example: The Career Counseling and Resources Center for the School of Continuing Education at New York University keeps a staff of 15, which serves university students and "people with job or education problems" from 17 and up. After taking a standardized test, the client has a series of interviews with a counselor.

"When we finish," the Center's Acting Director, Letitia Chamberlain, said to me, "the client knows to what he may reasonably aspire. He not only knows the field for which he has aptitudes and interests—say medicine—but how high he should reach: whether he should aim to be a doctor, or a therapist or a laboratory technician."

While most of the 1500 persons who are tested and advised at the Center each year are college students, many are between 30 and 40 and come for middle-age guidance.

At 36, Shirley, a supporting actress on Broadway and television, thought the time had come to shift to a career that would yield a more stable income and a more secure future; so she decided to consult a career doctor. A handsome woman with professional poise and a college degree, Shirley tested in a superior intelligence range and had a command of English and grammar equal to that of the top ten percent of college seniors.

The career doctor noted in his report that Shirley had talents for "public relations, sales and advertising." The job she landed combined all of these. She became a field representative for a cosmetics firm with the task of demonstrating new cosmetic products to distributors.

"The test results gave me the courage of my convictions," Shirley wrote to her career doctor. "I'm sure you appreciate how important that was at my age, especially since I was selling my *potential* to an employer, rather than proved performance."

Guidance experts make these points:

The aptitude test, alone, is not vocational guidance. Like an X ray, it must be interpreted by a specialist.

Don't come for guidance *only* at crisis points: when you've busted out of high school or college, or have lost a succession of jobs. Come at decision points: when it's necessary to choose between a vocational and an academic course in high school; when you must decide on a college major or whether to go on to graduate school—and if so, to what kind.

Ideally, the junior and senior high-school counselor should be the career doctor who can do most for your child. He has test scores, grades and teacher information from your child's earliest school days. In contrast to the counselor at the university center or voluntary agency who deals with a client for a brief period, the school counselor is involved in the child's continuous development.

To help parents get the most out of school counselors, the Minnesota Department of Education suggests:

Don't blow off steam at the counselor if he advises your son, whom you regard as engineer material, to drop math and take commercial courses instead. The counselor, free of the emotions in which parents wrap their judgments, provides an objective appraisal.

Should *you* see a career doctor? If you are in doubt, the answer is yes.

YOU *CAN* STOP BEING A PROCRASTINATOR

by NORMAN VINCENT PEALE, D.D.

THE most rewarding New Year's resolution that I ever managed to keep was one I made years ago: to stop being a procrastinator. In those days I was a confirmed putter-offer. I hated to make decisions, avoided difficult or unpleasant tasks. The more demanding a pressure or obligation became, the more I tended to delay facing it. I was in real danger of becoming completely swamped.

It took a few words from a level-headed friend to make me see the problem clearly. "Norman," he said, "you seem to think that this procrastination of yours is a built-in part of your personality or perhaps an incurable disease. Well, it's neither. It's a bad habit, and like all habits it can be broken. You had better break this one—before it breaks you!"

That warning got through to me. I resolved to work on the problem until I licked it. In the process, I hammered out some guidelines that any chronic putter-offer may find helpful. Here they are.

Stop regarding procrastination as a harmless little hangup. Businessmen fail because they put off making key decisions. Marriages sometimes disintegrate because a wife can't seem to get around to washing the dishes or making the beds. People die because they put off going to the doctor. Procrastination isn't just an inconsequential bad habit; it's a villain that can thwart your ambitions, destroy your happiness, even kill you.

Pick one specific area where procrastination plagues you—and conquer it. Quite often I get requests for speaking engagements that I know I cannot accept. But I hate to turn people down, and I used to put off such decisions—until it was too late to back out. When I finally forced myself to make a firm decision quickly, I was a much happier person—and so were the people who had to deal with me! If you can thus break the hold that procrastination has in one segment of your life, the sense of relief and triumph will help you eliminate it from others.

220

Learn to set priorities, and then focus on one problem at a time. Clutter and procrastination go hand in hand because each reinforces the other. A man with ten unfinished pieces of business on his desk wastes a significant part of his decision-making capacity merely attempting to choose between them. A housewife with ten chores left undone is likely to feel so overwhelmed that she may give up in despair and watch a soap opera instead of tackling any of them. Yet no two tasks, no two obligations, are of equal importance. Quite often, in my procrastinating days, I'd find myself doing optional or marginal things and neglecting essential ones. But no more. (Well, hardly ever!) Because I've learned to set priorities.

I do it by writing notes to myself all through the day about things I should attend to the next day. Then at night I list all the items in descending order of importance. That way I can tackle them in sequence the next day, joyfully crossing off each one as I dispose of it.

This may seem elementary, but it's astonishing how much time and energy you save by finishing one job before you move on to another. You have to make up your mind, though, not to let distractions creep in. Sometimes I have to talk harshly to myself: "You are going to sit in this chair until you have finished the job in front of you."

Once the mind accepts the discipline, the needed power will flow. Above all, it's necessary to concentrate. One day in Grand Central Station, I watched the man behind the information desk. People crowded around him, clamoring, demanding, but he never became flustered. He would pick out one person, look directly at him and answer his question slowly and deliberately. He never shifted his eyes, never paid the slightest attention to anyone else until he was finished and had singled out his next questioner. When my turn came, I complimented him on his poise and concentration. He smiled. "I've learned," he said, "to focus on one person at a time and to stick with his problem until it's settled. Otherwise, I'd go mad."

It's a lesson that all procrastinators might ponder with profit.

Give yourself deadlines. I don't mean secret deadlines that are easy to ignore, but deadlines that other people (your mother-in-law, for instance) know about and expect you to meet. Invite a couple over to admire that room you have been meaning to paint; your pride will make you finish it before they come. It's much harder to be a public procrastinator than a private one!

Don't duck the most difficult problems. To do so may be

human, but in the end it just leads to greater difficulties. Years ago, I would often sit down with a stack of letters. If the first one involved a particularly thorny problem, I would put it aside and look for an easy one to answer. Result: I would soon have two or three mailbags full of unanswered letters. I would have to make a frantic effort, working far into the night, in an exhausting attempt to catch up.

One day psychiatrist Smiley Blanton told me: "You're making a mistake. Don't duck the difficult letters. Tackle them head-on. The lift you get will carry you right through the remainder of the task." I tried it—and he was right.

Families sometimes slip into serious debt because they put off paying bills until the amount owed seems insurmountable—and then they stop trying to pay at all. Yet, when with experienced help they adopt a long-range, systematic plan to pay their debts, they find they can shake off the inertia that plagued them and start moving forward again.

Don't let perfectionism paralyze you. Lots of people fail to act because they're afraid they may not perform perfectly. Just the other day a woman said to me, "I've been meaning to write a note to a friend whose husband has died, but I don't know how to write a letter of condolence. I don't know how to express what I feel."

"How *do* you feel?" I asked.

"Deeply sorry," she said. "I've been thinking about that woman and loving her and praying for her."

I scribbled her words on a piece of paper and handed them to her. "That's all you need to say," I told her. "Your friend doesn't want a literary composition; she just wants a few words from the heart."

THESE, then, are some of the devices I used to rid myself of the hobgoblin of procrastination. What it amounted to in the end was a basic change in attitude. I finally realized that the rewards of achievement are far sweeter than the rewards of self-indulgence.

Look around and you'll agree that the really happy people are those who have broken the chains of procrastination, those who find satisfaction in doing the job at hand. They're full of eagerness, zest, productivity. You can be, too.

HOW TO BE YOUR OWN BEST FRIEND

by MILDRED NEWMAN AND BERNARD BERKOWITZ WITH JEAN OWEN

Q. People say they want happiness. Everyone reaches for it desperately. But for many it seems an impossible dream. What are we doing wrong?

A. It's not that bad. There are plenty of people who are having a wonderful time with their lives. But they don't talk about it much; they are busy doing it. Yet it's true; too few people have a sense of zest in their daily lives. Too few have mastered the art of being happy.

Q. You call it an art. Do you think it can be learned, like dancing or making pottery? I should think you're happy or you're not. I don't see how you can make happiness.

A. In a sense that's true. But the way you put it is part of the problem that many people have in their pursuit of happiness. They expect happiness to happen to them. They don't see it's something they have to do. People will go to a lot of trouble to learn French or physics or how to operate a car, but they won't be bothered learning how to operate themselves.

Q. You make it sound as if we should be standing at our own controls and pushing buttons. Shouldn't living be more natural than that?

A. Maybe, but for most of us it's not. We are not born with the secret of how to live. There are things we must learn.

Q. For example?

A. The first thing is to realize that we've probably been looking for happiness in the wrong place. The source is not outside us; it is within. Most of us haven't begun to tap our own potential for happiness. It's as if we're waiting for *permission* to start living fully, but the only person who can give us that permission is ourselves. We must realize that we are responsible for our own good time.

Q. If it is up to us, if we can push a magic switch and turn on happiness, why then doesn't everyone just do it?

A. There is no magic switch. But there is an attitude. To take responsibility for our lives means making a profound change

233

in the way we approach everything. Unfortunately, we do everything we can to avoid this change, this responsibility. We would much rather blame someone or something for making us feel unhappy than take the steps to make us feel better. We even talk about our own feelings as if they were visitors from outer space. We say, "This feeling came over me," as if we were helpless creatures overwhelmed by mysterious forces.

Q. But feelings come and go, and most of the time you don't know why. If I am angry or upset about something, I can't just stop being upset. If something has happened to hurt me, don't I have a right to feel that hurt?

A. Certainly. But too often people cling to unpleasant feelings. Without fully realizing it, they do things that make them feel bad and then say, "I couldn't help myself." What most people mean is "I *didn't* help myself." We can all help ourselves.

Q. How?

A. First, you have to make a very basic decision: Do you want to lift yourself up or put yourself down? Are you for yourself or against yourself? (These may seem strange questions, but many people are literally their own worst enemy.) If you do decide you want to help yourself, you can choose to do the things that make you feel good about yourself instead of the things that make you feel terrible. Why should you do what gives you pain when it is just as easy to give yourself joy?

Q. Can you be more exact?

A. Being aware of your own achievements is one thing. For example, when you do something you are proud of, dwell on it a little, praise yourself for it, relish the experience. It is up to us to give ourselves recognition. Why remember and dwell on defeats instead of victories?

Many people are under a kind of negative self-hypnosis. They put labels on themselves. They say: I am (a) a terrible person who (b) always does awful things and (c) can't possibly do better. Instead of convincing ourselves beforehand that something we want to do is impossible, we should spend those energies looking for ways to do it. We must encourage ourselves. You can't do anything if you believe you can't.

Another fundamental thing is to meet your own expectations. If you have work to do and are tempted to let it slide, ask yourself how you will feel if you put it off. If you sense that you will be a little disgusted, then go ahead and do the job, and let yourself savor the feeling of having done it, of being in charge of yourself. It's quite exhilarating.

Doing what makes you feel good about yourself is not self-indulgence. It doesn't mean gratifying an isolated part of you: it means satisfying your whole self, and this includes the feelings and ties and responsibilities you have to others. If we cannot love ourselves, where will we draw our love for anyone else? Love is an affirmation of the living, growing being in all of us. If you don't have it, you can't give it.

Q. A lot of us would rather do almost anything than change our habits, though.

A. Certainly, getting rid of bad habits takes a lot of perseverance. It's not just enough to want to change. You must want to want to, even when you don't want to. You have to watch what you're doing. Every time you catch yourself putting yourself down, just stop and turn around and push yourself up.

It takes realism, too. People often want to be perfect and become discouraged when they're not. They have to give that up. Perfection is not for human beings. Judging yourself by superhuman standards is another way of mistreating yourself, and a good excuse for giving up. Don't judge yourself at all; accept yourself and move on from there.

Q. What else can I do?

A. You must also learn to talk to yourself. You need to explain things, to reassure yourself. It can help you through all kinds of tough situations. When the child in you is up to mischief, you can stop and discuss it first; you can say no. At first it's hard, but it gets easier.

But when the child in you does misbehave, don't punish yourself. Forgive the child. Most of the things you feel terrible about weren't so bad to begin with. We often go on doing things against ourselves just to prove we are the terrible person we imagined we were as a child.

All the loving help you would give a child, you can give yourself. When you know a child well, you have a feeling for when to put on pressure, when to offer comfort, when to leave him alone. If you come to know the child in you, you can get that feeling for yourself. So, embrace the child in you; make friends with yourself. It gives you a reserve of strength to call on.

ORGANIZE YOUR WORRIES!

by JOYCE LUBOLD

FOR YEARS I was just an ordinary, run-of-the-mill circular worrier, like everyone else. No plan, no organization, pick up a worry here, drop another there, never *getting* anywhere, worrywise. I'd head for the grocery store, let's say, my mind clear as a bell, all ready to plunge into those tricky decisions between the Giant Economy Size at $1.99 cents and the Super Savings Size at two for $3.00. But the car would wheeze windily as it started, which would make me think of the cost of new cars (high) and the state of my bank account (low). Thinking about cars would bring on dark concern about the pollution problem, which would lead to fretting about the kind of world we'll be turning over to the young. By the time I got to the store I could hardly remember why I came, much less divide 16 ounces of tomatoes into 48 cents.

We're living, let's face it, in the Golden Age of Worry. Worry is everywhere these days, piling up—more solid, non-bio-degradable worry than most people can dispose of. It's a kind of mental pollution, and we're all showing the strain.

But then one day I began to discover that, like pollution experts finding ways to turn trash into treasure, I could turn my worry into work. After all, Ben Franklin found electric power at the end of a kite string. James Watt saw steam power in his mother's teakettle. So there's really nothing unusual in finding Worry Power in the odds and ends of worries hanging around the house. Here is what I've learned:

Concentrate your worrying. Worry power, like steam power, works only when you put a lid on it. I discovered this by accident the day my eldest son got his driving permit. I'd had a pretty busy summer, worry-wise. Between the state of the world, the dry spell, the funny noise the washing machine kept making, my young daughter's teeth and my husband's waistline, I just hadn't got around to worrying about my son's starting to drive. So it wasn't until they pulled away from the curb, my six-foot baby boy at the wheel, his father at his side, that the worry hit me. All at once. Talk about Watt's teapot blowing its top!

I went back in to start my chores, concentrating heavily on faulty brakes, tire blowouts and other things that could happen. Before I'd run through them all, I'd waxed and polished all the floors. Then, tensely, I began to review automobile accidents I'd heard or read about, as I cleaned three closets and my husband's bureau drawers. Then I turned to special hazards like drunken drivers, jackknifing trailer trucks, and icy patches on the road. (It was summertime, but worry knows no season.) When they came back, I had an immaculate house—and no memory at all of having done the work.

"He's going to be really good," my husband reported matter-of-factly. "He's got the touch." Then he looked around. "Wow! It's the Waldorf! What got into *you?*"

Worry power! It's the housewife's greatest help since somebody decided to pipe water right into the house.

Worry creatively. Worry doesn't have to furrow your brow and wear you out. Used imaginatively it can refresh and restore your strength. My husband took a plane trip recently. An ordinary, foolish fretter would have sat rigidly throughout the trip, listening to the shrieking argument in his brain: "This plane is going to crash.... Don't be silly, of course it won't.... It will *so....*" But my husband, a master at creative worrying, did it differently.

Even before he was airborne, he spotted a large rivet which he could easily believe held the whole wing together. It wasn't hard to imagine the bolt's working loose and being sucked into the jet engine, thus forcing a crash landing at sea. (The flight was entirely over land, which just shows you how creative a man he is.) Such an emergency would demand that some brave, quick-witted passenger (guess who?) would open the emergency door, thereby saving all the passengers' lives *and* earning the affectionate gratitude of the friendly stewardess, with whom he would then float cozily in a life raft just big enough for two until—well, until his plane landed in Toledo. By the time he deplaned, he was ready to lick his weight in corporate vice presidents.

If we can just break away from the "No it won't... Yes it will" pattern, imaginative worrying can make heroes of us all.

Don't call it worry if it's only procrastination. Once, in the middle of the night, I woke up coughing. I realized that I'd been coughing for weeks. "I wonder if I'm smoking too much," I worried to myself. "I'll bet I'm a mess in there."

Through the days that followed, I tried in vain to turn this into worry power, to use it, for example, to help me through two weeks' back ironing. But I simply stood weakly at the board, moving the iron slowly, slowly, as cigarette ashes fell on the clothes. I finally confided to a sympathetic friend, my fingers shaking just a little as I struck another match, "I'm so worried that I'm smoking too much."

"Then quit," she said.

She was right, of course. Whenever you find yourself agonizing over something you can actually do something about, you're not worrying—you're just kidding yourself.

Make a list. Most of us walk around with a large, foggy cloud of worries hanging over our heads, some of them old friends, some of them near strangers. If you sit down, make a list and really examine them, you may be surprised. For a month one summer I worried steadily about my second son, who was camping in the Canadian woods. Finally, when I wrote all the faceless worries down, I discovered that "appendicitis attack" was in the crowd. Since he'd had his appendix out years ago, I discarded that one—along with "typhoon," because you don't really get many typhoons in the Canadian woods. As I read down the list, I kept lightening my pack and feeling better.

Another day, weighed down with concerns, I made a two-column list: Worries, and What to Do About Them. My list of worries was a long one, ranging from "war" and "pollution" to "Jeannie's teeth." Then opposite each I entered something that was in my power to do immediately: "Write Congressman *today*"; "Call Boy Scouts about old newspapers"; and even that terrifying phrase, "Call orthodontist's office." The major worries I carried still, even after the small gallant actions had actually been taken. But at least some part of the worry had been turned into worry power.

If we can get our worries working for us, instead of the other way around, we may eventually find ourselves having less worry to work with. But let's not worry about *that* until the time comes.

BRING "THE RAINBOW" TO YOUR JOB

by JOHN KORD LAGEMANN

ALBERT ROGERS is an indefatigable shoeshine boy at a New York hotel whose rhythmic artistry with polish and brush leaves a shine that almost hurts your eyes. "Don't you ever get tired?" I once asked him. "No," he said. "But I would if I just shined shoes."

Albert has something in common with Will Edgers, a Vermont farmer who sells firewood. Some friends ordered half a cord one fall while we were visiting them. Will didn't just dump the wood from his truck. He made a small platform of stones, then carefully stacked the wood at a slant to keep rain water from standing on it. Then he surveyed his handiwork and said quietly, "Wood's a pretty thing now, ain't it? Growin', split or burnin'."

Albert and Will, each in his own way, have discovered a compelling secret that makes anything they do pay off in terms of greater satisfaction, deeper self-realization. Pablo Casals, the world-famous cellist, put it into words while giving a lesson to a young woman student. She played the notes just as they were written. Casals played the same notes, but they throbbed and glowed. He asked the girl to repeat the passage several times, each time demonstrating the special quality he wanted her to bring to it. "Bring to it the rainbow—always the rainbow," he said. When she finally did, her face lighted up in pure joy.

The "rainbow" is the glow that crowns an all-out effort to do a job, *any kind of job*, as well as it can possibly be done. It takes a shade more effort, a bit more time, but once you have experienced the mixture of elation, pride and relief that comes from creating rainbows, life is never quite the same. You can say with honesty, "This is good. It has a part of me in it." Then all tasks that once seemed boring and routine become meaningful and rewarding.

May I suggest some simple rules for bringing rainbows to our own work and life?

Give everything you've got. "The champion isn't necessarily the person who *has* the most," Dr. Laurence E. Morehouse, a professor at U.C.L.A., told me. "But he's always the person who *gives* the most. The champion is willing to risk all of himself on the task. The runner-up, who may have equal or superior potential, holds something back."

Often it's fear of failure that prevents us from going all-out. It's as if we were preparing to excuse our failure in advance, so that we can say, "I wasn't really trying." Paradoxically, losing oneself in the task at hand is the only way of finding oneself. The more you give, the more you have to give—and the more rainbows you create.

Give it one more try. To get material for a book, *How to Study Better*, Eugene Ehrlich, a professor at Columbia, interviewed hundreds of students, some with barely passing grades, some with average grades, some with A's. "There wasn't much difference in their native intelligence," he told me. "The one thing that distinguished the A students was the 'baker's-dozen complex.' After hitting the books as hard as they could, most students said, 'Well, that's that.' The A's, however, said, 'Let's give it one more for good measure.'"

It's hard to experience repeated failure and still go on trying. But sometimes it's even harder to go on after achieving limited success. It's tempting to say, "This will do." But Gustave Flaubert rewrote his great novel, *Madame Bovary*, at least three times, and was still so dissatisfied with it that he considered burning the manuscript. He gave it one last try—and the result is a classic.

Take a proprietary attitude toward your job. The electrical wizard, Charles Steinmetz, used to work on in his laboratory at General Electric hours after the rest of the staff had gone home. "Why do you do it?" a colleague asked him one day. "You don't have to prove anything. You'd get the same salary."

Steinmetz looked up from his workbench and said, "My friend, it doesn't matter how much you get or who pays you. You are always working for yourself."

Tackle little jobs as if they were big ones. Some people don't think their jobs are worth their best efforts. They are always saving themselves for the great break—which never comes. They don't realize that the big job consists of many little jobs, all of which have to be done well.

Some of the little jobs may seem thankless. But if they are consistently well done, "it is certain that," as Emerson wrote, "the secret cannot be kept. If a man has good corn or wood or boards or pigs to sell, or can make better chairs or knives, crucibles or church organs than anybody else, you will find a broad, hard-beaten road to his house, though it be in the woods."

Want to sign your work. Ask yourself when you finish a job, "Would I sign this?" One spring I hired a man with a bulldozer to dig out a pond in our woods. Frank, the operator, handled the huge machine as deftly as a sculptor wielding a knife. He was pleased by my approval, but he himself was harder to satisfy. Every now and then he descended from the cab, walked over to a high spot and surveyed what he had done so far. "We could curve it in among those trees," he said. "We could use some of the fill to raise up that low part."

Later, as the pond filled up, it looked as if it had been shaped by nature herself. Frank came back one day to inspect his handiwork—and to add a finishing touch: four white ducklings. "It needed something swimming on it," he said.

Create your own style. Style is perhaps the truest form of self-expression. "A man's style," said 17th-century author François Fenelon, "is as much a part of him as his face, his figure or the rhythm of his pulse."

In Tucson, I know a Navajo silversmith who goes right on creating fine jewelry while most of his competitors have compromised on workmanship and materials by making gewgaws for the tourist trade. One day I asked him why he spent so much time turning out little pieces of art when he could cash in so easily with inferior workmanship.

"I tried making junk," he said. "It was like making false money. It fooled other people, but it didn't fool me. I look at my bankbook maybe once or twice a month. But I have to live with myself every day."

Doing something he can call his own satisfies a deep need in man. The material world in which we live is stubborn and chaotic. All of us feel the urge to impose our own order on some small part of it. It is the way we discover who we are. It is the way we create rainbows.

CHAPTER 13
Out of the Rut, Into the New

EIGHT STEPS
TO A NEW LIFE
by NORMAN VINCENT PEALE, D.D.

FIFTY years of listening to troubled people has made me familiar, I think, with just about every human problem under the
sun. But there's one so prevalent that I consider it the basic
human sickness. It's the problem of the person who is living
far below his potential and knows it; who is deeply unhappy,
but can't seem to do anything about it.

Usually, from where the counselor sits, the person's difficulties don't seem so overwhelming—but the sufferer is convinced he can't cope with them. Although he seems to have
normal intelligence, adequate education and all the necessary
attributes for successful living, he can't summon them to his
aid. His life is blurred, out of focus, without power or purpose.

Always, you find three deadly characteristics in such people:
inertia, self-doubt and aimlessness. One autumn day, walking
alone around our local golf course (I was hoping to scare up
some sermon ideas), I came upon a young man raking leaves
off a green. I knew him slightly, and I asked how things were
going. He shrugged. "As you can see," he said, "I'm not getting
anywhere."

"Where do you want to get?" I asked. He looked at me
glumly. "I don't really know," he said.

"What do you do best?" I asked.

He shook his head. "I'm not sure that I'm much good at
anything."

"Well, what gives you the most satisfaction?"

He frowned. "No special thing."

"Look," I said, "I've asked you three of the most important
questions anyone can be asked, and I've had three completely
fuzzy answers. When you go home tonight, I want you to sit
down with paper and pencil, and don't get up until you've
answered my questions. Then let's meet here tomorrow at this
time, and we'll take it from there."

Somewhat hesitantly, he agreed. When we met the next
day, he told me that he liked to work with his hands, not his
head; that he thought he might have some mechanical ability;

234

and that what he wanted most in life was some sense of purpose or direction. Shortly thereafter, he got a job in a roofing-materials factory. Did he become president of the company? No, but today he is a foreman, living a happy and productive life. All he needed was a push to stop leading an unfocused life.

I meet people like that young man so frequently that I have developed a set of guidelines to help anyone, young or old, who feels the need to bring himself into sharper focus. There are eight points in all, and they add up to quite a stiff course in self-discipline. But anyone who makes a sustained effort to apply them will become a happier, more forceful, more effective person.

1. Pinpoint your primary goal in life. It's not enough to say, "I want to be happy" or "I want to make money" or "I want to be a better person." You must determine *exactly* what you want, and when. You need to say, "I intend to be a registered nurse in three years," or sales manager of this company, or editor of this newspaper, or buyer for that store, in four, five, or six years.

Write down a short summary of your goal and the achievement date; put it beside your bed and read it aloud to yourself every morning when you wake up. Vagueness is the invariable hallmark of the unfocused mind. Get rid of it.

2. Use imagination to fan desire. There's no use pinpointing a goal in life unless you want it enormously. Daydreams and wistful wishes are not enough; there must be intense, burning desire. Nobody can put this hunger into you; you have to develop it yourself by constant, vivid imagining of the benefits that achieving your goal will bring. Ask anyone who has achieved outstanding success in any field. He will tell you that clarity of purpose and intensity of desire are the chief ingredients of the magic formula. Unless you care, you won't get there.

3. Expect to pay for what you get. If you set a high goal, you will have to pay a high price. You will have to work, take chances, make sacrifices, endure setbacks. You won't be able to afford the luxury of laziness or the delights of frequent distraction. When setting your goal, remember that unless you're willing to pay the price you're wasting your time.

4. Send the right signals to your unconscious mind. This is crucial. The unconscious is a great dynamo, but it is also a computer that has to be properly programmed. If fear thoughts, worry thoughts, failure thoughts are constantly channeled into the unconscious, nothing very constructive is going to be sent back. But if a clear, purposeful goal is steadfastly held in the conscious mind, the unconscious will eventually accept it and begin to supply the conscious mind with plans, ideas, insights, and the energies necessary to achieve that goal.

5. *Be willing to fail—temporarily.* A man who made a long-term study of highly successful men in various fields told me that he noted they had only one trait in common: persistence. They kept picking themselves up and returning to the fight long after most men would have given up.

In a sermon not long ago, I condensed the life history of such a man. This man failed in business in '31. He was defeated for the state legislature in '32. He failed again in business in '34. He had a nervous breakdown in '41. He hoped to receive his party's nomination for Congress but didn't in '43. He ran for the Senate and lost in '55. He was defeated again for the Senate in '58. A hopeless loser, some people said. But Abraham Lincoln was elected President in 1860. He knew how to accept defeat—temporarily.

6. *Believe in the power of thought to change things.* It's very hard for most people to realize that the most powerful force in the world is an idea that has taken root in a human mind. But it is.

Some time ago in Australia, I met a remarkable man named Bert Walton. He told me that he had started out in life by failing at one school after another, then at one job after another. He was working for the Australian division of an American corporation—and going downhill at that—when a man came out from the parent company to talk to Australian employes. One sentence in the man's talk struck Walton with enormous impact: *You can—if you think you can.*

"I suddenly realized," Walton told me, "that the reason I was a failure was my habit of thinking of myself as a failure. The concept created the condition—not the other way round. So I decided to change the concept. I said to myself: 'I think I can become manager of this company for New South Wales. In fact, I think I can become manager for the whole of Australia.' Well, it took a long time and a lot of work, and there were a lot of setbacks, but that's the way things turned out. Then I got into the department-store business, and I said to myself, 'I think we can build this business into one of the big chains in Australia.' And eventually that happened too. I'm a very ordinary man, but I got hold of one extraordinary idea, and hung on."

What happened to that man? The idea, like a burning glass, focused the rays of his personality on a definite goal with such intensity that hitherto inert elements burst into flame. The idea is not a new one. The Bible says over and over: "If ye have faith, nothing shall be impossible unto you." A staggering promise, certainly, but profoundly true.

7. *Never build a case against yourself.* Just last week, a man came up to me and asked if we could talk. He had a stooped, dejected look. And he sounded defeated. "I'm a salesman," he said. "I make a living at it, but my work is of no importance. I'm depressed and miserable most of the time. Can you help me?"

"No," I said. "I can't crawl into your head and rearrange the machinery. But perhaps I can tell you how to help yourself. In the first place, stop cringing. Stand up straight. Next, stop running down your profession. In our society, salesmen are the ball bearings on which industry moves; without them, the economy would grind to a halt. Finally, why don't you stop looking at yourself from a worm's viewpoint and look at yourself from God's? You are His child. If you are important to Him—and you are—what gives you the right to go around proclaiming your unimportance?"

We talked a bit more; then he thanked me, and went away looking thoughtful. I hope he had learned, or begun to learn, the importance of not building a case against himself.

8. *Stop short-circuiting yourself with alibis.* Unfocused people do this constantly. They say, "The timing is wrong" or, "I'm not really qualified." They play the if-only game: "If only I had more money, or more education . . . if only I weren't so tied down . . ." The alibis go on and on, and they just reinforce the three deadly characteristics—inertia, self-doubt, aimlessness. To become a focused person you have to control self-limiting thoughts. "I don't believe in circumstances," George Bernard Shaw once said. "The people who get on in this world are the people who look for the circumstances they want, and if they can't find them, make them."

PLATO once said that the unexamined life isn't worth living. The statement is as true today as it was 23 centuries ago. So, examine your life. If it is out of focus, make up your mind to get it into focus. And start today.

GRASP THE NETTLE, NOW!

by OSCAR SCHISGALL

"DO EVERY DAY or two something for no other reason than that you would rather *not* do it." Thus William James, the American philosopher, emphasized a solemn, eternal truth that has been the very basis of man's progress, the ladder by which man has climbed to new heights.

James has plenty of supporters. "It's the hard jobs we tackle daily that get us places," the late Sen. Irving Ives once said. "Easy roads all seem to lead downhill."

Years ago I went to Boston to visit Dean Roscoe Pound. At 90, long since retired as dean of the Harvard Law School, he still worked eight hours a day in his office at Langdell Hall. His secretary told me, "He's become quite weak. But every day he forces himself to walk the two blocks from his hotel to his office. It takes him an hour, but he insists on doing it because it gives him a sense of achievement. He wouldn't dream of taking a taxi."

Just then a burdened and annoyed-looking law student came out of the dean's office. "It's always the same," he muttered. "I ask a simple question, something the dean could answer with a yes or no, and he hands me a dozen books. 'You'll find the answer here,' he says."

Later, Dean Pound said, "It's the way I myself was taught to study—the hard way. If that boy digs into those volumes, he'll end up with a real knowledge of the subject. He might one day become a good lawyer."

Top-rank professionals and noted achievers almost inevitably turn out to be men who tackle the difficult task head-on, without procrastination. One morning when I went to keep an early appointment with my friend and literary agent the late Carl Brandt, he asked, "Mind waiting while I make one phone call? I have a distasteful job to do; I'd like to get it over with."

I remarked later that most of us are inclined to put disagreeable chores off as long as possible.

"I've learned to grasp the nettle," Carl answered. "When I have something hard to do—which happens practically every day—I get it out of the way first. Then I can go through the rest of the day in much better spirits and get more done."

Once we confront a difficulty, we may find it less trouble-some than it appeared. A man whom I will call Henry Jones started years ago as a Washington newspaperman—an extremely shy newspaperman. He was appalled when his boss told him to go get an interview with the late Supreme Court Justice Louis Brandeis on a speech he had made. "How *can* I ask for an exclusive interview?" he said. "Justice Brandeis doesn't know me; why should he take the time?"

Whereupon a fellow reporter picked up the telephone, called Justice Brandeis's office and spoke to the secretary. "This is Henry Jones of the *Star*," he said (while the real Henry Jones gasped). "I've been assigned to interview the Justice. Would it be convenient for him to give me a few minutes today?" He waited. Then, "Thank you. One-fifteen. I'll be there." Putting down the phone, he told Jones, "You have your appointment."

Years later Jones said to me, "From that I learned to take the direct approach. It has been a hard thing to do, but useful—and every time I overcome this sort of timidity it is a little easier to do it the next time."

Timidity manifests itself in other ways, too, as in the reluctance to voice a difference of opinion. Most of us hesitate to stand up in public and say *nay* when all others are saying *aye*. Why? Is honest dissent really so dreadful? Emerson wrote, "Whoso would be a man must be a nonconformist." He was writing not of eccentrics or freaks but of men who fearlessly speak their minds. For many of us, the "something hard" we do could be simply speaking our plain thoughts.

Yet, there are things more difficult than speaking out. Albert Einstein, asked what he would say to science students, replied without hesitation, "I would advise them to spend an hour every day rejecting the ideas of others and thinking things out for themselves. This will be a hard thing to do, but rewarding."

The human brain can be an amazing instrument when it is *forced* to function. It can create a Beethoven sonata, a Hamlet, a rocket to the moon, television, the sculpture of Michelangelo, skyscrapers, pyramids, Hoover Dams—but never until it is driven to the hard job of thinking.

Countless areas offer challenges. "Doing something hard every day" could mean reading a profound book, forcing one's mind to stretch to its utmost capacity. As learned a scholar as Charles Darwin once said he regretted the lack of attention he had given to stretching his own mind with unfamiliar interests. "If I had my life to live over," he said, "I would have made a rule to read some poetry and listen to some music at least once a week; for perhaps the parts of my brain now atrophied would thus have been kept active through use."

The late Franklin P. Adams, one of the country's most popular columnists, was asked by a journalism student, "When you sign a contract to do five columns a week, how can you be sure you'll get five fresh ideas every week?"

FPA answered, "If it were so easy that I could be sure, there'd be no fun in this job. It's having to find an idea every morning that makes me feel I'm earning my salary."

"What if no ideas come?" the student persisted. "Then I sit down and start writing anyway," said FPA. The difficult task of *starting*, of launching a chain of thought, was his way of grasping the nettle.

Obviously there are as many daily nettles to grasp as there are people. The calmest men I know, the happiest, and by and large the most successful, are those who grapple with their problems as quickly as they appear. This practice of grasping the nettle is, in the long run, the surest way to peace of mind.

NEVER SAY "NEVER"

by MICHAEL DRURY

FEW people set out deliberately to miss the wonder and richness of living, but it is treacherously easy to do. A postponement here, a sidestepping there, a hesitant retreat—and behold a life dried up behind a wall of negatives: No, I can't; I won't; it can never happen; I never go to big parties; I'll never marry a career woman; I'll never speak to him again.

I know a brilliant woman who has led a fascinating and rewarding life, and once I asked her if she could select the single most important lesson she had learned. She was silent a moment, then said, "Yes. That all the things you think can never happen, *will* happen. And that all the things you think you'll never do, you probably *will* do."

She did not mean, of course, that one should not make choices, pro and con. Without some rejections, some boundaries to give pattern to life, every minor decision would become a major crisis: whether to come or go; whether to act or wait; whether to speak or to keep still.

But *never?*

Never to venture beyond the boundaries and try ourselves against experience? Never to read a book we are not predisposed to like? Never to ride in planes because people sometimes get killed in them?

"Never" is a cunning thief that impoverishes a spirit. We are all born to unspecified possibilities. They are ahead of us, waiting. Yet too often the simple recognition of fact digs in as a practice and a principle, and the possibilities narrow and stop. To say, "I have never been to Europe," is harmless; but the moment it becomes, "I never go to Europe," and then, "I will never go to Europe," we are being robbed under our very noses.

A friend whose work sometimes takes her to foreign countries used to languish in hotel rooms during her leisure hours. "I had an elaborate list of reasons for not going out," she says now. "I didn't know the language; I was a woman alone; I was working, and I thought I had no time for me. Oh, I had it all built up like the Berlin Wall."

One day in Athens, a hotel clerk, taking for granted that

she would want to explore his city, gave her a local map. It was in English, with the hotel and the great historical sites clearly marked. My friend looked at it and thought, "Why, that building is only three blocks from here. I couldn't possibly get lost, and I can come right back."

In a sense, she never came back. The wall was down, and her particular world grew wider. She has learned to know not only the foreign cities but their people. She has discovered that real communication goes much deeper than language.

That is one of the satisfying aspects of ending self-imposed negation; more than release from something, it is release *to* something—to fulfillment, to self-possession.

Once, my mother and I decided to ride the aerial tramway from Palm Springs in the California desert to the top of 10,805-foot San Jacinto Mountain. At a gas station where we stopped for directions en route, the attendant said, "You'll never catch me riding that thing."

"Why not?" I asked.

"I run my life on hunches," he said. "And I just have a hunch about cable cars."

I confess that the experience itself—the swift, silent rise in a glass-sided car that put one in a new, untried relationship with one's world—was not every moment comfortable. Yet it was exhilarating, a taste of a new dimension.

Our gas-station man could have been right—for him. But hunches can so easily become hedges unless we re-examine occasionally.

That is the key word: *re-examine*. Plainly, negatives are sometimes suitable and necessary. Any position, however, may be outgrown. The child who says, "Grownups never have any fun; I'm never going to grow up," one day perceives that he not only must grow up but desires to.

Life is a process of finding out who we are and what we may become. It is quite possible that the thing we say so flatly we will never do is the very thing we need for completion. That is why the effort to break out of the pattern exhilarates us; it is a creative act.

If you would make yourself felt in the world and known to yourself, say "yes" to life.

TURNING FAILURE INTO SUCCESS
by FREDELLE MAYNARD

VICKY—beautiful, talented, very bright, voted "Most Likely to Succeed" in college—got a promising job with a large specialty store after graduation. Then, after two years without promotions, she was fired. She suffered a complete nervous breakdown. "It was panic," she told me later. "Everything had always gone so well for me that I had no experience in coping with rejection. I felt I was a failure."

Vicky's reaction is an extreme example of a common phenomenon. In a society that places so much emphasis on "making it," we fail to recognize that what looks like failure may, in the long run, prove beneficial. When Vicky was able to think coolly about why she was fired, for example, she realized that she was simply not suited to a job dealing with people all the time. In her new position as a copy editor, she works independently, is happy and once again "successful."

People are generally prone to what semanticist S. I. Hayakawa calls "the two-valued oriention." We talk about seeing both sides of a question as if every question had *only* two sides. We assume that everyone is either a success cr a failure when, infact, infinite degrees of both are possible. As Hayakawa points out, there's a world of difference between "I have failed three times" and "I am a failure." Indeed, the words failure and success cannot be reasonably applied to a complex, living, changing human being. They can only describe the situation at a particular time and place.

Obviously no one can be a whiz at everything. In fact, success in one area often precludes success in another. An eminent politician once told me that his career had practically destroyed his marriage. "I have no time for my family," he explained. "I travel a lot. And even when I'm home, I hardly see my wife and kids. I've got power, money, prestige—but as a husband and father, I'm a flop."

Certain kinds of success can indeed be destructive. The danger of too early success is particularly acute whenever a child demonstrates special talent. I recall from my childhood a girl whose skill on ice skates marked her as "Olympic material." While the rest of us were playing, bicycling, reading, making things and just loafing, this girl skated—every day after school and all weekend. Her picture often appeared in the papers, and the rest of us envied her glamorous life. Years later, however, she spoke bitterly of those early triumphs. "I never prepared myself for anything but the ice," she said. "I peaked at 17—and it's been downhill ever since."

Success that comes too easily is also damaging. The child who wins a prize for a dashed-off essay, the adult who distinguishes himself at a first job by lucky accident faces probable disappointment when real challenges arise.

Success is also bad when it's achieved at the cost of the total quality of an experience. Successful students sometimes become so obsessed with grades that they never enjoy their school years. They never branch out into tempting new areas, because they don't want to risk their grade average.

Success may, quite simply, cost too much—in strain (infighting at the job, keeping a cheerful public face while your personal life falls apart) or loss of integrity (flattering, lying, going along with questionable actions). Above all, it may be too costly if the end result is fear—fear of not repeating the success. One of the most successful hostesses I know has come to hate entertaining: "I've acquired such a reputation," she explains, "that my friends expect me to outdo myself. I can't disappoint them—and I'm worn out before my guests arrive."

Why are so many people so afraid of failure? Quite simply because no one tells us *how* to fail so that failure becomes a growing experience. We forget that failure is part of the human condition and that, as family therapist Virginia Satir observes, "every person has the *right* to fail."

Most parents work hard at either preventing failure or protecting their children from the knowledge that they *have* failed. One way is to lower standards. A mother describes her child's hastily made table as "perfect!" even though it wobbles on uneven legs. Another way is to shift blame. If John fails science, his teacher is unfair or stupid.

When one of my daughters was ten, she decided to raise money for charity by holding a carnival. Proud of her, we rashly allowed her to put posters all over town. We realized too late that she couldn't possibly handle all the refreshments, shows and games promised in the posters. The whole family pitched in to prevent embarrassing failure—and the next year she advertised an even more ambitious event. Why not? We had kept her from discovering her limitations.

The trouble with failure-prevention devices is that they leave a child unequipped for life in the real world. The young need to learn that no one can be best at everything, no one can win all the time—and that it's possible to enjoy a game even when you *don't* win. A child who's not invited to a birthday party, who doesn't make the honor roll or the baseball team feels terrible, of course. But parents should not offer a quick consolation prize or say, "It doesn't matter," because it does. The youngster should be allowed to experience disappointment—and then be helped to master it.

Failure is never pleasurable. It hurts adults and children alike. But it can make a positive contribution to your life once you learn to use it. Step one is to ask, "Why did I fail?" Resist the natural impulse to blame someone else. Ask yourself what *you* did wrong, how *you* can improve. If someone else can help, don't be shy about inquiring.

When I was a teen-ager, I failed to get a job I'd counted on. I telephoned the interviewer to ask why. "Because you came ten minutes late," I was told. "We can't afford employes who waste other people's time." The explanation was reassuring (I hadn't been rejected as a person) and helpful, too. I don't think I've been late for anything since.

Success, which encourages repetition of old behavior, is not nearly as good a teacher as a failure. You can learn from a disastrous party how to give a good one, from an ill-chosen first house what to look for in a second. Even a failure that seems definitive can prompt fresh thinking, a change of direction. After 12 years of studying ballet a friend of mine auditioned for a professional company. She was turned down. "Would further training help?" she asked. The ballet master shook his head. "You will never be a dancer," he said. "You haven't the body for it."

In such cases, the way to use failure is to take stock courageously, asking, "What have I left? What *else* can I do?" My friend put away her toe shoes and moved into dance therapy, a field where she's both competent and useful.

Oddly enough, failure often brings with it a peculiar kind of freedom. Even a major life failure can be followed by a sense of "It's happened. I wish it hadn't, but it's over now—and I survived."

Failure frees one to take risks because there's less to lose.

Often there's a resurgence of energy—an awareness of new possibilities.

If faced, absorbed and accepted, failure contributes to personal growth and often leads to improved personal relationships. The officially "successful" person often remains closed off and self-protective, but simple human vulnerability is revealed in failure. A woman who recently ended what seemed like a perfect marriage says her friendships have a new closeness and warmth since her divorce. "I used to hear other people's troubles," she said, "but never tell my own. Now I can let it all out. The other day someone told me, 'I used to be put off by your superwoman act. You seem softer, more open now. I like you better this way.'"

Though we may envy the assurance that comes with success, most of us are attracted by gallantry in defeat—ideally exemplified by Adlai Stevenson's response after he lost the Presidential election in 1952; he said that he was "too old to cry, but it hurt too much to laugh." There is what might be called the noble failure—the special heroism of aiming high, doing your best and then, when that proves not enough, moving bravely on. As Ralph Waldo Emerson said: "A man's success is made up of failures, because he experiments and ventures every day, and the more falls he gets, moves faster on. . . . I have heard that in horsemanship he is not the good rider who never was thrown, but rather that a man will never be a good rider until he is thrown; then he will not be haunted any longer by the terror that he shall tumble, and will ride whither he is bound."

COPING WITH FUTURE SHOCK

by ALVIN TOFFLER

A STRANGE new society is erupting in our midst. Its conceptions of time, space, work, religion, sex are all incessantly changing, with a resulting mass disorientation. Much conflict today— between generations and cultures, between parents and children—can be traced to the acceleration of change.

We are now undergoing a world urbanization so rapid that the earth's city population has increased by about one-third in the past ten years. Economic growth is so fast in some countries that the child reaching teen age is surrounded by twice as much of everything newly man-made as at his birth. The time between an original technological concept and its practical use has been radically reduced: the Stanford Research Institute found that for a group of appliances introduced before 1920—including the vacuum cleaner, electric range, refrigerator—the average span between introduction and peak production was 34 years. But for a group that appeared in 1939–1959—including the electric frying pan, television receiver and washer-dryer combination—the span was only eight years. Today, the transistor, the cassette-player, and other devises sweep through society at an even faster clip, changing lives and changing people.

Already, within the main centers of change, in California and Cambridge, Mass., in New York and London and Tokyo, millions are living the life of the future. What makes them different? Certainly they are richer, better educated, more mobile. But what specifically marks them is the fact that they "live faster."

To survive in such communities, however, the individual must become infinitely more adaptable than ever before. Above all he must understand *transience*. Transience is the new "temporariness" in everyday life. It can be defined as the rate a which our relationships—with things, places, people and information—turn over. Let's explore life in a high-transience society.

Things: The Throw-Away Society. More and more of th

products we use are made for one-time or short-term use. In today's home, bottles, bibs, paper napkins, facial tissues, towels are all used up quickly and ruthlessly eliminated. TV dinners are cooked on throw-away trays. In fact, the home is a large processing machine through which objects flow at an ever-faster tempo. The same is true of our relationships with autos: we hold onto them less long—or rent them for short-term use. Across the board, we make and break our ties with the things around us at a faster pace than ever before.

The transience of our relationships with objects is also linked to their proliferation and variety. Between 1950 and 1963, the number of different soaps and detergents on the American grocery shelf increased from 65 to 200; frozen foods from 121 to 350; baking mixes and flour from 84 to 200. We are, in fact, racing toward "over choice"—the point at which the advantages of diversity are canceled by the complexity of the buyer's decision-making process. High-speed turnover of the things in our lives, along with greater complexity of choice, confronts us with the need to make increasingly rapid, frequently trivial decisions.

Places: The New Nomads. Just as things flow into and out of our lives at high speed—so, too, places. Americans travel faster and farther than ever before. Moreover, between March 1975 and March 1976—a single year—35.6 million Americans changed their place of residence. This is more than the total population of Cambodia, Ghana, Honduras, Israel, Mongolia, Nicaragua and Tunisia combined. It is as if the entire population of all these countries had suddenly been relocated. In each year since 1948, one out of every six Americans changed his address.

The professional and technical populations are among the most mobile of all Americans. (It is a house joke among executives of the International Business Machines Corp. that IBM stands for "I've Been Moved.") This moving of executives from house to house as if they were life-size chessmen on a global board has led one psychologist to propose facetiously a money-saving scheme called "The Modular Family." Under this system the executive could leave not only his house behind, but his family as well. The company would then find him a matching wife and children at the new site. No one appears to have taken the idea seriously—yet.

Such frequent relocation breeds the "loss of commitment"

that many writers have noted among the high mobiles. The man on the move is ordinarily in too much of a hurry to put down roots in any one place. Thus an airline executive is quoted as saying that he avoids involvement in the political life of his community because "in a few years I won't even be living here. You plant a tree, and you never see it grow."

Yet if one does withdraw from participation, what happens to the community and the self? Can individuals or society survive without commitment?

People: Early "Disaffiliation." People flow through our lives at a faster clip, too. We form limited-involvement relationships and easily abandon friendships—it's too difficult keeping in touch when jobs, status, locations change. Compared with previous generations, whose personal ties were relatively few and stable, we deal with many more people in the course of our daily lives and the cast of characters changes frequently.

Today, training for "disaffiliation" begins early. Ask a class of children how many have lost a best friend in the past year because the friend's family moved away—and watch the hands go up. In earlier generations, a "best friend" lasted a long time. Today our children, caught up in the rapid pace of our culture, turn over their friendships at a frenetic speed, with staggering results in terms of loneliness, isolation, and loss of deep satisfying emotional involvement.

Information: The Kinetic Image. We not only turn over things, places and people at high speed; we are continually under pressure to get rid of obsolete ideas and facts. Communications expert Robert Hilliard says, "By the time the child born today graduates from college, the amount of knowledge will be four times as great." This affects everyone's life, for every person must carry within his head a mental model of the world. If we are to function, even to survive, our model must bear some resemblance to reality. But, in a fast-changing society, yesterday's truth suddenly become today's fictions. An example is the constant radical change in the "rules" for correct child-rearing, emerging from the convulsing social sciences, and producing vast confusion among parents.

Today, surrounded by print, the average American adult ingests thousands of edited words per day. He also spends several hours a day listening to the radio and watching television—add several thousand more words. He is assaulted by hundreds of advertising messages each day. All this cannot leave us unaffected, and more and more we suffer from information overload. In the brain's neural system there are, in all likelihood, inherent physical limits to the amount and speed of image processing. How fast can a human being keep revising his inner images of the world before he smashes up against these limits? Nobody knows.

We do know that people often get sick when they are asked to change again and again—and can't keep up. How does change produce illness? A change in stimuli—visual, auditory, tactile—triggers in us a complex, massive bodily response. If the environment is overloaded with novelty, it can produce the equivalent of anxiety neurotics—people whose systems are continually flooded with adrenalin, whose hearts thump, whose hands go cold. And prolonged stress produces illness.

But future shock attacks the psyche as well: anxiety, confusional breakdown, extreme irritability, violence and apathy. Today, there are striking signs of breakdown all around us— the spreading use of drugs, the rise of mysticism, the politics of nihilism, the sick apathy of millions, old and young alike. Affluence makes it possible, for the first time in history, for large numbers of people to make this sort of emotional withdrawal. The family man who retreats into his evening with martinis and televised fantasy withdraws part-time. For other dropouts, withdrawal is full-time and total. It is impossible to produce such future shock in large numbers of individuals without affecting the rationality of society as a whole.

How, then, can we deal with future shock? At the most personal level, we can improve our our ability to cope with change by doing consciously some of the things that we already do unconsciously. In the words of Dr. Hans Selye, whose works on stress opened new frontiers in biology and psychiatry, the individual can "consciously look for signs of being keyed up too much." Heart palpitations, tremors, insomnia or unexplained fatigue may well signal over-stimulation. By asking ourselves if we are living too fast, we can attempt, quite consciously, to assess—and change—our life pace.

We employ a de-stimulating tactic, for example, when we turn off the stereo unit that has been battering our eardrums, or search for solitude on a deserted strip of beach. But we have stronger ways of coping with the threat of over-stimulation. We can, for example, refuse to purchase throw-away products.

We can hang onto the old jacket for another season; we can stoutly refuse to follow the latest fashion trend. We can resist when a salesman tells us it is time to trade in our automobile. In this way, we reduce the need to make and break ties with the physical objects around us.

None of this is to suggest that change can or should be stopped. The problem is not to suppress change, but to manage it. A broken engagement probably should not be too closely followed by a job transfer. The recent widow should not, perhaps, rush to sell her house.

In the past, ritual served as an important change buffer. It still can. The sending of Christmas cards, for example, is an annual ritual that not only represents continuity in its own right but also helps individuals prolong all-too-temporary friendships. So do celebrations of birthdays, holidays and anniversaries.

But all such personal efforts are not enough. It is hard to live a sensibly paced life when society is running away with itself. That is why we also need social and political strategies for the prevention of future shock.

First, society must create a "super-industrial" education system—one that enhances our ability to adapt. In the technological systems of tomorrow, machines will increasingly perform the routine tasks; men the intellectual and creative tasks. For education, the lesson is clear: it is no longer sufficient for Johnny to understand the past. It is not even enough for him to understand the present, for the here-and-now environment will soon vanish, to be replaced by something new. We send Johnny to school "to help him lead a better life in the future." But how many of us have taken the time to think seriously about what that future will be like? Most of us, teachers included, assume that today's way of life will be repeated in the future. Yet all the evidence points toward a radically changed tomorrow. Johnny must learn to anticipate the directions and rate of change. All of this will require broad, imaginative innovations in our educational system.

It means, for example, that nothing in the curriculum should be required unless it can be strongly justified in terms of future usefulness. This is not intended as an "anti-cultural" statement or a plea for total destruction of the past. Nor does it suggest that we can ignore such basics as reading, writing and math. What it does mean is that tens of millions of children today are forced by law to spend precious hours of their lives grinding away at material whose future utility is highly questionable. Why, for example, must teaching be organized around such fixed disciplines as English, economics, mathematics and biology? Why not around stages of the human life cycle? Or around contemporary social problems? Or around "the future of the family" or "life-styles of tomorrow"?

There are encouraging signs that higher education is beginning to treat the future with new respect. This fall American colleges will offer as many as 300 varying courses about the future. Our lower schools, too, must begin to introduce the student to tomorrow. After all, as one 17-year-old recently wrote to me, "Young people are the major shareholders in the future."

Another powerful strategy in the battle to prevent future shock involves the taming of technology. The pace of change is force-fed by technical innovation. We cannot and must not turn off the switch of technological progress. Only middle-class romantics with full bellies babble about returning to a "state of nature" in which, as Hobbes reminded us, the typical life is "poor, nasty, brutish, and short."

At the same time, it is undeniably true that we frequently apply new technology stupidly and selfishly. In our haste to milk technology for immediate economic advantage, for example, we have turned our environment into a physical and social tinderbox.

What we desperately need is a worldwide movement for *responsible* technology. First, we must submit new technology to a set of demanding environmental tests before we unleash it in our midst, so that we stop adding to pollution, noise and filth. Second, and much more complex, we must question the long-term impact of a technical innovation on the social, cultural and psychological milieu, as well as on the physical environment. The automobile, for instance, is widely believed to have changed the shape of our cities, shifted home ownership and retail-trade patterns, altered sexual customs and loosened family ties. We can no longer afford to let such secondary social and cultural effects just "happen." We must attempt, as best we can, to anticipate them in advance. And where these effects are likely to be seriously damaging, we must also be prepared to block the new technology.

This is why the recent public controversy over the supersonic transport was so healthy. It was the first time that a large sector of the public asked questions about a major piece of technology *before* its arrival on the scene instead of after. This is the beginning of a much-needed future-consciousness and the first step in shifting control of technology out of the hands of scientific, corporate or political elites into the hands of the public itself. Only by following this course can we guide technology into more humane channels and *pace* its arrival so that it does not produce mass future shock.

In short, future shock—the disease of change—can be averted. To do so, the individual must become infinitely more adaptable and capable than ever before. He must search for totally new ways to anchor himself; for all the old roots—religion, nation, community, family or profession—are now shaking under the hurricane impact of the accelerative thrust. But if we are to avoid a massive adaptational breakdown, we must learn to control the rate of change not only in our personal affairs but in society at large.

THE SHOCK OF HAPPINESS

by GEORGE KENT

FOR EIGHT months the girl lay in a Swiss tuberculosis sanatorium making virtually no progress. One day her father arrived and, after a worried look at her, departed for a talk with the physician in charge. A half-hour later, a horsedrawn sleigh, jingle bells and all, was at the door. The girl was bundled in blankets and carried down—and away they went, up and down the snow-covered mountain roads, with a stop for chocolate and cakes, another for a gape at an Alpine valley, then off again for another 20 minutes.

No miracle happened, but it is on the record that from that moment recovery started. Less than a year later, the girl was home, well along the road to normal health.

This is as good an example as I know of what may be called cure by the shock of happiness. Webster defines a shock as "a sudden and violent agitation of the mental or emotional sensibilities." In other words, a brusque upsetting of routine, a rock tossed through the gray window of boredom. Let the upset be joyous. The old wives have always known that happiness is a medicine. Administered sharply and dramatically, it can work wonders.

The business of living calls for an occasional squeal of delight, and that comes only from being brought up short by something we may have dreamed about but certainly did not expect. We all tend to get into ruts. Marriage counselors tell husbands to surprise the little woman with flowers; they tell wives to offer a new trout fly or a golf gadget. Gifts on birthdays, on anniversaries and at Christmas—of course! But the present that shakes awake the sagging spirit is one offered for no reason at all except tenderness, and on any old ragamuffin of a day.

Good advice, not only for husbands and wives—and why not turn a simple surprise into a jolt of joy by making the gift dramatically different or outsize? Calling on a woman friend, a man I know brought a bucket of freesias, 50 at least, enough to adorn and perfume the house for weeks. They are still remembered. On another occasion he came bearing a box of candy with a single white orchid caught in the twine. The rule about giving is to give more than expected. Knock the postman, the waiter, the cleaning woman off their feet with a haymaker of a tip. You won't go bankrupt, and you'll get the money back in smiling service. And ditto for gifts to anyone at any time. The annual necktie from Aunt Emma always got a thank-you note, but the Christmas she sent a hydraulic jack, the house was lit up by the sparkle in papa's eyes, and instead of a letter she received a telephone call that rang with hosannas.

An evening out that follows a sudden impulse is worth a dozen carefully planned affairs. One night a friend, a business executive, telephoned his wife: "I'm waiting for you in the lobby of the St. George Hotel. We're having dinner out—I've found a swell new steak house." You could almost hear her stammer, "But the dinner—it's all ready.". "Stick it in the icebox; we'll eat it tomorrow," said the brute.

The woman was rocked by vertigo, but secretly happy; it was as if they were back in the old days of courtship when nothing mattered except being together. And after dinner, instead of a sedate dancing spot, they went to a discothèque where, in shock abandoned, they rocked and twisted, imitating the youngsters about them. At one o'clock the husband moaned with a grin, "Oh, my aching back!" "Oh, my darling!" said the lady, and the glow of the moon was in her eyes. As marriages go, this is one of the best, because the shocks come often and never fail to evoke delectable pins and needles.

"Every evening should have its menu," said Balzac. It may be an hour of skating under the moon on a remote lake. It may be exotic food. Instead of a show, why not go to a political meeting and get up and express your opinion? In a word, explore the possibilities—you will find they are as varied as your wit and imagination.

And let the daring young man remember to keep doing this after marriage. Once joined in wedlock, he usually falls off the trapeze; the inventor of surprise and tingling forgets what made him a hero. At work, he will still pummel his brains, but home becomes for him a place for *not* thinking. Not thinking can become a habit. Brilliance, too, is a habit and can be cultivated. If you create high-voltage shocks at home, you are more likely to shine at the office.

With children, shocks of happiness can even be a cure for misbehavior. Take a three-year-old who won't stay in bed and keeps coming downstairs. He is prepared for a scolding, or at best a quick trip back to his cot. One evening I tried a new maneuver. I heaved the boy up on my shoulders and walked outside. The sky was a snowfield of stars. There was a fingernail of a crescent moon. The boy had never seen the night before, and he was awed, thrilled, frightened and elated all at once. I pointed out the few constellations I knew: Orion with his Belt, and the Great Bear with its Big Dipper. I reassured him that the strange sound he heard was an owl, the bird that works a night shift. As to the rustling,.that was the leaves whispering in their sleep. This excursion did not put an end to the trips downstairs. But they became less frequent, less often the result of a bad dream or of lying awake alone in a dark room. Another cure or near-cure through the shock of happiness.

For some men and women, lack of self-confidence is almost pathological: the man who freezes when asked to address an audience, the woman who falls to pieces when there are more than four people for dinner. For such persons, the simple shock of sudden change may be better than shock treatment by electricity.

I have in mind a timid soul who lived in a small house in the suburbs. He had two children and a wife who ruled him in a peevish, unintelligent way. His job as an accountant gave him a knowledge of all aspects of the company for which he worked; one day, safe in the routine of memo-passing, he sent a suggestion to the general manager. It was a good idea, but it required investigation, and so our Mr. Milquetoast was asked to pack his bag and tackle it. He wanted passionately to refuse the assignment but, standing on the executive carpet, he did not dare.

The news that this mild creature of routine was going on an unexpected out-of-town trip was like the explosion of a bomb in the little suburban house. The shock waves went on spreading as he settled in a first-class seat on an airplane, put up at the best hotel, made telephone calls and appointments. Overnight our man became a man of the world. Life in the suburbs was never the same again. He bought a new car and gradually assumed command of his home. His wife, who secretly wanted nothing better than a dominant male, brightened up and rediscovered the joy of laughter. The explanation: a shock of happiness that came *from inside*, by the man's own efforts.

It is possible for all of us to create the shock that can change our lives. It may take a little courage to shake oneself out o the pajamas of habit. But it can be done, and it's easier than you imagine. In Finland, one rushes from the superheated sauna bath for a plunge into the icy waters of a lake. Stop to think and you won't do it—ever. Dive in without hesitancy, and after the shock you feel more wonderful that you have ever felt before.

Everybody wants to know how to get more out of life. The answer is to make greater use of the power that drives us— our emotions. By agitating them in a wise but ruthless fashion, we can acquire the self-confidence and the feeling of power that will lead us to a life packed with interest, excitement and love of beauty. Franz Kafka once said, "We need an ice ax to break the frozen sea within us." The best ax is a shock of happiness.

"IF I SHOULD DIE BEFORE I WAKE"
by ARDIS WHITMAN

> *Now I lay me down to sleep,*
> *I pray the Lord my soul to keep;*
> *If I should die before I wake,*
> *I pray the Lord my soul to take.*

WHENEVER I said that prayer as a little girl, I thought not of death but of life, not of sleeping, but of waking up the next day. And what a waking it was! The sun blazing through the windows like a trumpet of the dawn, the cheerful cackling of the kitchen fire starting, the fragrance of coffee and the voices of my parents at ease with each other, all seemed to welcome me to the celebration of another day.

Our life was frugal but our house was a very center of life, not death; of waking, not sleeping. We had no money but we had almost everything else. In particular we had the glowing vitality of my mother. I can see her now, running upstairs and down, even up the attic stairs, to look at the wind in the trees from some special vantage point. She read enormously, piling books around her. Music, too, was her great love; it poured through our house. She seemed to turn in every direction, holding out her hands for life's treasures.

My mother's special gift to me as a child was this sense of vivid delight in everything. I still remember the vividness—the smell of burning leaves and dusty haymows, summer afternoons when I climbed to the treetop to rock with the winds through the fragrant hours. The freshness, the aliveness, the *awakeness* of these memories! So it is no wonder that when I said my prayer each night—*if I should die before I wake*—I thought not of dying but of waking; of tomorrow and the next day and the unending years.

That childish petition had not crossed my mind for years. Then, recently, I learned what it has to say to us who are grown up. I was in the hospital in the midst of a life-threatening illness when one evening I found myself saying inwardly the little prayer's most poignant line: *"If I should die before I wake."*

Suddenly, I knew that what was troubling me was not so much the thought of dying—but of dying before I had fully waked from the slumber of my life. I realized that what the prayer says is: "Wake up and live, for time is flying." I promised myself passionately that never again would I take a moment of life for granted.

In that flash of illumination, I thought of what a profound word "waking" is, how close to the roots of life. The dictionary says that "to awaken" means not only "to be roused from sleep," but also "to rise to action." In short, it is to be born again into life.

The adult, like the child, *should* rise from sleep with spring in his heart; should, and so rarely does. Suppose we counted how many hours there were in a recent week when we moved about like children, antenna out for the winds of heaven, touching, hearing, looking, as though morning had just dawned on the earth for the first time. How many would there be?

True, it is easier when we are children. Then we ran, wakeful as the blazing sun, through our days. Everything was possible and life was forever. We cannot get back to those magical, wide-awake joys of childhood. But we have journeys of our own to take, and the joy of the adult when it comes, rises from deeper reasons than the child's; it is informed by greater understanding; it is freighted by longer, more poignant experience.

I remember a day in early spring. For weeks, New England had been its coldest and rainiest. Suddenly, there was sunshine like the hand of God on the land. Red buds appeared on the maple; robins hopped on the lawn; and, by happy coincidence, it was a holiday for my teacher husband.

We got into the car and drove to a state forest which was empty of everything except birds and chipmunks. We came to the river. The sand on the shore was hot in the sun, and we stretched out on it, side by side, holding hands. The air was full of the smell of sun on pine trees and the soft sounds of running water. We spoke little; but no child's joy could have contained so much.

Out of nowhere, these waking moments come like a benediction; moments when, like children, we are all of a piece, responding to life totally. It's like going back to the child in us but going back with understanding. It is to be alive, first of all, to the lovely world around us. Just to have been born here, to have lived at all, how wonderful that is!

With all its flaws, the world around us is, indeed, lovely and worthy of our gratitude. Yes, and so are its people. If human beings often hurt each other, they as often pity and sympathize. When they are not kind, it is often because they are overwhelmed by their own troubles. We are most awake when we realize this and, forgetting ourselves, pour out our love.

I remember a spring afternoon in Paris, years ago. Saddened by what seemed to be betrayal by a trusted friend, I walked the lovely streets alone, oblivious to the day, hurt by the happiness of the people who passed me. Ahead of me loomed the towers of Notre Dame. The cathedral's darkness appealed to me, and I trudged in at a side door and found myself being guided around by a tiptoeing old man, round as an apricot, and bursting with knowledge.

I struggled to listen, but sorrow grew and engulfed me. Suddenly, to my horror, I found myself beginning to weep. Appalled, my little guide stepped up his eloquence. At last, when it must have seemed that the tears were destined to go on forever, he stopped suddenly in a remote aisle where a shaft of sunlight fell from arched windows—stopped and reached out his hand. "Hold to me," he said softly in his quaint English. "Hold to me. I am here."

We stood so in the pouring light, and for that instant sorrow gave way to understanding. In a rush of joy and tenderness I saw and felt the love in the world, the goodness of human beings, the reaching of hands to each other; saw it and felt it as though it were a palpable presence flooding the ancient church.

All this is what it is to be awake; and it is the task of all of us before we die. But few people live their lives so. Instead, we drift along on the surface of things, dazed and confused like dreamers, only half-alive. Then, there comes a day when the shortness of time is upon us like a dark end. What we hoped to do with our lives has not been done; the things we wanted to say have not been said; the people to whom we wanted to express our love have never received it; the wrongs we have done have not been made up for; the talents we have, have not been used.

It almost seems as though we have done it on purpose; as though drifting is what we really want. But it is not. What we really want is to live while we live. We want to wake before we die.

How can we do it? How shall we come out of the dream while we still have time?

First, we must stop shutting out the light of the morning. Ask yourself *why* you are running from life. Is it just to save yourself from effort—from the true waking which challenges, illuminates, enlightens and stimulates? No one can help feeling fear; but try to cut down the number of times you act on it. Reach out for life's experiences.

Another way to wake is to accept who we are, imperfect but unique. Once you realize that since the beginning of time there's never been anyone like you, that the world will never again be touched by that very voice which is yours, by just these views, by this special tenderness, this particular insight, you will not want to spend your life following others.

Look for the glimpses of your true self. Spend time alone; identity is found in silence and solitude. Risk fulfilling what you really are.

The most important way to wake is to return to the wonder of the child. Seek the occasions and seize the day, as a child does. Rise before dawn some morning and see the miracle of creation all over again. Rise, too, at night, and see moonlight in the empty streets. Watch how the wind plays with the bright leaves of a maple tree in the spring.

"Use your eyes," wrote Helen Keller, "as if tomorrow you would be stricken blind; hear the music of voices, the song of a bird, as if you would be stricken deaf tomorrow. Touch each object as if tomorrow your tactile sense would fail. Smell the perfume of flowers, taste with relish each morsel, as if tomorrow you could never smell and taste again."

Inevitably we live between light and dark, life and death. Daily we come out of the thicket of darkness, live in the bright bowl of the sun and return again to the fall of night. *"Now I lay me down to sleep."* It is about this immemorial rhythm of life that the little prayer speaks.

When we have lived a day richly and warmly, running in the sunlight, laughing and loving, then night comes sweetly and without regret. Perhaps that other night, that longer night we call death, will come sweetly, too, if we have spent our life so that it blessed us and the others around us; come sweetly and bring, like all the nights we've known, a new and fresh awaking.

Great Reading on the World's Most Popular Subjects From America's Most Trusted Magazine
READER'S DIGEST

I AM JOE'S BODY   06548-0/$2.95 _____

is based on the most popular series in DIGEST history, in which the various organs of the human body explain themselves

SECRETS OF THE PAST   05765-8/$2.75 _____

explores ancient mysteries and tells about man's earliest adventures.

THE ART OF LIVING   05891-3/$2.75 _____

contains practical and heartwarming advice, designed to help make life richer, more enjoyable, and more meaningful

TESTS AND TEASERS   05730-5/$2.75 _____

is brimful of brain-wracking puzzles, quizzes, games, and tests. It promises hours of escapist fun and mental gymnastics

Berkley / Reader's Digest Books

Available at your local bookstore or return this form to:

 BERKLEY
Book Mailing Service
P.O. Box 690, Rockville Centre, NY 11571

Please send me the titles checked above. I enclose _____
Include $1.00 for postage and handling if one book is ordered; 50¢ per book for two or more. California, Illinois, New York and Tennessee residents please add sales tax.

NAME _____

ADDRESS _____

CITY _____ STATE/ZIP _____
(allow six weeks for delivery)   44M